RICH BROTHER
RICH SISTER

Other Books by Robert T. Kiyosaki

www.richdad.com

RICH BROTHER
RICH SISTER
*Two Different Paths
to God, Money and Happiness*

ROBERT KIYOSAKI AND
EMI KIYOSAKI
(Venerable Tenzin Kacho)

Vanguard Press
A Member of the Perseus Books Group
New York

Designed by Anita Koury
Set in 12 point Bembo

Kiyosaki, Robert R., 1961-

Rich brother rich sister : two different paths to prosperity, God, and happiness / by Robert Kiyosaki and Emi Kiyosaki.

p. cm.

ISBN 978-1-59315-493-6

1. Wealth. 2. Faith. 3. Happiness. I. Kiyosaki, Emi H. II. Title.

HB251.K59 2009

650.1—dc22

2008045713

Vanguard Press books are available at special discounts for bulk purchases in the U.S. by corporations, institutions, and other organizations. For more information, please contact the Special Markets Department at the Perseus Books Group, 2300 Chestnut Street, Suite 200, Philadelphia, PA 19103, or call (800) 810-4145, extension 5000, or e-mail special.markets@perseusbooks.com.

All photographs accompanying the text are courtesy of Robert Kiyosaki and Barbara Emi Kiyosaki.

10 9 8 7 6 5 4 3 2 1

To Mom and Dad

"The test of a first rate intelligence is the ability to hold two opposed ideas in the mind at the same time and still retain the ability to function."
—F. SCOTT FITZGERALD

"My religion is simple: my religion is kindness."
—His Holiness the Dalai Lama

CONTENTS

Special Thanks

We extend our heartfelt thanks to Kathy Heasley and Mona Gambetta.

Kathy stepped up to the daunting task of drawing out the stories and life experiences of a brother and sister with very different points of view—siblings who grew up in the same house but whose questions and quests in life have, in many ways, been worlds apart. Kathy's patience, thoughtful probing and ability to clarify subtle nuances gave life to this book. She searched for—and found—many of the things that are often unsaid within families and brought spirit to the messages of God, money and happiness.

And in true Rich Brother Rich Sister *spirit, offering complement and counterpoint, Mona drew upon her eight years of experience with The Rich Dad Company to bridge the worlds of material wealth and spiritual wealth—the bridge that leads to a rich life.*

BARBARA EMI KIYOSAKI   ROBERT KIYOSAKI

PREFACE

Two Worlds Collide

We are born with two families. The first family is our biological family, the family we are born into. The second is the spiritual family, the community that beckons us to that place where we can contribute and grow . . . that space where we can live the life we were born to live.

We were raised in a family of Japanese descent in the small town of Hilo, Hawaii, shortly after World War II and in the midst of the Cold War. With a home on the Big Island, we grew up in a community that dealt with devastating tidal waves and violent volcanic eruptions.

Our father, Ralph Kiyosaki, was the state superintendent of schools, a leader in the local Civil Defense chapter, and was active in disaster relief efforts that frequently took him and our mother, Marjorie, away from the family for days at a time.

Mom was a registered nurse and worked with the American Red Cross. A faithful member of the Hilo Methodist Church, she had a special love for music and at Christmastime often gravitated to

Dad, Robert, and Emi (at ages three and two). Dad's large hands always protected us. Notice his cigarette. As much as he loved his family, his addiction to smoking took him away from the family he loved.

whichever church had the best choir and choir director. She also had a heart condition—rheumatic fever—from which she had suffered as a child. It had weakened her heart and contributed to the heart failure that took her life at the age of forty-nine.

The Kiyosaki family believed in finding and supporting "solutions," in offering assistance and being of service. Instead of *talking* about the importance of education, our father studied and served others. Instead of *talking* about religion, our mother practiced her faith at church and in life. Instead of *talking* about public service, they volunteered in their community. They provided a home, a shelter from the storms of life, and did their best to protect their children.

But they could not shelter us from the world, and the world came at them from all directions. In 1962 Robert was fifteen years old,

Emi was fourteen, their brother Jon was thirteen, and the youngest, Beth, was eleven. The whole family was watching television when a bright flash caused Beth to shout.

"Oh, my god. Look out the window!"

We all rushed into the dining room and looked out at the night-time sky as the flash faded to an angry orange, then to swirling bright red to dark purple and, finally, back to black. We didn't know it at the time, but what we were witnessing was an atomic bomb explosion spreading its wrath across the Pacific sky.

The next day the local paper said that the United States atomic bomb test, one of a series that took place on Christmas Island, looked like someone had poured blood across the sky. A local newscaster described the experience much more graphically, saying it looked like someone had slit the throat of an animal and let the blood gush out across the sky. At first the blood was bright red, he wrote, frothy because it was still alive with oxygen. As the blood began to die, it began to coagulate, become thicker, transitioning from dark red to purple. Eventually dark purple gave way to black, and the twinkling of stars finally pierced the blackness.

The times themselves, combined with witnessing that atomic blast, contributed to the decisions—the actions and reactions—of the entire Kiyosaki family. In 1964, Ralph and Marjorie quit their jobs and volunteered for President Kennedy's Peace Corps, taking substantial cuts in pay. The two sisters joined the peace movements, protesting against the Vietnam War in school and in the streets. And the two brothers volunteered and served in Vietnam: Jon in the Air Force and Robert in the Marine Corps.

In our own way, ironically, each of us was working for peace.

From an early age, though biological siblings, we were a study in contrasts. To the casual observer, our differences may seem more apparent than our similarities.

Emi (Tenzin Kacho) Kiyosaki and Robert Kiyosaki .

The contrasts run deeper, however, than the image of a smartly dressed Robert Kiyosaki juxtaposed with his sister, clad in her monastic robes. Deeper than the juxtaposition of material wealth and spiritual riches. Deeper and more profound than choices related to war and peace ... scarcity and abundance ... questions and answers.

Family number two is our spiritual family, the family that draws us with its call, the promise of acceptance, true understanding, and happiness. It is a community in which we know the power of unconditional love and find that which we know, in our hearts, is missing from our life.

Our spiritual family is our true home, an environment where we can live the life we are born to live and gain the perspective and ability to accept and appreciate other thoughts and points of view. There are many paths to finding your spiritual family: marriage, education, religion, career, friends, teachers, and even crisis and despair.

Finding your spiritual family in marriage is finding your soul mate. There is no more powerful union than two people who find each other to share another life together. As we all know, divorce rates are high. While there are many and varied reasons for divorce, one is loneliness—the loneliness and emptiness of being married to a person who is not your soul mate. There is a big difference between loving your spouse or partner and loving a soul mate.

Many people search for—but few ever find—their second family, their spiritual family.

This book is about a brother and sister, two people born into the same biological family, and their parallel but divergent paths to god, money, and happiness through knowledge and self-discovery. It is a story of our support of each other, in the face of contrasting points of view and conflicting ideologies, in the search to find our spiritual families.

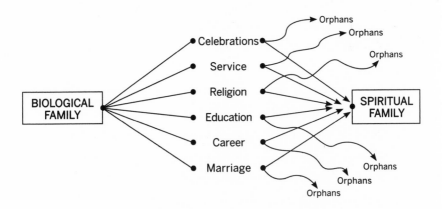

Many people spend their entire lives searching for their spiritual family ... and never find it. Many people feel empty and lonely—wandering through life, feeling like orphans, searching for their true home and family. They often ask themselves "Does my life have meaning?" as well as "What is the meaning of life?"

It is also the story of our search for a spiritual teacher. Life is filled with teachers. Very few are spiritual teachers.

When a spiritual teacher touches your heart, your mind opens to another world, another way of thinking ... of living. The Dalai Lama touched Emi Kiyosaki's heart, and she became a Buddhist nun and took the name Tenzin Kacho. Dr. R. Buckminister Fuller touched Robert's heart, and he found a path to support his search for understanding, education, and answers.

It is important to note that neither of us were great students in the traditional sense of the word. We did not excel in school. Nevertheless, once these spiritual teachers touched our hearts and opened our minds, we both became students—students who excelled, studying the subjects we were born to study. Today we are dedicated students using our gifts, the genius we were born with, the type of genius not always recognized in the realm of traditional education.

When children lose their biological mother and father, they are called orphans. In today's world, there are many spiritual orphans still seeking their spiritual family. For many, it is a lifelong journey; others find their spiritual family early and know that their search is over—that they have found the home and the family that will allow them to lead the life they were born to live.

Spiritual orphans often find themselves drawn to organizations in which they feel accepted and valued. Some find relief from their loneliness in church communities, patriotic groups, organizations that support a cause such as the environment or animal rights. Others become die-hard fans for whom sporting the team colors and cheering them on to victory fills that empty space in their heart and soul. There is a basic human need for acceptance and, for many people who have not found a soul mate, they search to find that space, that place, they can call home, that they can call their spiritual home and family.

Many people work for big corporations—orphanages that are filled with people who work for money and security, but not for love. We see this in the changing trends related to employment where decades of service, loyalty, and a bond that goes beyond a paycheck have become values of the past. How many of you know, first hand, the sick feeling in the pit of your stomach on Sunday evening when you think about the week ahead? For many, this is a reflection of a void in their life. They are not using their special genius, nor have they found a spiritual connection within their career or job.

They are not doing the work they were born to do.

Although busy and often surrounded by others, many people are lonely. After work, they seek their spiritual family in a church or an organization that matches their heart, their mind, and their spirit's mission, their spirit's reason for being born, for being here on earth. Today, growth in church attendance reflects the growing need for people to find their spiritual family.

Barbara Emi Kiyosaki never dreamed that one day she would be a nun. Once she found this spiritual family, her choices to forsake material wealth in favor of a lifelong quest for spiritual riches took her down a path that led to a monastic life—the seclusive life of a nun—in which living below her means seemed *suitable* for a nun.

When this high school graduation photo was taken, there was no way
Barbara Emi Kiyosaki could know what the future held for her.

Two worlds collided for Tenzin when the need for lifesaving medical treatment meant confronting the realities of a material world that she had, long ago, determined would not motivate or rule her. She came to learn that there is a difference between "living below your means" and putting yourself, your very life, in jeopardy.

The reality of the role that money plays in our lives—like it or not—hit hard and fast when life-threatening illness and the need for medical treatment resulted in a mountain of bills and limited financial resources. This spiritual woman, disciplined in both diet and spiritual focus, confronted these life and death choices. At the same time she dealt with the question of how a hard-living brother who had chosen a different path could recognize and appreciate her burden and offer opportunities that would lighten it.

Tenzin searched for a way to resolve the apparent conflict between her monastic life, her medical debts, and her future health needs. In doing so she came to some interesting and sobering conclusions. Those conclusions fueled her ability to look within, to see strengths as well as weaknesses, and muster the courage and the commitment to change.

Robert Kiyosaki never dreamed he would one day be a teacher like his dad. He failed English twice in high school because he could not write. Today his books are read in countries and languages all over the world. *Rich Dad Poor Dad* has been on the *New York Times* best-seller list for nearly seven years. Only two books in history have been on that list longer.

He found his spiritual family when he joined the Marine Corps, and again when he followed in the footsteps of his rich dad—his best friend's father, who guided him in learning about finance and investment.

In 1981 the course of Robert's life changed when he met Dr. R. Buckminster Fuller—considered one of the great geniuses of our

Robert takes a break in Vietnam.

time—who revealed to him that he could become rich by being generous, and with this new way of thinking Robert went on to create The Rich Dad Company. Both the Marine Corps and The Rich Dad Company are driven by very strong missions. Strong missions attract spiritual family members ... members looking to fulfill their life's purpose, their life's mission, performing the tasks they were born to do.

Have you found your soul mate? Have you found your spiritual teacher who will lead you to your spiritual family? Have you found your spiritual profession? In other words: Are you doing the job you were born to do?

That is what this book is about.

It also is about two journeys. It is about a brother and a sister, very different people though born to the same biological family, supporting each other to find their spiritual families, and living the lives they were born to live. The lives of these siblings are testimony to the resilience of the human spirit and the powerful and heartfelt connection that went beyond the obvious bonds of shared family and childhood to encompass a life of searching and realization and a future that would bring fulfillment to each of its protagonists.

This book is about the events, in many ways triggered by an atomic blast, that led Robert Kiyosaki and Tenzin Kacho to—and through—their leaps of faith. *Rich Brother Rich Sister* is about their different paths and different philosophies, in search for answers to the same questions. It is about a search for happiness and meaning in life.

The story of *Rich Brother Rich Sister* is one of contrasting worlds: material and spiritual, war and peace, questions and answers, divergent points of view. This book is about how lives can be separated and come back together in the service of a higher spiritual power.

INTRODUCTION:
ROBERT

For Love and Money

People often say, "Never discuss religion, politics, money, or sex." As you know, these are all highly charged, emotional subjects with almost everyone having their own, and sometimes irrational, personal point of view. This book does not follow this advice and discusses two of the taboo subjects: money and religion.

In the summer of 2006, my wife, Kim, and I flew from Phoenix, Arizona, to Los Angeles, California. The day trip was to attend a conference where His Holiness the Dalai Lama was to speak. My younger sister Emi Kiyosaki—going by her Buddhist name Tenzin Kacho—had invited us to the event. Kim and I are not Buddhists. Neither was my sister Emi, at least not when we were kids. The four Kiyosaki children had been raised as Christians. Emi became Tenzin in her mid-thirties, and if you had known my sister when she was a kid, you would never have guessed she would one day become a Buddhist nun.

At least *I* would never have guessed it.

Our limousine driver pulled up in front of the Gibson Amphitheatre. For miles, we had driven past lines of humanity walking toward the same destination. When I say "humanity," I use that word to include the wide spectrum of characters that included hippies, yuppies, techies, urban gangsters, and other more average-looking people. The crowd was a broad spectrum of races: black, white, yellow, red, brown, and golden. We saw a range of strange and conservative hairdos, as well as a number of shaved heads, people who looked like my sister. There was also an interesting array of clothing, some looking like it came from a church thrift shop and others from the most expensive shops of Rodeo Drive, just a few miles away.

I felt a little self-conscious—out of place—when the limo driver pulled up to the front entrance. He opened the door and let Kim and me out in front of the gathering crowd. A limo entrance might have been appropriate for a Hollywood film premier, but we weren't in Hollywood for that reason.

We were there to see one of the most influential religious leaders of our time.

As the limo drove away, Kim and I were lost in a sea of people. We did not know where to go. My sister wasn't able to greet us since she was busy backstage, and all we knew was that someone would meet us with our tickets. Suddenly, a nun of European ancestry—with shaved head, dressed in burgundy robes—greeted us. She guided Kim and me around the crowd to a side entrance where VIPs entered. Soon we were ushered to our seats, front row, center stage, right next to a number of Hollywood celebrities. Kim sat near Sharon Stone.

The audience took their seats, the lights in the auditorium dimmed, and the crowd hushed. As the curtains opened, I was surprised to see my sister step forward to open the program and introduce His Holiness the Dalai Lama. I had no idea she was part of the event.

In the morning session, we had attended a traditional Buddhist teaching. Although I did not understand the rituals, the entire hour-and-a-half program was dramatic. The stage was beautifully lit and filled with monks and nuns. When His Holiness spoke, there was no talk about sin or hell and damnation. He didn't say that the love of money was the root of all evil. He did not endorse any political candidate. He did not pass the offering plate. He simply spoke of the trials and tribulations all of us—including himself—face as everyday people. He did not put himself on a pedestal.

Since Tibetan Buddhists do not believe in god, he did not claim to have god's private cell phone number. He spoke in simple, everyday words about, essentially, everyday events. His words filled the auditorium with kindness, compassion, and humor. Thousands of years of wisdom and compassion swirled around the hearts and minds of those who had gathered there.

Toward the end of the program, another nun came to get Kim and me. This nun led us backstage where I finally saw my sister, standing

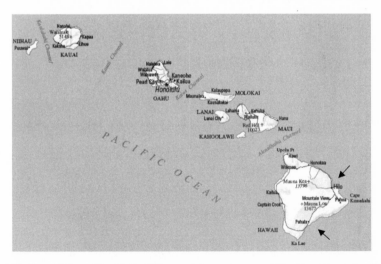

A *National Atlas of the United States of Amercia* map of The Hawaiian Islands. Of interest are Hilo, the home of the Kiyosaki family, and Pahala, where parents Ralph and Marjorie Kiyosaki met, where Emi lived to begin her Buddhist studies, and where Robert saw Dr. R. Buckminster Fuller for the last time.

between two towering stage curtains. She beamed, her smile bright and beautiful, and beckoned us toward her. It had been months since we had last seen each other. As Kim and I drew closer, my sister's love reached out and touched us from across the distance.

Once we were next to her, she asked in hushed tones, "Would you like to meet His Holiness? He'll be coming off stage soon."

"You've got to be kidding," I replied. "You can arrange that?" Tenzin—or Emi as I was still calling her—smiled and answered in a teasing tone.

"I'll see what I can do."

There are four children in our family. We are fourth generation Japanese American. Our ancestors arrived in Hawaii in the 1880s to work in the sugar and pineapple fields. Although raised in both cultures, being the fourth generation in the United States, I believe we are more American than Japanese. Although our mom and dad could speak Japanese, none of the children learned the language.

As most of us know, even though they may be born to the same family, children are often very different. Even identical twins can develop different personalities, temperaments, and interests. All four children in the Kiyosaki family are very different, including my sister, Barbara Emi Kiyosaki. Emi is her Japanese name and the name we used as kids. Growing up, she was always a kind, joyful, happy person. Today, she is even *more* so. In fact, I would say she is the most loving and joyful person I know.

I would say I am her polar opposite. While I do have a kind side, I have to fake being nice. While she will do anything to avoid conflict, I have always loved a good fight. During the Vietnam War, my sister was working for peace, and I was working for war.

This picture shows three of the four kids: myself, Emi, and brother Jon—the third of the four Kiyosaki children. It is a glimpse of the future. Years later, Jon joined the Air Force, and I joined the Marine

A picture of the future: Robert, Emi, and Jon.

Corps. We both fought in the Vietnam War. My sisters, Emi and Beth, worked for peace. My mom and dad joined the Peace Corps.

While we stood backstage, the Dalai Lama continued to speak. He did not speak about peace. He spoke *from* peace. He spoke with compassion. As I listened to him, I wondered if I could live and speak from so kind a space. After four years in military school and six years as a Marine Corps pilot, I had grown used to much harsher words and environments.

It was interesting to observe him as he continued his address. From our vantage point I could observe him and the audience. He was elevating them spiritually.

Suddenly, the program was over and His Holiness was ushered offstage, followed by more senior monks, nuns, and devotees. Seeing the crowd swarming around him, I did not have much hope of meeting him. As he headed toward his dressing room, two lines of people formed to silently honor him, clasping their hands in a praying position and bowing respectfully as he went past.

Wherever he goes, the Dalai Lama says, "It's like meeting old friends."
He is remarkable in making people feel loved and welcome. Here Tenzin
was part of a meeting to plan a future event.

As he came closer, smiling, the Dalai Lama saw Tenzin and walked toward us. She gently guided him to where we were standing. I was overwhelmed. I was impressed. I could not believe my little sister was inviting one of the most influential religious leaders of our time to meet us.

After Tenzin introduced us, we stood talking with His Holiness the Dalai Lama for a few priceless minutes. And then he was gone. I thought about never washing the hand that shook his. I felt blessed. Not only was I impressed with my sister, but I was proud of her. The more impressed I became, the more humble she grew.

I knew my sister had become a Buddhist nun, but beyond that I had not a clue what she did or who she was or what she had become. I knew she had searched for years to find her own life, her own calling, and her own path. Being Asian, Western, Christian, and a single mother had not been easy for her. As her older brother, standing next to His Holiness and Emi, I was much happier for my sister than for my opportunity to meet the Dalai Lama. Emi had found her place in the world. In her very humble way, she had found her power via the very gentle power of love. She had accomplished life's greatest achievement: she had grown up to become the person she was born to be.

Success does not always mean we become what we were born to be. Graduating from college does not necessarily mean we have become who we are born to become. Just because someone is professionally successful—as an attorney or doctor—does not mean they are doing what they were born to do. The same is true for money. Just because you are rich does not mean you have succeeded in becoming who you were born to become.

And just because my sister had become a nun, it didn't necessarily mean she had become who she was born to be. Becoming who you were born to become goes beyond success and attainment. Becoming who you were born to be is rediscovering your path and getting back on that path.

It is about life's journey, not life's destination.

A Christian preacher whose church I once attended said, "We are born human beings. This means we are both humans and beings. Some of us are more human than beings." Explaining further, he went on to say, "Humans have limits. Beings do not. Beings are limitless. Humans get old. Beings evolve."

He continued, "Humans die. Beings do not. Humans need jobs. Beings have missions." I had just returned from Vietnam and was in my twenties when I heard this preacher's message. Since I had faced death so many times in combat, his words had an immediate impact. While in Vietnam, I witnessed events that are not explainable within the traditional context of life and death. As a classmate of mine who also served in Vietnam said, "I am alive because dead men kept fighting." In Vietnam I came to know the difference between body and spirit or—as that preacher was defining it—the difference between humans and beings. Once I was touched by the power of our spirits, I came back a different human because I was a different being.

Obviously, this difference between humans and beings and body and spirit caused many problems in my life. Once you are not afraid of dying, you can begin to live. The problem with that transformation is that it becomes difficult to tolerate people who live with limits, live in fear of dying, live in fear of making mistakes, live in fear of being criticized, and live for security rather than for a rich, fuller life.

In 1974, I left the Marine Corps to begin my life back in the world of civilians. I had been in a military environment for nearly ten years. That year, I was hired by the Xerox Corporation in Honolulu and began sales training. Learning to sell was terrifying for me, but at least I knew I could learn to overcome my fears and my lack of skills. If I could learn to fly and learn to survive in a combat situation, I knew I could learn to sell.

I knew that one day I would learn to be an entrepreneur.

In 1974, I began to notice how many people in the business world were more humans than beings and more body than spirit. I became acutely aware of how many businesspeople were willing to say, "I can't do that."

Or, "The task is too hard."

"I would do it if I had more money."

"What if I fail?"

"What if I make a mistake?"

"I can't afford it."

"Will you pay me overtime?"

Wimpy things like this wouldn't have been tolerated in the Marine Corps. In combat, when my commanding officer gave a direct order such as, "Take out that machine gun nest," we weren't allowed to say, "But what if I get hurt?" Or, "I'm not feeling well. I have not had a day off. Ask someone else." All we were allowed to say was "Yes, sir."

And if we succeeded—and lived—we weren't allowed to brag. We were disciplined enough to simply ask, "What's the next mission?"

There are many similarities between the military and religion. At the military academy in New York, our first task was to memorize the mission of the United States Merchant Marine Academy. In the Marine Corps, the mission is more important than life.

In religions, true disciples are called missionaries. Unfortunately, in the real world, most people have jobs, not missions. People with jobs work for money, and people with missions work for a spiritual calling. In 2006, when I saw my sister standing next to the Dalai Lama, I was a proud and happy brother because I knew my sister had become who she was born to be. She had found her spiritual path, a path she had probably been on before. She had found her spiritual home and her spiritual family . . . again.

As I have said, there are four children in our family, and all four are very different. I suspect we are different because each of us has a different mission, a different life's work. My younger brother, Jon, is a mechanical genius. When he was a kid, he constantly brought home old radios, clocks, and engines, spending hours trying to fix them. Today he works with a large real estate company in Honolulu in the property management division. His job is to make sure the properties are well maintained and in good working order. He and I could not be more different. If you put a screwdriver in my brother's hand, it is used as a tool. If you put a screwdriver in my hand, it becomes a weapon. When he picks up a hammer, things get repaired. When I pick up a hammer, things break.

Our youngest sister, Beth, was born an artist. Throughout school she excelled in art, from paints to clay to weaving. Her gift was recognized early, and she sailed through college, even completing two years of graduate work. Today she is an artist in Santa Fe, New Mexico. Once again, she and I are complete opposites. She produces one-of-a-kind originals. She is a true artist. I suspect she would rather starve than turn commercial and sell her artwork to the mass market.

On the other hand, I am 100 percent commercial. I love the mass markets. I want my work mass-produced. I love having my books in Barnes and Noble, Amazon.com, Borders, Wal-Mart, and Costco. I love seeing them on the best-seller lists all over the world. I would rather sell than starve.

Until 2007, I just lived my own life, focused only on what I was doing. I had very little contact with my brother and sisters. I lived in my world and they lived in theirs. We rarely saw each other. That year, with the realization that we were now all adults, I began to wonder how my brother and two sisters were doing financially, as well as medically. I wondered if I would be the one who had to care for them as we all grew older. None of them had ever asked for any financial support, but we were all growing older and, if we are lucky, we will live long lives in good health.

In 2007, I found out that my sister Tenzin needed a heart operation. Her arteries were blocked, and she needed three stents to keep her blood flowing. Having had cancer a number of years earlier, she was having difficulty with her medical insurance. They were not willing to cover the cost of the heart surgery.

I hadn't known about her earlier bout with cancer. She never told me about it. Somehow, friends in Seattle helped her out. Now, with this heart surgery looming, she needed help.

Learning about her medical challenges shocked me. It was the first time any of us four children had faced a life-threatening disease of our own. Mom and Dad had passed on years earlier. Dad died of lung cancer at age seventy-one. He had smoked for most of his life. Mom died from heart disease at forty-nine. Being the oldest child—and the one with the most money—I felt I had an obligation to my sister that went beyond just being a loving brother. In Sunday school, I had been taught the words, "Am I not my brother's keeper?"

With Tenzin's cancer, those words took on a deeper meaning.

America is a great country if you have money. If you are poor, America can be a tough place to live. Taking a moment to look at my sister's life, I realized she was the only one of the kids without a home she owned. Though approaching sixty years of age, she has always been a renter. As a Tibetan nun, she did not have enough money to buy a home, especially in the Los Angeles area where she lives. As a nun, she is paid a small stipend and has a second job to cover her expenses.

My wife Kim and I sent her money to help with her heart operation. We offered to share what we know about investing and bought a condominium for her in Arizona. Even though Tenzin would not live there, at least for the moment, she receives some rental income and knows that she has a home of her own.

Tenzin's second life-threatening ailment caused me to pause and ask myself questions I had not asked before. What happens if she has no more money or insurance to cover additional medical expenses? What happens if her next medical emergency requires more and more money? What happens when she is no longer able to care for herself? Am I responsible?

Obviously, my answer was "Yes."

Readers may find it interesting, as I did, that my sister has been a vegetarian for years. She does her best to live a simple, stress-free life. She meditates religiously. She does not drink or smoke.

I, on the other hand, am a meat-eating, hard-drinking cigar smoker. I thrive on stress. If you ask most doctors, they would tell you that I am the one who should have the cancer and heart disease. Yet that is not the case. And while I do have my health challenges—I was born with a birth defect, a weak heart that was passed on to me from my mother's rheumatic fever, which almost kept me out of the military—I also have the money to spend on preventative healthcare that medical insurance does not cover. That is a big difference.

I do my best to stay away from medical doctors and hospitals. I would rather see chiropractors, natural health doctors, acupuncturists, and travel overseas to see alternative physicians not allowed to practice in the United States. I am into health, not medicine. If you have no money, it's hard to have good health. Good health can be expensive.

As I thought about the problems of love, family, and money, I realized that the problem my family was facing is a problem people all over the world face, even in America. In 2008, the first of 78 million American baby boomers begins to receive Social Security and soon, Medicare benefits. I wonder how the richest country in the world can afford 78 million aging baby boomers who are becoming more and more dependent upon the government for medical and life support. If each of those 78 million requires $1,000 a month from the government, the monthly bill will be $78 billion a month.

Who will pay the bill? And what happens to the families that do not have enough money to cover what the government will not? In Sunday school, I learned that giving a person a fish feeds them only for a day. It is better to teach a person to fish than to give a person a fish. While this bit of wisdom makes sense to me, it seems as if our government system believes in *giving* people fish rather than teaching people to fish.

This may be why our schools do not teach much about money.

So while Kim and I can afford to care for my sister's long-term health, I thought it better to assist her in fishing for herself. After all, I am a capitalist. I am very commercial. I am mass-market. My business, The Rich Dad Company, was formed to teach people to fish. When it comes to money, while I do support charitable causes, I do not think financial handouts work. I believe that giving poor people money only keeps them poor longer. As my rich dad often said, "Money does not cure poverty."

From a very young age, I had two dads, both offering me advice. My biological father is the man I call my poor dad. He was highly educated and intelligent, yet he struggled financially. My rich dad, the father of my best friend, never finished the eighth grade. He was fanatical, however, about exercising his mind. My rich dad said, "My brain gets stronger every day because I exercise it. The stronger it gets, the more money I can make."

So rather than give my sister more money, I decided it might be better to assist her in learning to fish. That is one of the reasons we decided to write this book—for money. This book is a money-making project. It is my way of sharing with my sister what I have spent my life studying, the study of how to be a capitalist. I am fairly confident that I can guide her to become a multimillionaire, if she wants to earn that much money. As a Buddhist nun, she has not taken a vow of poverty, as many other religious orders require.

When I asked her if she wanted to be a millionaire, she just smiled and said, "Right now, I just want to be able to pay my medical bills."

The second reason I decided to write this book was for love. It's not that I don't have love in my life. I have a lot of love. I feel blessed to have a loving, happy, and prosperous marriage with Kim.

Kim is my soul mate. She is very much like my sister, a person who comes from love. I simply wanted a deeper sense of love, a love that radiates through joy and happiness, the joy and happiness my sister has attained in her life. Being a capitalist, I thought it would be a great deal if I could give my sister the ability to create the money she wanted and needed, and she could give me a deeper sense of love, the love of this gift called life.

Those are the two reasons I decided to write this book. One is for love, and the other is for money.

It was war that separated my sister and me years ago, and when our paths crossed again it was as if we both searched for god, all the while not knowing if there really was a god. In many ways this book is more about finding our paths in life than it is about god—finding our spiritual work, home, soul mates, and family.

This book may challenge many religious beliefs. I know encouraging my sister to turn "commercial" may offend many people, especially those who believe that the love of money is the root of all evil. Personally, I do not think that money is evil. Money, in and of itself, is neutral. What is evil is how we make our money. For example, if I robbed banks, or worked for a company that killed people, or destroyed the environment, that would be evil. But to me, money is just money and, given the choice, I would rather have a lot of it than be poor.

Nor do I think that god loves poor people more than rich people. I do not think poor people go to heaven and rich people go to hell. I think it cruel—*and* evil—that our educational systems do not teach people about money. It still breaks my heart to see people struggling financially—it reminds me of my mom and dad. If I thought giving poor people money would solve the problem, I would. But instead I have chosen financial education as my life's work. That is why The Rich Dad Company was created.

In Sunday school I also was taught that Christ's last words on the cross were, "Forgive them, Lord, for they know not what they do."

Unfortunately, in my world, the world of money, no one forgives you for not knowing what you do not know. In my world, if you do not know what you are doing, then the world of money punishes you severely. With her health challenges, the world of money was pounding my sister. Again, I could help her by teaching her to learn to fish.

I got rich when I started thinking more about giving than receiving.

One of the most important lessons I learned in Sunday school was to "give and you shall receive." When I find people who are struggling financially, it is often because they are focusing on receiving and not giving. If I want more, all I have to do is give more. One way for my sister to become a multimillionaire is for me to teach her how to give more of her gift.

While my sister's faith does not teach the belief in god as many of us think of god, she has taught me a lot about living a more loving and enriched life. I believe in god, or what the American Indians call the Great Spirit. My life changed when I stopped working for myself to become rich and began working for everyone to become richer.

And that is the message at the core of this book. It is about the struggle many of us face, the struggle between being humans and being beings. It is about the gap between our body and our spirits. It is about kindness and the power in our hearts.

It is about finding our spiritual family and the life we were born to live.

INTRODUCTION:
EMI

Sound Body, Healthy Spirit

I never had any doubts as a child that we were loved.

My parents, our large family clans, the community, and the country were starting fresh again after World War II. Everyone had high hopes, as though all the fighting, anger, and hatred of war had purged the world, and people could set out to build their families, careers, and their fortunes once again.

Our parents were young, smart, and well-connected, and they were eager to start their family and life together. Robert, Jon, Beth, and I were born into this bubble of hope and determination. We were loved and greeted into the world with all the fanfare and joy that the birth of a child brings to a family. With great-grandparents proudly looking on in their new home country of the United States, Robert was the first great-grandson, first grandson, and first son on our father's side of the family. His birth was a cause to celebrate.

I arrived one year later, Jon a year after that, and Beth two years after Jon was born. Life became busy—busy, hectic, and challenging. Our early years were fraught with illnesses, and, living on a small

This family photo was taken at Grandpa's photo studio on Maui. Left to right: Barbara Emi, Marjorie, Jon Hideki, Ralph with Beth Teru, and Robert Toru. Emi loves this photo because it was fun to wear matching dresses with Mom and Beth. Mom is wearing the most amazing balsa wood mobile earrings that Dad made for her. The family was very close during these years.

income and getting little sleep, life for our parents became strained and difficult.

A family life that began with high hopes and the aspirations of living one's dream was tested. The challenges of life startled us and crashed into our dreams with a force that left us devastated. Even the most realistic of us can recall a time when wide-eyed optimism— unbridled hope for the future—fueled our existence. We are not always prepared for life's harsher realities. Our reactions to life's problems remind me of a wife I met through my hospice work. Her husband was dying, leaving her with young children, and she said to me, "This is not what I signed up for."

We are born, we live, and we face death; it is inevitable. And on our life's journey come sickness and aging as well. Starting a family, raising children, and life itself reveal this painful realization. Every person wants happiness and sets out with the hope of accomplishing their dreams. Our American society supports this dream, and we paint rosy pictures of our futures. Yet the realities of life find a way to tap us on the shoulder, reminding each of us of their nature.

While our parents dealt with their challenges, Robert and I—as with every younger generation—headed out with our own plans and dreams and traveled to lands and places we had only imagined when we grew up in our small island town.

I chose the path of a spiritual renunciation, yet through firsthand experience I had to learn not to ignore my health and financial well-being. This should have been readily apparent, since the Buddha's first teaching was the Four Noble Truths, and the first truth is the truth of suffering. Life is impermanent; because we are born, we face aging, sickness, and death. Nevertheless, I thought that if I practiced sincerely and served my teachers well, life would be good. So when I got cancer, and then heart disease, I found myself quietly bemoaning, "This is not *fair!*"

This was my own naïve thinking. My teachers have been telling me this all along, and so has Robert. Dealing with the medical challenges of my aging body and the financial horror created by a bad insurance plan, my eyes opened to the world that many Americans—particularly many baby boomers—are facing today.

Robert is always exhorting, "Mind your own business!" In Robert's world, that means making your life's business—your businesses of living and crafting your future—a high priority. Even in my simple world, I should have been minding my own business—paying attention to it. In seeking an individual insurance policy, I had been turned down by some of the more familiar carriers because of a pre-existing condition of leg edema that occurred, not so much from a health failure, but because some lymph nodes had been removed to see if cancer had lodged in those glands. It had not. Still, I did not research the insurance company that I finally signed up with, nor did I examine my policy well. I was hurriedly trying to get into retreat after a busy couple of years, and I thought anything was better than nothing, assuming that I would be fine anyway.

Without creating a better health-care package, not having a good retirement package, I lived as a nun, focused on day-to-day affairs and fulfilling the needs of others. This had been a pattern that worked for decades. I accomplished and learned a lot, but the system broke down.

Working with Robert has been an eye-opener, and the process of "righting my ship" has been essential, exhilarating, and difficult. When awareness dawns, exposing unhealthy patterns and blind spots in one's life, we can stay stuck and complain, or we can make the choice to change. For me, it's been a combination of both. Because of ingrained patterns, the journey has been one of leaps and stalls, but the decision to change is the driving impetus that keeps me going. Nevertheless, there are times when I fall asleep or want to go back to the way things were because breaking out of old patterns is hard.

What I faced was more than just a situation of getting good health insurance. It has been the changing of a calcified mind-set, a way of thinking and relating to life. The game of life is not easy, nor is it fair, and it is up to the individual to become aware of where you are on the game board, what kind of chips you have, what you need, and how you want to play.

At one of Robert's seminars, we broke up into groups that had to work together over the course of a few days. One woman on my team was a smart, pretty, very accomplished person. She seemed to know well the concepts that Robert spoke of, and let everyone know so. On Saturday Robert told us to show up that evening to a street address he gave us, and he told us to wear clothes we wouldn't mind never seeing again. We wondered what we were getting into!

We ended up at a paintball arcade, after hours, and had the place to ourselves. Each team had to face off against another team in a game to capture the other team's pennant and bring it back to base. There were obstacles, bunkers, and hiding places where people could fire their paintball guns or escape being hit. We wore padded garments and masked helmets, so I couldn't see very well. The helmet squashed my glasses and fogged them up. We battled in the dark with an annoying strobe that lit the arena in staccato flashes. Robert threw us into the fire of the game.

That accomplished woman had been so proud and confident throughout the seminar. Yet here at the paintball arena she got hit in the back and soon was crying on the sidelines. She whimpered, "They aren't playing *fair*!" I could hear Robert yelling over the din from across the room.

"Life is not fair!"

Our team did not work as a team; it was every person for himself. In retrospect, we could have covered and helped each other, but everyone wanted to be the star and get the pennant. We had no strategy to work together.

Our lives are nuanced by so many facets, and the things to which we do not pay attention will manifest at some time or another and will need to be reconciled with the larger picture. While taking good care of my studies and practice, I had ignored my health and personal welfare. Each time I hesitate, my mind flashes back to scenes of Robert exhorting, "Mind your own business!"

We all have our own life lessons.

After the angioplasty procedure to care for my heart and endless communication with the insurance company, doctor, and hospital, I faced an out-of-pocket bill of more than $17,000. At the time of writing this, the insurance company I so hurriedly chose has come back to me again—a year and a half after the procedure—reopening the file and reexamining the same bills I had paid and thought were behind me. The company is charging me another $8,000, forcing me to write still more letters. Either this insurance company is not clear in its own policies, or it is trying to simply squeeze more money out of me.

Robert and Kim helped me with my first bill, sending me $10,000 so that I did not have to worry or take out a loan. Robert does not like to just give money away, though. He lives by the familiar Christian saying, "Give a man a fish, you feed him for a day. Teach a man to fish, and you feed him for his life." This nasty situation of getting sick and having huge bills has been my wake-up lesson—to "mind my own business."

In doing so, I'm honing my chaplaincy and teaching skills, working with an excellent hospice team, and taking care of my life. My safe, secure world of the Buddhist center, while providing an excellent refuge for practice and study, has had to expand. I've had to polish other facets of my life and learn new lessons. I am embarking on new horizons for dynamic, viable avenues for monastics in the twenty-first century.

Robert called me recently and told me a story he hears again and again. Someone asked him about the floundering economy and stock market and wanted to know what to do. Robert told them, "It's time to rely on your savings."

"They're all used up," was the answer.

"Stay with your job then," Robert replied.

"I don't have a job."

"Then you're sunk," Robert said.

While it seems coldhearted, Robert was stating the facts, the unvarnished truth. His bottom line was that you have to find a way to provide for yourself!

This is my story, too, and at age sixty, I forged my way back into the working world. I have to "take care of business" of developing the means to take care of myself. Robert says that while the baby-boomer generation has produced an incredibly rich group of people, it also produced a host of welfare dependents and an even greater cross-section of people living paycheck to paycheck and in credit card debt. This stance—our position in life—is coming first from our mental attitudes and then from how we follow through and engage in the world. When you live like this for years, you've etched out your reality.

The beautiful thing about being human beings is that we have the opportunity to change. We don't have to live in a rut. Our mind is powerful and can *create* the change. Even with my hospice patients who are facing terminal sickness, I tell them, "Your mind is powerful. Call on empowering thoughts. Don't dwell in, 'I wish I could be around to see . . .' or 'I should have . . .' or 'I will miss. . . .'"

Even at life's end we can say, "May my family live on well."

"May my children be successful."

"May our leaders benefit others."

"May there be peace in the world."

Robert and I share our adventure with you because it is not just a physical journey, but a spiritual one, too. Our lives have been ones of searching for an outward life that would reflect and mesh with our inner journeys, our quests of the heart.

We write of the contrast between the school of life experience and meeting our spiritual teachers, those who give us ballast and direction in life. In many ways, our search is everyone's search. And it is a search for meaning, belonging, success, and understanding—a search for contentment and peace. Through collaborating on this book, Robert says he gained a greater understanding of kindness, kindness that grows in the heart. Our hearts are home to our most precious gifts, and kindness is key among them.

I, on the other hand, have learned to have more courage. Like the journey to the Land of Oz, this story was my quest for courage, and in writing and sharing my life and journey, I found courage. Robert, venturing into new and uncharted territories in writing a book with his sister about the spiritual view of his journey, found more kindness in his heart.

1

Born into History

Every generation of people is shaped by the history into which they are born. As history unfolds we see how events and the stories surrounding them impact and shape lives and decisions and families.

The World War II generation was shaped by war and the Great Depression. This generation's new technology was the radio, and World War II ushered in the nuclear age with the destruction of Hiroshima and Nagasaki. Politically, the Great Depression brought us Social Security, Medicare, and the idea that government should take care of its citizens for life.

Today's generation—the Iraq War generation—is born into a history marked eternally by the events on September 11, 2001. They deal with the ramifications of the Worldwide Web, the shift of power to China, the end of oil, accelerated global warming, and global terrorism. Today's generation is faced with a thousand-year-old Holy War, massive government debt, and paying for Social Security and Medicare passed on from the World War II generation. The Iraq War Generation will be asked to resolve problems that previous generations failed to solve.

The baby boomers—the Vietnam War generation—were born into the Cold War, marked by the pervasive fear of humanity's extinction due to a nuclear holocaust that could destroy the world in minutes. When Russia placed missiles on the island of Cuba, giving the former Soviet Union a strategic first-strike advantage—an advantage measured in minutes—President Kennedy blockaded Cuba. The naval blockade took us to the brink of war, yet it prevented a global nuclear war and humanity's extinction.

The boomer generation's technology was television. In the 1960s these people watched The Beatles on The Ed Sullivan Show *as they ate frozen TV dinners in their living rooms. They also watched the assassinations of their much-loved President John F. Kennedy, civil rights leader Dr. Martin Luther King, Jr., and presidential candidate Robert Kennedy, also from their living rooms. As the Vietnam War was waged, instead of obediently marching off to war as their parents had, many burned their draft cards, embraced the "hippie" lifestyle, staged love-ins, and rejected many of the values their parents had fought for.*

The baby boomers also became the richest generation in the history of the world, starting with their Davy Crocket coonskin caps and the Volkswagens they drove during their college years, stepping up to BMWs, Porsches, Mercedes, and private jets in their middle years. Many of this generation were not content to have just one place to live, instead buying second homes in Aspen, Maui, or in the south of France.

For the World War II generation, age was an asset as they climbed the corporate ladder. Instead of accepting their parents' lifestyles and values, the boomers let the world know that the young now ruled the world. This idea is even more prevalent in today's Iraq War generation. For today's generation, old is thirty, especially in the corporate world. Today we have twenty-year-olds becoming billionaires, taking their Web companies public while their parents—those of the Vietnam era—struggle to save a few dollars in their retirement plans, and their grandparents cling to Social Security and Medicare as they watch inflation wipe out their savings.

While the World War II generation enjoys Social Security and Medi-

care benefits, it is doubtful that the following generations will have the same financial and medical security.

Starting with the baby-boomer generation, the gap between the rich and everyone else will widen. As capitalism spreads the American Dream worldwide, and evolving into the International Dream, many Americans will notice they are falling behind, rather than leading the world in economic lifestyle. Many baby boomers and their children will work all their lives—not for financial freedom but for financial survival. In fifty years, America has gone from being the richest country in the world to becoming the biggest debtor nation in the world. Instead of the American Dream, it is bye-bye American Pie.

Instead of heaven on earth, for millions of people it may soon be hell on earth.

With the loss of financial security, increasing global competition, and rising prices—especially in health care—there has been a renewed interest in spirituality and religion, a search for life's answers that aren't being provided by our schools, churches, businesses, or politicians. With so many eras of history colliding into one, old questions require new answers. In fact, old answers, such as Social Security and Medicare, are the cause of many of today's problems.

It is this collision of generations, histories, cultures, and technologies that defines the history we are a part of today. If we do not change our answers, we will not change our futures.

ROBERT: TURNING POINT

In the summer of 1962, when the United States exploded that atomic bomb near Christmas Island—a small atoll south of the islands of Hawaii—we lived in Hilo, Hawaii, a little town on the Big Island, the southernmost point of the United States.

The four children and our mom and dad had just finished dinner and were watching *The Adventures of Ozzie and Harriet* on our

Junk Bonds

The January 11, 2008, issue of *Financial Times* ran a headline that stated, "US's Triple-A Credit Rating Under Threat." In other words, the once-powerful U.S. Bond market might become downgraded and was headed for junk bond status.

Most of us are aware of the subprime credit mess. This mess was created when people who should not be borrowing money were offered teaser interest rates to buy a new home or borrow money on their existing home to pay off credit card debt. The significance of the *Financial Times* headline was that, according to the credit rating agency, Moody's, the U.S. government's credit worthiness might also be rated subprime.

One of the primary reasons for Moody's warnings about America's financial problems had to do with Social Security and health care. The article stated, "The combination of the medical programs and Social Security is the most important threat to the triple-A rating over the long-term."

In other words, too many people are expecting the government to take care of them and our government cannot afford to do so.

black-and-white television. There was no squabbling about what show to watch because there was only one channel. We had no choice, no VCR, no DVDs, no Tivo—and no color. The broadcast went off the air at 10:30 every night since there were so few shows being produced for television. Programming didn't resume until 7 o'clock the next morning.

Suddenly, halfway through the show, a harsh, blinding white flash lit up the sky—and our entire living room—for a split second, so intense, so bright white that it washed out everything else in the room, including the TV screen.

"What was that?" someone shouted.

"Did someone snap a picture?"

"What *was* that?"

On that summer evening, my family witnessed something that remains vividly etched in my memory . . . as clear and powerful as it was forty-six years ago. For Emi and me, it impacted our thinking about god, war, peace, health, and money. It affected our choices, our actions, and our futures.

"Oh, my god. Look out the window!"

It was Beth, our sister and the youngest, who turned our attention to the spectacle unfolding before us. As each of us reached the window, we uttered the same words: "Oh, my god."

For the next few hours, while other Americans simply went on watching television, our family stood in front of our dining room window, watching the sky as it changed from an angry orange flash to swirling bright red to dark purple and, finally, back to black.

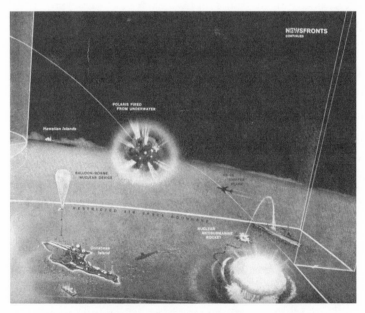

Life magazine image depicting various forms and locations
of Christmas Island nuclear testing.

In the summer of 1962 I was fifteen years old, just about to enter high school. Being close in age, my brother, sisters, and I were well aware of the atomic threat and possibility of war with the Soviet Union, Communist China, or both, and we were all old enough to understand the far-reaching implications of the angry sky framed by our picture window. While the potential for atomic war was far, far away from the living rooms of most U.S. citizens, we had ringside seats in our own front yard.

At school, there were nuclear attack drills. A siren would sound, and we were trained to crawl under our desks. A few families actually built fallout shelters in their yards and held parties to christen their new home improvements.

The Kiyosaki family did not build a fallout shelter.

Instead, my father, Ralph Kiyosaki, became a leader in the local Civil Defense chapter. My mother Marjorie was a registered nurse and joined the American Red Cross. If an atomic war did occur, both would be active in disaster relief.

Thankfully, there was never an atomic war, although Hilo, Hawaii, was hit by a number of natural disasters, including disastrous tidal waves. In the 1960s an especially large wave struck at night, wiping out the low-lying parts of the town, killing about fifty people.

Local disasters also involved volcanic eruptions. During World War II, the military actually bombed a large lava flow, hoping to divert it before it destroyed the city. In those days, there was an additional fear that the light from the lava would serve as a beacon for the Japanese to attack our town. While most eruptions were contained and safe if viewed from a distance, a number of them did extensive damage, even threatening the entire town. In the 1960s, lava flows destroyed papaya and orchid farms, as well as the homes of many local families.

As community leaders, our father and mother were often gone for days, providing much-needed government and medical services to fellow citizens. That was the example they set. It didn't matter if

We moved to this big, rambling house in 1959 after Dad was appointed as the school superintendent for the Big Island. Notice the tree with no leaves on the left. After the long volcanic eruptions, that tree lost all its leaves. But the next year, it bloomed spectacularly—just that one year—and we think it was because of the volcanic ash. We had our best years here at this house. About once a year, we'd have the house cleaned and throw a big party for people from the department of education.

the cause was public education, health care, tidal wave, lava flow, or threat of nuclear war, the four Kiyosaki children grew up in a family environment in which there was more than merely talk about community service and civic responsibility. We grew up with parents who said very little, but who acted a lot.

In that regard, they were great role models.

During the disastrous 1960 tidal wave, our parents were involved with disaster relief for days. Our home was on a hill and was not affected by the wave, so they knew we would be safe. I vividly remember my dad shaking me awake in the middle of that disastrous night.

"Take care of the kids," he said. "The town has been destroyed, and many people have been killed. Mom and I may not be home for a while." I was thirteen years old.

We grew up in a family that was actively involved in finding and supporting "solutions," in the giving of assistance and being of service. They volunteered in their community. They provided a home,

Dad points to two chairs that the tidal wave had deposited on top
of the Hukilau Restaurant, which was one of our family's favorite restaurants.

a shelter from the storms of life, and they did their best to protect us.

But they could not shelter us from the world. And the world came at us from all directions.

For young people of the 1960s, it was exciting and frightening and confusing and challenging. This era of history was known as the atomic age. At times we reveled in national pride in what America was accomplishing, especially in the space program. Yet in that glow of patriotism, we wrestled with the reality of nuclear war delivered from space. There was a very big difference between hearing about the threat of nuclear war in the news and actually witnessing an atomic explosion with our own eyes.

Hiding in a fallout shelter and crouching under our desks didn't seem to make much sense, yet the climate of fear and uncertainty created doubts and questions about the future. Being of Japanese descent, and being fourth-generation Americans, the pictures of attacks on Hiroshima and Nagasaki added to our turmoil.

For me, it was nearly impossible to fight off the sense of futility, a "What does it matter?" outlook on life. I know I wasn't alone in my feelings of pointlessness. Many parents reported children shaken by nightmares of death by an atomic blast or from the fallout from nuclear winter—a term used to describe our globe shrouded by a cloud of radioactive dust. Many children of this era, from the 1960s through the 1980s, experienced feelings of a childhood lost—a future that might never be. It's hard to have dreams of tomorrow when you're not sure there will be one.

Witnessing that atomic bomb explosion contradicted the very foundation of what we had all learned in Sunday School, as well, where we were told, "Thou shalt not kill." But maybe what we were witnessing was more like "Onward, Christian Soldiers," the title of a well-known Protestant hymn.

It was a frightening and confusing time to be a child. Mom always said I had a mean streak, and the times only reinforced what I already had begun to feel and to experience. At the age of fifteen, the same year as the atomic blast, I bought a rifle for $81 from a mail-order catalog. I paid for it with my own money. My dad hated the fact that I owned a gun—almost as much as I loved firing it.

When I was sixteen, a kid pulled a handgun on me in a movie theater. I don't know whether that gun was loaded or not, but the incident was a psychological and emotional rush. I felt fear, but that fear grew into excitement. It was a high—a thrill—that spiked my adrenaline and toughened me.

I had a "nice boy" exterior, but behind that was emerging a side of me my mother didn't want the neighbors to see. It was a side that Sunday School tried to quiet in me at the same time that America was calling us all to arms. Even then I could see the contradictions. What was right, and what was wrong? It was impossible to tell, and I began to question the commandment, "Thou shalt not kill." I began to wonder if the commandment should be changed to, "Kill or be killed."

In church I listened to the lessons and knew they were important, but I had trouble believing the stories that surrounded them.

A future marine in training.

Creation, Noah and the Ark, the virgin birth of Jesus, his walking on water. . . . I just couldn't buy these incredible tales. My attitude and questions didn't sit well with my mother or the women who I came to term her "Church Lady Friends," women who just believed the dogma without question.

"That's what faith is," they would say, "and if you want to go to heaven, you must believe."

I could not "drink the Kool-Aid," as some would say. I couldn't buy the stories without questioning them. Many of us are familiar with the phrase, "drink the Kool-Aid." It entered common usage after a preacher named Jim Jones took his flock to Guyana in 1977 and had them drink Kool-Aid laced with poison. It was a mass-suicide in the name of god, and its gruesome pictures were broadcast throughout the world.

Even though this Kool-Aid, this flavor of dogma, wasn't my drink, I remained a nice, polite young boy and didn't challenge the Church Ladies. I made my way by putting one foot in front of the other, taking in what made sense, and leaving behind everything that didn't. I don't know if it was a path I knowingly chose, or if it was one that the times had chosen for me. Either way, I knew where I was going and what I needed to do. I knew my time would come.

Each of us four kids went in a different direction in the search for our own answers, about god, war, money, religion, school, and careers. And even though our parents often didn't approve of our choices, they made sure we had the freedom to choose.

That bomb blast gave me the license to pursue my dark side, and within ten years my rifle had become a marine helicopter with six machine guns and two rocket pods. The Bible says, "You were born for a time such as this." Perhaps we all were. I knew I was—and my dark side was coming to light.

Those times, combined with that atomic blast in 1962, contributed to the decisions—the actions and reactions—of the entire Kiyosaki family. In 1964, Ralph and Marjorie quit their jobs and volunteered for President Kennedy's Peace Corps, taking substantial cuts in pay. My two sisters joined peace movements, protesting against the Vietnam War in school and in the streets. And the two brothers volunteered and served in Vietnam: Jon in the Air Force and me in the Marine Corps. In our own way, ironically, we were all working for peace.

The reason this book begins with war is because war was instrumental in defining our values and each person's individual quest. Without the specter of a global atomic war, and the Vietnam War as a backdrop to this era of history, it's impossible to know whether Emi or I would have gone in search of own answers to god, each in search of our own separate peace.

EMI: EYES OPEN

It wasn't just the sight of the blood-red sky or the difficult contradictions we faced that made it challenging to be a kid in the sixties,
it was also the ever-present, emotional dark cloud hanging over us.
The threat of nuclear war with the Soviets, the possibility of fighting enemies with terrifying weapons, and the untold consequences
of death and devastation were on the news every night. The proof
of that reality occurred right before our eyes.

As a child living in Hilo, facing the realities a child should not have
to face, there was no way I could forget the nebulous but ever-
present cloud of nuclear holocaust, of mass destruction caused not
by god, but by man killing man. It left as strong an imprint on me
as it did on my brother Robert. We did our best to live normal lives,
but at times we would least expect it, the nuclear threat would become real again.

Parks were meant for playing. But in one park, in the middle of
town in Hilo, the city constructed a model bomb shelter as if to show
everyone "how it's done." You couldn't miss the formidable structure and, of course, it was open to the public. I remember my brief
tour well. The tiny, cramped space was damp, cold, and dark. It
smelled of earth, mold, and wet concrete. I couldn't imagine staying in it for more than ten minutes, let alone living in it with my
family for weeks, if not months.

The air raid drills we had in school seemed important then. One
minute we'd be struggling through a math problem and in the next,
sirens would sound, and all the kids would dutifully hide under our
desks. Today we know how pointless the exercises really were. But
then we were told ducking under our desks and covering our heads
could save our lives.

Our parents protected us from the world as much as they could.
They did their best to shield us from the news of escalating global

tensions and potential conflicts. They knew—and we sensed—that war and strife could arise anywhere and thrust us into harm's way, even in a remote town on a distant Hawaiian island.

There seemed to be something noble about it all. Fighting for "truth, justice, and the American way," as the announcer said on *Superman*. It seemed as if we were in a fight of good versus evil, and we were the good guys. We were all being called to arms, even as schoolchildren.

Our dad answered that call by becoming a leader in the local Civil Defense chapter, and Mom put her nursing skills to work and joined the American Red Cross. Because they were involved with community activities, the kids were carted off to all kinds of events with them. I remember one evening when we drove to another little town where three families had pooled their resources and built a network of adjoining, underground rooms and passageways. It was our first "fallout shelter" party. These friends were so proud of their massive space—a shelter that could accommodate more than a dozen people in the event of an emergency.

While others were marveling, I was becoming more and more concerned. Why weren't we doing this? Didn't our family need one of these shelters? In an attack, would we have time to drive to a shelter? Would others who were already safe and secure let us in?

Then there was the real issue: I still could not imagine cowering like a trapped animal in a cold, dark, dank bunker. Nor could I, even at such a young age, grasp that a cement hive would protect me, given what I had seen from our picture window that summer evening.

And, furthermore, would I want to live in a world destroyed by atomic weapons?

This bleak prospect of being lonely survivors on a wasted earth was compounded by the play we were reading in school: *No Exit* by Jean-Paul Sartre. I found my high school English teacher's choice of literature almost prophetic in that *No Exit* was the story of three people who were trapped in a room with no windows and one locked door. The people expect their captors to torture them, only to find out that their torturers are each other.

Perhaps I was ultrasensitive at the time. Or maybe our teacher was trying to tell us something through the voice of a great writer. Regardless, Sartre's message—or my teacher's, perhaps—wasn't lost on me. What I never could have seen coming, though, was how this piece of literature, when combined with the events of 1962, would pull me toward my destiny.

Another kind of "war" we dealt with growing up involved developing a peaceful coexistence with Mother Nature. Even today, the Big Island of Hawaii experiences growing pains with active volcanoes while, at the same time, settling and slowly sinking. Located in the midst of the largest ocean in the world, the island is vulnerable to tidal waves and the effects of global warming.

The beautiful town of Hilo was devastated in 1960 by a tidal wave that hit at 1:05 in the morning. We lost a childhood friend. They found her body three days later when they cleared away the rubble of their home. She was still in her bed. Friends woke up in the middle of night treading water, grabbing onto whatever they could. One elderly friend said she had grabbed onto some "bushes" and when the water subsided found herself high in a tree with several other people. Fire truck ladders assisted in their rescue.

Stores, houses, industries, a hospital, and a school were completely destroyed. One wave killed sixty people. The huge wave, thirty-five-feet high, raced across our sleeping town, churning and destroying everything in its path, dredging up boulders and debris from the ocean floor then belching them onto the land. The force of the wave was so strong that parking meters were bent like putty, houses and cars heaped upon one another other like a bored child's discarded toys.

Living as we did on the Big Island of Hawaii, the forces of nature were ever-present in our family life. Volcanic lava flows, such as this one destroying a friend's house, couldn't be diverted, so people were evacuated and could only watch in awe.

Mom and Dad woke us in the middle of the night to say they were leaving us alone at home while they went to help the rescue-and-relief teams. We lived several miles from the ocean and we were unaffected by the wave, but Mom was a nurse and Dad had to open up the schools for evacuation centers.

The entire town was shut down for weeks, and all the townspeople pitched in to help. Mom took us to help wash out bolts of fabric from a dry goods store. I remember unrolling the fabric to dry in long rows on the lawn of a park and marveling at the patterns and colors that were so beautiful in the sunshine.

There were also times when Dad had to go to sites where lava was flowing and burning entire small towns. A classmate and her family had to move because, after weeks of steam venting from the ground, the farm plot in back of their house had become a sunken volcanic crater. Another family friend lost their beachfront property when it became a clinkery lava field, rough and jagged, after a flow rolled over their property and into the ocean. Fortunately, volcanoes in Hawaii are generally not explosive.

As a counterpoint to the destruction, we were fascinated by these natural volcanic displays, and Dad would drive us to the nearby volcano areas to see majestic shows of nature. Robert and I, as well as our siblings and friends, grew up with very real and powerful expressions of earth's impermanence.

Conditions of war, strife, loss, and change swirled around us. There was nothing to hold onto except family, and there, too, we experienced sickness, loss, and change. During those formative years, we lost our grandmother in Chicago, then our great-grandparents on Maui. With those losses came the shifting powers in family hierarchy as strength and position ebbed and changed.

2

War and Peace

As mentioned earlier, this book begins with war and images of war because war was instrumental in defining the values of our biological family and our personal search for personal answers to old questions.

Like so many, we struggled to understand the values of our parents, and the way to find our spiritual family. Growing up Japanese American, we frequently dealt with the ramifications of war, in particular World War II. Ironically, war would help us find answers, conquer fear—including the fear of dying—and discover that there are things worth dying for.

In 1962 we witnessed an atomic explosion. At the time, the event triggered as much excitement as fear. It triggered questions that we've asked time and again over the course of our lives. The sight of a sky going from bright red to deep purple illuminated more questions than answers and caused us to wonder how humans could invest so much technology into killing our fellow humans.

And to what end?

ROBERT: LESSONS OF WAR

As early as the age of fourteen, I knew I was going to war. I do not know why. I just knew. Call it intuition. At that age, I asked my mom and dad if I could volunteer for the Marine Corps. When my dad asked me why the marines, I said, "Because they are the first to fight. They are the first to land on the beaches."

My dad just shook his head and suggested I wait until I was eighteen to make that decision.

I had seven uncles in my family who went to war. Four fought in World War II in Europe, members of the most highly decorated combat unit in U.S. military history, the 442nd Regimental Combat Team of the army. Members of this unit, mostly of Japanese American heritage, earned more than 18,000 individual decorations, including 9,486 Purple Hearts, and 4,000 Bronze Stars. There were twenty-one Medals of Honor, and the 442nd RCT earned five Presidential Citations in twenty days of Rhineland fighting, the only military unit ever to claim that achievement.

Their bravery helped stem much of the prejudice caused by the Japanese attack on Pearl Harbor. Many of the men in this unit had much to prove about their loyalty as Americans. This may be why they fought so hard and suffered such heavy casualties. Thankfully, all four of my uncles returned safely.

Two other uncles fought for America against the Japanese. One was taken prisoner in the Philippines and was part of the infamous Bataan Death March. Like many who were part of the one-hundred-mile trek, he was severely tortured by his captors and very fortunate to have survived. A book was written about his capture and his ordeal at the hands of the Japanese. The book is titled *A Spy in Their Midst*, written by Wayne Kiyosaki, my father's youngest brother. That uncle spent the rest of his military career in the U.S. Air Force in Japan and in the United States, working in the Office of Special Investigations. He even later worked with some of his former captors, forgiving them by saying, "The war is past, now" and "We do terrible things in war."

My uncle Wayne also served in the Korean War. He was fluent in a Chinese dialect and spent his time during that war interpreting Chinese message traffic, which flowed during that conflict.

Although I had seven uncles go to war, they did not affect my decision to fight, since they rarely spoke about the war. My father did not serve in the military. He volunteered but was classified unfit for the service because he had very poor eyesight, was too tall, and was underweight. Instead of going to war, he took a job as a schoolteacher in an extremely remote town on the Big Island of Hawaii. There he met my mom, who was a nurse in that sugar plantation town. Had he gone to war, he might not have met my mother or fathered four children or shared the life we had together.

When I graduated from high school in 1965, the specter of war affected my choice of schools. I applied to and received two congressional nominations: one to the U.S. Naval Academy at Annapolis, Maryland, and one to the U.S. Merchant Marine Academy at Kings Point, New York.

I accepted the appointment to Kings Point for four reasons: number one, my dad wasn't going to pay for my education. He felt I was such a bad student that paying for my college would be a waste of his money.

Number two, I found out Kings Pointers were some of the highest-paid graduates in the world, much higher than Naval Academy graduates, and even at a young age, money mattered to me.

Third, I knew I needed a very strict, disciplined environment. The University of Hawaii, where many of my friends went, would have been a big mistake; I would have flunked out immediately.

And number four, I wanted to travel the world by ship, to follow in the footsteps of the great explorers like Columbus, Cortez, and

Left to right: Robert, mother Marjorie, father Ralph, and sister Beth at Robert's graduation from the Merchant Marine Academy, on June 4, 1969. It was a proud moment. Emi noted, "I so wished to be there for Robert's graduation, too, but I was at home preparing for Erika's birth the following month."

Magellan. I got my wish, sort of. A year later, at the age of nineteen, I sailed into Cam Ranh Bay, Vietnam. The U.S. Merchant Marine Academy sent students to sea for a year on board merchant ships such as tankers, passenger liners, and freighters. During that year, students traveled throughout the world. I had hoped to be assigned to ships traveling to Europe and South America, but my first assignment, however, was on board a freighter carrying bombs to Vietnam, where I witnessed the Vietnam War firsthand.

Experiencing war that way, rather than from the movies or on television, deeply affected my outlook on the world. I wondered how we, as humans, could put such massive amounts of time, money, effort, and technology into killing each other.

While in Vietnam in 1966, I saw my first Buddhist monks. There they stood in their robes, holding their rice bowls and gathering handouts of food from people on the street. Give them food, and the monks would pray for you. If the rice bowl remained down, the monks would not receive anything from you, and you would not receive the monks' blessings. That's what we were told, and it bothered me.

In Sunday School we had been taught to "love your neighbor as you love yourself." There's nothing about whether the neighbor gave you food or not. I didn't understand what I saw, and considered it hypocrisy. It reminded me of my childhood church experiences where I'd watch people be pious in the sanctuary, and then cut each other off when leaving the parking lot.

Returning from Vietnam in 1966, I saw my first hippies in San Francisco. I didn't understand them either. Little did I know that my sister would later make both these paths—Buddhism and the peace movement—her own.

By 1968, around the time of the Tet Offensive in Vietnam and protests in the streets of America, dinner at home was an interesting affair. Mom and Dad were working for peace through the Peace Corps, my sisters were definitely against the war, and my brother and I were preparing to join up. Although we respected one another's points of view, there were differences in opinions. Mom and Dad were more or less neutral, allowing the children to form and hold their own opinions. I was less neutral. I thought my sisters were dreamers and traitors. I thought the guys they dated were draft dodgers, cowards, or hippies—certainly not "real men."

Although I loved my sisters, I did not really have much to say to them for years. War had split me apart from my family.

Two years later, in 1969, I graduated from Kings Point as a third mate and accepted a high-paying job with Standard Oil of California on one of its tankers. It was a good job with lots of security, just like my mom and dad wanted for me.

That lasted only six months.

Back in San Francisco, I saw the hippies' Summer of Love evolve into a life of drugs and angry protests. I carried a vivid memory of being spit at twice for wearing a military uniform, as well as recollections of long, scraggly-haired men and women coming up to me, offering flowers and saying, "Peace, brother." I thought all of them were cowards and losers. I thought they were wrong. Feeling an obligation to take a side, I gave up a high-paying job as a ship's officer with Standard Oil of California on board an oil tanker and volunteered to serve my country.

With the line drawn in the sand, I drove from California to Pensacola, Florida, to begin flight school. By 1971, I was back on the West Coast at Camp Pendleton for advanced training aboard helicopter gunships. In 1972, at the age of twenty-five, I was in Vietnam again. This time it was as a Marine Corps lieutenant and pilot of a helicopter gunship.

I volunteered for many reasons. Even though I was exempt from the draft because my classification as Non-Defense Vital Industry—namely oil—I decided it was my duty to fight for my country. I also volunteered because my younger brother Jon had done so. And, ultimately, I volunteered because I wanted to go to war. The mean streak in me, my dark side, wanted to fight. *I* wanted to fight. I wanted to know what "kill or be killed" felt like, and I wanted to get back to the rush I had felt at sixteen in that movie theater. I wanted to know if I had the right stuff. This was the war of my generation, and I didn't want to miss it.

Maybe it had something to do with the fact that my family on my father's side is from the Samurai, the warrior class in Japanese culture. Perhaps I believed I had a family tradition of the Samurai to uphold. Whatever the source of my commitment, I had drunk the military Kool-Aid, and felt I was carrying on the family tradition.

I continued to wonder how humans could put so much time, money, technology, and effort into killing, but deep inside I understood that killing is and would always be part of human make up. There have been wars throughout history and, unfortunately, there will be wars in the future.

Every society throughout history has had a warrior class. Cultures that are weak have always been conquered by cultures that have stronger armies. A warrior's job is actually to keep peace by being ready to go to war.

This is my way of saying that I am not against war. I am in favor of peace, and willing to fight for peace, as insane as that may sound to some people. To survive, to keep peace and flourish, a civilization needs warriors. In every city there will always be a need for the police, firefighters, doctors and nurses, civic leaders, workers, professionals, educators, and business people who are warriors at heart. People who go in there and fight to save a life—even give their own lives—when others cut and run to save themselves.

I began to believe peace and prosperity depended not just upon peacekeepers, but upon strong warriors. This, of course, was at odds with the beliefs of my parents and my sisters.

In the movie *Saving Private Ryan*, director Steven Spielberg portrayed the horrors and the heroics of war. It was nothing like the John Wayne, Hollywood-glamorized movies. We do not wear white hats in war. Had I known the realities, I might not have volunteered.

A highly decorated World War II veteran told me just before I left on my tour of duty that in his day, when a new guy joined the squad, that soldier had to be ready to shoot a prisoner in the face. It was an unpublicized rule of the battlefield. "Take no prisoners," a saying we use in business or life all too casually, meant "shoot the prisoners." Of course, that went against all the rules of war as we were taught. But in the war zone, where you are face-to-face with the realities of life and death, you do what you must to save the lives of the guys in your squadron, and your own life.

Thankfully, I never had to pull the trigger, but I was prepared.

In *Saving Private Ryan*, Tom Hanks's character could not kill the German prisoner, and the German prisoner ended up killing him.

In a way, this happens in business and in life every day. Beyond the brutal realities of survival, war taught me many things—more than I could have realized at the time. Over the years, I've been able to boil them down to three important lessons.

While at war, I painfully learned that *talk is cheap* and that *actions speak louder than words.* I know, those are sayings we've all heard before, but again, those were just words. I learned this truth through action. Many young men died because people on our side did not keep their word. They asked us to fight a war we had no reason to fight. Today, while I support our troops, I feel the same sense of betrayal from our leaders— leaders who are my age and of my era. Leaders who did not fight in Vietnam and did not learn the lessons we learned from fighting in the war of our generation. It seems to me as if many of those who ordered the invasion of Iraq conveniently missed the Vietnam War. Were they hippies in San Francisco or bureaucrats in Washington?

Again, I am not against war. There is a time and a place for war. What I am against is failing to learn the lessons—lessons that others died for decades ago—and are once again being ignored. Playwright George Bernard Shaw once wrote, "If history repeats itself, and the unexpected always happens, how incapable must Man be of learning from experience."

Another lesson that underscores the reason I am not against war is that, eventually, *war leads to peace.* England was our enemy on a number of occasions. Today, they are our strongest ally. The same is true for France, Germany, Italy, Mexico, and Japan. The United States had its own war between the North and South. Today we are all at peace and are all trading partners. War is often a precursor to trade, and trade brings peace.

It is generally bad for business to shoot your customers.

However, when wars are not fought to a conclusion—with a decisive winner—there is no peace. Instead, the war goes on for years, as it did between East and West Germany, North and South Korea, and North and South Vietnam. Today, East and West Germany are united, and North and South Vietnam are united and becoming prosperous. North Korea remains terribly poor and continues to be an unstable threat. Although costly in many ways, war—fought to a conclusion, it seems—is a faster way to peace.

Unfortunately, the Iraq war is not a war between nations; it is a war of nations, a war amongst tribes under the banner of religion. It's a thousand-year-old conflict, a re-run of the medieval crusades, except this time it is fought with updated weapons. And it will continue.

The third lesson is this: *Peace comes through prosperity*. Even though more people have been killed in the name of god and for national patriotism, most of us know that the real cause of war is money. As most of us know, the real issues underlying the Iraq war are not freedom or democracy, but oil and profit. War is very profitable. Many people and companies make fortunes on war.

That is why in 1974, I left the Marine Corps. I had had enough of war, and knew there had to be a better road to peace than war. Until 1974, I had spent my life studying to be a warrior. The government had spent a lot of money training me to be a warrior and to supply me with the tools of war. It was time for peace, and my search began.

It was this search for peace, and for answers to spiritual questions, that brought my sister and me back together again, many years later.

Today, I remain grateful that I did go to war and for the experiences fighting in a war offered me. In the Marine Corps, I gained a level of discipline and maturity I had not found, even at military school. As a marine, I met some of the finest men, both officers and enlisted, that I have come across in my life. Because of my wartime experience, I gained a deeper level of meaning for the words honor, courage, duty, respect, and integrity. I search for those same qualities in the people I do business with today.

War also taught me a lot about people and character. When we're faced with tough situations—in war and in life—our true colors show, and you will see that it brings out the very best in people. Or the very worst. We witness someone's true character and their strengths—or weaknesses—when they are faced with adversity or stress or the prospect of a life-or-death battle.

War is a true test of character.

In 2007, with a small group of friends, I met with Shimon Peres, winner of the Nobel Peace Prize, former prime minister of Israel and, at the time of the meeting, the president of Israel. During the nearly hour-long meeting, Mr. Peres said, "War unites. The price of peace divides." Explaining further he said, "Governments can only make war. We cannot make peace." He then talked about the privatization of peace, stating that it was in the best interest of business to keep the peace. It was his hope that by countries having a strong military, business could strengthen the peace process via business relationships between countries. As a Nobel Peace Prize winner, he was talking about peace through prosperity.

I came away from that meeting sensing that he held little hope of peace via government or religious efforts. As he said, "War unites." Unfortunately, I believe he meant that although people do not wish for war, they will rally *behind* a war and raise money to support that war.

When President Perez said, "The price of peace divides," I believe he meant that keeping the peace is expensive. The problem is this: No one wants to pay for peace. They want someone else to pay for it. So we keep having wars because war is profitable. It is easy to raise money for war. War creates jobs and brings prosperity.

As we know, the Iraq War is extremely expensive. Every state in the United States has at least one business that profits from this war. These are the businesses that build the weapons and supply the troops

Robert and Kim with Shimon Peres—president of Israel and winner of the 1994 Nobel Peace Prize, along with Yasser Arafat and Yitsak Rabin, for efforts to create peace in the Middle East.

with the tools of combat. For businesses such as Halliburton, Boeing, and General Motors, their biggest customer is the government, funded via the taxpayers' money.

To me, this means that businesses that work for peace need to work a lot harder. When talking about the privatization of peace, President Peres was saying that for there to be peace, peace needs to be a function of the business process because most businesses want prosperous customers, not dead ones.

Fast forward to September 11, 2001.

My wife Kim and I were in the air, making a final approach to Leonardo da Vinci airport in Rome at the very moment American Airlines flight 11 crashed into the World Trade Center.

Three days later, we were in Istanbul, Turkey, speaking to a group of Muslim businesspeople. I began my talk with these words:

"I was raised a Christian. I really do not know what the Muslim faith is about. I believe this is part of the problem, and I apologize for my lack of knowledge about your culture and your religion."

The title of my talk, which had been chosen several months earlier and well before 9/11, was "World Peace Through Business." It was either the best title or the worst title for this moment in history.

I began my talk about the importance of financial education, co-operation, and capitalism. It was about pulling people up via financial education rather than with government handouts. It was about peace through prosperity. It was not a talk about religion or war.

Standing on that stage in front of hundreds of Muslim men and women, I noticed three distinct styles of dress in three separate areas of the room: the clothing of the West, the colorful garments of the modern Middle East, and the black garments of the Muslim fundamentalist movement. I realized that my entire lifetime of experience up to that point had prepared me for that moment.

I could not speak as a warrior for war, but I could speak as a warrior for peace.

EMI: MYTH OF THE SAMURAI

I may hold an idealist's view of life. I've always revered my parents, family, and my teachers, expecting people to be noble, to fight the *good* fight.

At the same time as there are wars over boundaries of countries, there are wars inside of each of us, every day. I believe that these internal struggles are centered around our faults and delusions—those mental acrobatics that prevent us from finding peace and living the good life, however you choose to define it.

The good life is a simple one with inner peace, and it has been something I've been striving for since my teens. I expect people to value others and hold them as precious, to respect one another's differences, to work to benefit those around us, and to become the best we can be. Whatever our lifestyle and culture, what better challenge is there than this?

Many life lessons are still ahead for me, but those are the truths I believe in.

One of the first sayings of the Buddha is, "Hatred does not end by hatred; hatred ends by love." While this may seem simplistic in light of the complexities of war, it bears the seed needed for understanding and peaceful coexistence between warring factions across borders and between the warring factions within ourselves.

With naïve innocence, I trusted that my parents would protect us. I was confident that our country was good and would do things to benefit mankind. War and the threat of war evoke fear and suspicion in our minds. It is unsettling, polarizing, and heightens emotions, both good and bad. Perhaps it gives us greater meaning, stoking the fire of life into our otherwise complacent beings, helping us realize that life really *is* impermanent and could be snuffed out in an instant, in a flash.

And while the leaders of nations determine strategy in war, young men filled with bravado and purpose carry out orders for the love of country. Perhaps for each of us, our entire life's ancestry prepares us, sometimes in seemingly roundabout ways.

The Kiyosaki family is of the Samurai lineage and, in sharp contrast to my nonviolent views, I was proud of this. But my pride came from the sense of upholding righteousness over wrong, helping the oppressed, and being the noble keeper of peace. That was part of the Samurai tradition, and to me, the sword represented *this* power, rather than the violence that comes from greed and hatred.

Our parents did not speak of World War II very much, although the remnants of it and the military presence were all around us in Hawaii. Every island had military bases placed in strategic locations. Sometimes people would comment that the military had the best real estate in Hawaii.

It must have been extremely hard for people of my parent's generation to be of Japanese ancestry at that time. Still, our parents and friends shielded us from that stigma by being model citizens and community leaders. We Japanese have a strong, deeply conditioned manner of being reserved, yet a huge aspect of our culture is to be

The last samurai. This photo, of our great-great-great-grandfather, was taken around 1860. It was the end of the samurai as a noble class and the beginning of the gunpowder era. The sword and the samurai code have been handed down from first son to first son for generations. Our dad passed the sword down to Robert, just as his dad passed it on to him. The warrior's code lives within us all. All we have to do is call on it.

of service to others. Like so many my age, I held a childlike awe of the people around me and took pride in my family.

In Hilo, where we grew up, a large percentage of the population was Japanese, so perhaps I never really felt prejudice or discrimination, though over time and with the shifting trends of immigration, the Japanese Americans have become a minority today, even among the percentages of Asian Americans. We grew up in what we called the "melting pot of the Pacific" where all the different races and peoples lived together. With that base of experience, I could never understand why people had to fight and kill each other to resolve differences.

Occasionally, my father and brothers would go on hunting trips with other fathers and sons, loading up camping and hunting gear and taking off for weekend outings. Robert pursued this more than Dad or Jon and sometimes packed bows and arrows or fishing gear and spears and took off with his buddies. The guns and spears scared me the most, and I had an aversion to them. I found offensive the smell of killed game they brought back.

One day, I took out one of my brother's BB guns, and when no one else was around, I sat in our driveway playing with it. There was an empty lot across the street, so I took aim at a few bushes and branches and fired the gun. Then I spotted an unsuspecting bird sitting on the telephone wire and fired at it. The bird flapped its wings as it dropped to the ground. It shocked me so much, I raced over to the tangle of brush where I thought it had fallen, but I never found it. I hoped it was not hurt and was only hiding from me.

From then on, I never picked up his gun again.

I do not condone war, yet we do need mighty peacekeepers. The Tibetan people, whom I have been studying with since 1972, lost their country to Mao Tse-tung and Communist China in 1959 because they did not have a military force and were not prepared for the onslaught of an invasion. They enjoyed being left peacefully alone, which later rendered them vulnerable.

As my brother has said, "There had to be a better road to peace than war." But for the Tibetans, it begs the question posed in 2007 by the former Tibetan Cabinet Minister Kalon Pema Chhinjor: "Was it the Tibetan's insular focus on isolation and spiritual practice that caused the loss of their country?"

Applying this premise to my own life, I then must ask myself these questions: "Is my own insular focus on spirituality and avoiding conflict causing a war within me? Do we as individuals, as nations, become so involved and focused in one direction that we handicap ourselves?" These questions and the inevitable answers have brought me closer to Robert's world.

This book opened with a quote from F. Scott Fitzgerald:

The test of a first rate intelligence is the ability to hold two op-posed ideas in the mind at the same time, and still have the ability to function.

This is the challenge for each one of us and for communities and nations as well. How do we balance our worldly and spiritual aspi-rations, needs, and actions? Or is the reality more as Jacob Needle-man states in *Money and the Meaning of Life*:

Will is the power to live and be in two opposing worlds at the same time.

Can we live whole and free within these seemingly centrifugal forces of opposites: war and peace, wealth and spirituality?

I mentioned the pride I feel in being of the Samurai lineage. That emotion comes from viewing those traditions, in large part, as be-fitting the noble keeper of peace. We always had a huge, beautiful Samurai sword in our house. Dad, as the first son of the first son, must have inherited it from Grandpa and Grandma when he married Mom. I remember the occasion when we gathered around, and Mom and Dad gave the sword to Robert, because he, too, was the first son of the first son.

The informal yet pervasive dignity and power was imparted to us as being of Samurai lineage. Yet this holds a double-edged history. How could we have pride in being swordsmen? Samurai were esteemed as the protectors and defenders of our land, people, faith, and leaders, but they could also be marauders, thieves, and drones following corrupt warlords. Essentially, they kept the peace and held status.

Grandpa left the island Kyushu with his cousin to enter medical school in Tokyo. When they arrived and there was only one spot left,

Grandpa encouraged his cousin to take that one remaining spot. Grandpa eventually found passage with my grandmother's family on board a ship bound for Hawaii. Robert jokingly says it would have been a natural transition for a swordsman to become a surgeon, but that wasn't to be, in Grandpa's case.

Our roots developed in Hawaii; Great-Grandpa and Grandpa carried on the patriarchal lineage, and our family flourished. When the Samurai sword was transferred into Robert's hands, he also received a brass mirror for his future wife, which had been made before the time of glass production.

What did I receive?

Nothing. I was a girl. In this traditional hierarchy, only the first son received the inheritance. The place for women was not esteemed, and as young Japanese girls in Hawaii, we were taught this old school view from ancient Japan.

With little emphasis on church or school, though, and little attention in coaching us, helping with homework, or learning of our parents' aspirations for us, we enjoyed a lot of leisure time and freedom in our childhood. We were impacted more by events unfolding in our lives and the world around us than by being prodded toward particular life goals or directions.

I was always interested in psychology and ethics and received my undergraduate degree in psychology with an emphasis in gerontology—the study of aging. Early in my studies, Dad encouraged me to take another direction when he said, "Why do you study such pseudo-sciences like psychology? Why don't you go into the pure sciences, which are more exacting?" Dad was a mathematician and scientist, and those were the subjects he taught before he became an administrator.

I recall Dad asking similar questions of Robert over the years—why he wanted to go to war, why he *didn't* want one of the secure government jobs my dad had held for most of his working life. . . .

I had little understanding of the political reasons behind the war in Vietnam, but I was against violence as a means to resolve issues. Classmates were either being drafted or enlisted. Most of my friends were doing everything they could to avoid the draft or to get out of serving any way they could. There was so much polarization, and the lives of my two brothers in the midst of war seemed worlds away from me.

War and peace for me were internal struggles, and struggles I believe *everyone* faces.

I did not actively protest against the war in Vietnam because it caused me confusion and uncertainty. The reality of war fans our fears, driving us to engage in heinous acts justified and encouraged in the heat of battle. Too many people endure shocking atrocities because of aggression, hatred, greed, and acquisition. The sights of war—death, destruction, and violent protests—poured into our living rooms through television. I took the view of peaceful resolution, and held to the belief that conflict could be resolved through negotiation and non-aggression. "Hatred does not end by hatred; hatred ends by love" (Buddha).

But war ends when one side is overpowered and concedes to the victor, or through concessions and resolutions. Before that happens, though, chaos reigns in war, and we engage in the most heinous acts. I recall Robert's comments about the Vietnam War: "The reality there was that many young men died because people on our side did not keep their word."

Or, in the words of war correspondent Chris Hedges:

> *War exposes a side of human nature that is usually masked by the unacknowledged coercion and social constraints that glue us together. Our cultivated conventions and little lies of civility lull us into a refined and idealistic view of ourselves. But modern industrial warfare may well be leading us, with each technological advance,*

a step closer to our own annihilation. We too are strapping explosives around our waists. Do we also have a suicide pact?

Hedges states in his book *War Is a Force that Gives Us Meaning,* "Not less than 62 million civilians have perished" in the twentieth century, and "43 million military personnel [have been] killed" because of war.

I was stunned to learn how many more civilian casualties there were, and this does not include those who have been crippled and maimed by war, nor those emotionally scarred by loss, displacement, sickness, rape, poverty, and witnessing war's atrocities. How high the cost of this greed, fear, and hatred of others, each combatant holding to the view of that his side is more important, worthy, and right.

Delusions hold strong sway over us. According to educator and writer William James Durant, "There have been only twenty-nine years in all of human history during which a war was not underway somewhere." That is a sad testimony to humankind, when we think of the great things we have accomplished and our potential to achieve even greater benefits for our world. In the time encompassing "all of human history," could we not have resolved conflict with less grotesque means than war?

The outlook is not good and impels us to annihilation of the human race by our own hands. Aggression and hatred, old wounds, and the deluded thought that one can overpower another by building an arsenal and troops through military and political might, all perpetuate the delusion.

3

New Answers to
Old Questions

---

*War and natural disasters forced their way into our family. Their images
and realities influenced and defined each of us, and in many ways the nuclear blast we witnessed made life more precious and not something to be
taken for granted. Without the backdrops of the specter of global destruction and the Vietnam War, in this era and our lives, we might not have
begun our personal searches for our own answers to life and god . . . if
there was a god.*

*Although we were all baptized Christian, there wasn't much talk about
god in our home. We reserved prayer for before meals and for those special occasions such as Thanksgiving, Christmas, and Easter.*

*Mom went to church faithfully, but she went to different churches dur-
ing her lifetime. Although she spent most of her time at the Hilo Methodist Church, at Christmastime she gravitated to the church that had the
best choir and choir director. Mom especially loved that season and loved
singing Handel's* Messiah. *For a month before Christmas, the Kiyosaki
home reverberated with a 33 rpm record playing the "Hallelujah Chorus,"
over and over again.*

'A helping soprano'

Superintendent's wife's interests run from basketball to classical music

By Ligaya Fruto
Star-Bulletin Writer

To an interest in young people, a love of singing and an ability to adapt to any situation, add a pixie sense of humor and you get the essence of Mrs. Ralph Kiyosaki's personality.

The wife of the head of the State Department of Education is a nurse by training, but her life has been spiced with more variety than befalls the lot of a nurse or a housewife.

She has done private duty nursing and has worked with the Board of Health as a plantation nurse and as a doctor's clinic nurse — "all within three years," she chuckled.

After the former Marjorie Ogawa married Ralph Kiyosaki in 1946, she was able to do "only an insignificant amount of work — between babies."

She graduated from the St. Francis Hospital School of Nursing and was on the staff of the hospital for a while.

Then in Hilo, Hawaii, her home for 13 years, she got a job that she remembers as a highlight in her career.

"That Peace Corps job was such a pleasure," she said during an interview at her office at Chaminade College. She started as Chaminade's nurse and job placement counselor this fall.

"I love working with young people. They keep you on your toes. It's so stimulating.

"At the Peace Corps training center in Hilo, I learned to speak Malay and Thai, I learned greetings in Indian, Nepalese, Korean, and I even learned a Filipino song.

"Alicia (Mrs. Richard) Koller, who was born in the Philippines and had nine children at the time — she has 10 now — would sometimes leave all her children at home, come to the dispensary and we'd be singing away.

"The job itself was not interesting, just giving inoculations, treating ingrown toe-nails and common colds. But the people . . . You meet young people from different places, including such far away areas as Indonesia and Thailand and the Philippines. They come to teach languages and job in the training of American Peace Corpsmen.

"These Asian leaders have such wonderful ideas. Mostly young, they're just starting on their way up. You don't know where they'll end up, how high they'll go."

When asked the inevitable question of what she thought of her husband's job as school superintendent, she hesitated. "I am very confident of his abilities," she said.

"I feel that it is a great honor, his being selected for the job. But I was a little afraid when I first found out

GIFT FROM A FRIEND—Mrs. Ralph Kiyosaki smiles at the quietest member of her household, a stuffed blue-neck pheasant shot by a friend on Hawaii and presented to her and her husband when they left Hilo.

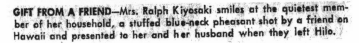

A news clipping from the *Honolulu Star-Bulletin* on Marjorie Ogawa Kiyosaki.
Mom managed to accomplish a lot while she was busy raising us.

Dad went to church only on rare occasions, the most memorable being those holiday times when Mom was singing with the choir. He enjoyed working in the garden, doing his art, and reading books. He seemed to find peace in the solitude.

Our parents emphasized education about as much as they emphasized religion. Even though our dad would one day become the superintendent of education for the State of Hawaii, he didn't push the importance of school on any of us children. If we came home with bad grades, he didn't

*say much. He made sure he was there to help us with our homework—
but only if we asked. We didn't even have the common parental pressures
of going to college to become a doctor or lawyer. Our parents let us each
search for our own answers according to our own interests.*

*This was the family environment that shaped the future of the four
Kiyosaki children.*

ROBERT: LOSS AND BETRAYAL

In 1970 our Dad—then the superintendent of schools—took the
biggest step of his life. He ran for lt. governor of the State of Hawaii
as a Republican. It was a suicidal step because Hawaii has for decades
been a stronghold for Democrats and labor unions. There was little
chance of his winning.

Before making his announcement, he called all of us kids and explained why he was taking such a politically disastrous step. It was
a tough decision because he was running against his boss, the governor of the State of Hawaii. If he lost, he was out of a job as the
head of education, a position he had dedicated his life to attaining.
Nevertheless, he went over the reasons with his wife and his four
children.

"There comes a time in each of our lives when we stand up and
do what is right . . . or we do nothing." He went on to say, "I can't
just keep doing my job and not say anything. This political machine
is very corrupt. If I win, I have a chance to make some changes. If
I lose, at least I can look myself in the mirror and know that I stood
up for what I believe is right."

He explained that this was the reason he would give up his job
and risk everything he had worked to achieve. He warned us that
the campaign would probably get nasty, even dirty, and that things
would be said that weren't true. He anticipated attempts to discredit
him and perhaps the entire family.

Schools Chief Quits to Run for Lt. Governor

By Tom Coffman
Star-Bulletin Writer

In an announcement surprising the political and education worlds, State Superintendent of Schools Ralph H. Kiyosaki revealed today he will run for lieutenant governor on the Republican ticket.

He submitted his resignation effective "as soon as possible."

Kiyosaki sent resignation letters to Gov. John A. Burns and the Board of Education. Kiyosaki, superintendent of education for three years, said, "I admit I am scared." "I am not a politician."

In the primary election he will run against Richard Sutton, a perennial candidate who has some following in the conservative wing of the Republican Party.

IF KIYOSAKI wins the primary, his presence could considerably strengthen the Republican ticket in the general election.

He said he knows and respects both Republican can-

didates for governor, D. Hebden Porteus and Samuel P. King.

There is evidence that the real relationship may be with King.

King and all of King's managers were on hand for the press conference.

He flew to Honolulu from Reno, Nev., where he is lecturing on family court law, just to be on hand for Kiyosaki's announcement.

KING, STANDING next to Kiyosaki before the opening of the conference, said, "I'm here to give moral support."

One of Porteus's aides was on hand, although Porteus wasn't. The aide said, "We weren't invited."

Kiyosaki said a lieutenant governor "should be more than a supervisor of elections — or a seat warmer in the Governor's absence.

"I believe the lieutenant governor should have a close, daily working relation-

Turn to Page A-19, Col. 1

Ralph Kiyosaki

Continued from Page 1

ship with the chief executive.

"I would expect to be the Governor's right hand man, his helper, and his principal administrator.

"I would expect to be in his confidence and by his side right down the line.

"I AM NOT interested in the office on any other terms."

Kiyosaki took office June 1, 1967, as superintendent.

He said he decided several months ago to quit the school department, but was unsure where he wanted to go.

He said, "I am seeking

elective office for a simple reason."

"IT WAS Republican Party friends who approached me and offered their support.

"And I agree with them that it is time for a change in the influences that move our State.

"I agree it is time for a change in attitudes. It is time to re-order our thinking."

Kiyosaki has never had a strong partisan identity, and today he appealed for the campaign support of "all my friends, whether they wear a political label or not."

This is the news clipping from the *Honolulu Star-Bulletin* announcing that Ralph Kiyosaki had resigned his post as state superintendent of schools to run for lt. governor—a race nearly impossible to win. He always wanted to give his best to the community. This event changed Dad and the family forever.

In spite of all this, he asked, "Do I have your support?"

We were all in agreement: we were with him, win or lose.

The Republican Party assured him that, if he were to lose the election, they would get him a high-paying job. After he lost, the job never materialized. At the age of fifty-one, he was out of work. Soon after the election, his wife Marjorie, our mother, died at the age of forty-nine. It seemed she took the defeat—and Ralph's fall from political prominence—harder even than her husband.

The loss of the election and the loss of his wife seemed to be more emotional trauma than he could handle. Although still a relatively young man in his early fifties, he never got his professional career back on track.

Until the election, his life had read like a textbook on success. He was a straight-A student, class president, valedictorian, and obtained his undergraduate degree in just over two years. As he climbed the ladder of the educational system, he continued his graduate studies by attending Stanford University, University of Chicago, and Northwestern University. He came close but never quite finished his Ph.D.

Losing the race for lt. governor was his first real setback in life. Until then, all he had known was success. After politics, he entered the world of business and soon found that success in academics is not the same as success in business. In a few years, both his early retirement payout and savings were depleted.

He died in 1991, at the age of seventy-two, having paid a very high price for standing up for his convictions. Just before he died, Dad was awarded an honorary doctorate degree from the University of Hawaii and was recognized as one of the top-two educators in Hawaii's history. Although weak from chemotherapy, he insisted on attending the award ceremony and wept as he thanked his fellow teachers for remembering him.

Dad's election loss and Mom's death took place in 1971, just as I was being sent to Vietnam. I wished I were at home to help with the campaign and be of moral support, but flight school in Florida didn't allow much time off. I got five days of official leave to attend Mom's funeral in Hawaii.

My father's political undoing sent a somber message to the family. More than just losing the election, it was one more example of how powerless people are to change things, to wrestle power from those *in* power. As most of us know, politics can be a very corrupt system. When our father ran for office, we knew he was a good man attempting to change things for the better. He was tired of the

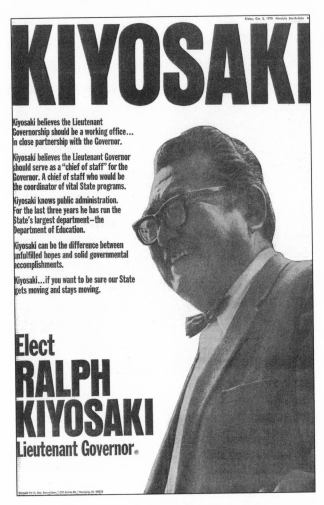

Campaign poster for Ralph Kiyosaki's ill-fated run for
lieutenant governor.

behind-the-scenes corruption running the State of Hawaii. His
crushing defeat signaled the harsh reality that being a good person
with good intentions isn't enough, especially when it pits you
against rich and entrenched power structures.

In January 1972, I was assigned to an aircraft carrier in the South
China Sea. School was over, and my real education began. A year

later, by January 1973, I was a different person. After a year of combat, I returned to the United States deeply disturbed from the experience of war. I wasn't traumatized by the war. I didn't have any emotional scars. Although I know that people had died due to my actions, I never killed anyone directly. From the point of view of a helicopter pilot, the war can be sterile, almost surreal. I never saw my enemy face to face. I didn't see their bodies once the battle was over. Every night, I flew home to the aircraft carrier, had a warm shower, a hot meal, watched a movie, and slept in a cozy bed in an air-conditioned room at sea far away from danger.

Yet I found myself disturbed by it all. I believe some of the same issues that caused my dad to run for politics were bothering me in Vietnam. About halfway through my tour, I got the sickening feeling that we were being lied to. I realized then that the United States did not wear a white hat. We weren't the good guys. We were not innocent. The Vietnamese were not welcoming us with open arms. I was not John Wayne, and we were not the heroes.

I felt as if my blind patriotism had been taken advantage of, and my ignorance was being exploited. The questions that assaulted me were unrelenting.

Was I fighting for America, or was I fighting for multinational corporations and their investors?

Was I fighting for freedom or was I killing for money?

Was I doing to the Vietnamese the same thing soldiers before me had done to the American Indians or the Hawaiian people?

Were we no different from a Christian Crusader and an Arab Muslim from the Dark Ages, killing each other in the name of the same god?

In our newspapers, the political spin was that we were fighting for the hearts and minds of the Vietnamese people, not for god or money. As combatants, we did our best to befriend and be kind to the Vietnamese people. They are truly wonderful people. The problem was, we never knew who the enemy was. This wasn't World War II. The enemy didn't have to wear uniforms and fight according to the rules. It was tough being kind to a child or a woman and at the same time being ready to kill them.

North Vietnamese men fought us while wearing U.S. uniforms. Many times, flying with Vietnamese on board, my crew chief had to keep a close eye on the troops we were carrying, never knowing which side the soldiers were really on. And I began to wonder, "If we are the good guys, why do the Vietnamese hate us? Don't they understand that we are fighting for their freedom?"

One day, after a particularly disastrous battle, I asked my commanding officer, "Why do their Vietnamese fight harder than our Vietnamese?" In a ready room, filled with about forty pilots, all exhausted and discouraged from our losses, my question was not well received.

A few days later, in a similar briefing, a pilot said, "Don't worry, we'll win this war. God is on our side."

Immediately, another pilot chimed in. "Well you'd better hurry and tell God. We're getting our butts kicked."

The room full of pilots laughed nervously.

Besides the patriotic philosophy that said we were fighting for democracy and freedom, there was always a religious undertone to our mission. Before arriving in Vietnam, we were told that we were fighting communists and that communists did not believe in God. Many of the pilots *did* believe that we were fighting for God, and that God was on our side. One pilot went so far as to wear an embroidered patch that read, "Kill a Commie for Christ."

Our squadron commander had him remove the patch.

With my own eyes, I could see that most of the Vietnamese were very religious people. They may not have believed in the same god we did, but they appeared to believe in god. Most homes prominently displayed different religious symbols. There were magnificent Catholic cathedrals in the major cities.

After a while, I also began to wonder who was pulling the strings. Who was stirring things up? Who were the master puppeteers? Who could get sane men to kill each other? The more I thought about it, the less I hated my enemy. I realized the enemy soldiers were just like me, fighting out of fabrications of patriotism, never knowing the whole story. Most were fighting me because I was there fighting them. I thought I was right. They thought they were right. It became obvious to me that for many, war is caused by our need to be right—and make someone else wrong.

Sitting alone late at night, on an aircraft carrier at sea, gave me a lot of time to think. I realized how wrong I had thought my draft-dodging classmates were. I *made* them wrong for seeking any way possible to avoid serving their country. I realized how wrong I had made my parents for joining the Peace Corps, and my sisters for protesting the war. I realized how right I thought I was: right for being brave, patriotic, and fighting for my country.

One night it dawned on me that we were all working for the same thing—peace. I realized that my enemy was also fighting for peace. Sitting alone that night, it seemed insane that we—as humans—would invest so many of our resources into fighting and killing for peace.

The more I contemplated the subject of war, the more I realized that war would always be a part of the human condition. As long as we thought in terms of right and wrong, there would always be wars, fights, disputes, and arguments. If not wars against countries, then wars in politics, religions, and business. Even between husband and wives, friends and families.

On that very dark and windy night, sitting on the deck of the aircraft carrier, my war against the Vietnamese ended, and my search for my own personal peace began. That night, I knew that for me to find my own peace, I needed to control the war raging in me.

In 1974 the Marine Corps brought me up on charges and threatened me with a court-martial. By this point, I was done being the good boy. I had worn a military uniform for nearly ten years—four years at the academy and six years as a marine—and I was tired of following orders. I had become emboldened after flying in combat for a year, facing death for a year, crashing my helicopter three times and surviving. I believed I was invincible, super human, overconfident in my abilities, or should I say, overconfident in what I could get away with.

The charges I faced didn't seem all that serious to me. I was a party animal just having fun. Instead of the quiet, polite boy who left Hilo in 1965, I was a man with my dark side in full view. My crime was that I would go into Waikiki, strike up conversations with attractive young women at bars, and ask if they wanted to take a helicopter ride to a deserted island. At first they would think I was joking, but it wasn't hard to convince them that I was dead serious, especially since all the other guys at the time had long hair and I had a marine crew cut.

On Friday evenings I would check out a helicopter from the squadron, fly to a beach nearby, and load the aircraft up with beer and women. Fifteen minutes away—a short flight across the water to a remote island—my co-pilot and I would land on the most beautiful deserted beaches in the world. It was heaven on earth, the lifestyle of the young and delirious!

We'd return on Sunday night.

One Sunday night, after dropping the girls off, I landed back at my squadron. As soon as I shut the engine down, three MP squad cars pulled up. I opened the door of the helicopter, and the first things that fell out were beer cans that then rolled across the tarmac. The next thing that fell out was me—a U.S. Marine who, instead of being dressed in a fireproof flight suit with boots, was wearing swim trunks and rubber slippers.

It was pretty bad, and it quickly got worse when the MPs discovered a cooler full of lobsters, a dead deer I had shot from the air, and women's underwear in the passenger compartment. For some reason they didn't see any humor in the situation.

I was immediately removed from flight status and placed under house arrest—which wasn't so bad because I lived in Waikiki, which most would agree is close to paradise. For five months, the military attorneys prepared their case against me, occasionally calling me and asking questions. The problem was that I lied. In fact, I had to lie over and over to cover my earlier lies. Pretty soon I couldn't keep my story straight.

The marines taught me how to willingly give my life for a higher purpose, and to have no fear. They gave me strength of character, but what was considered bravery in Vietnam was deemed recklessness back at home. My strength of character had become my character flaw. My personal checks and balances were gone, and I lived my life with complete disregard for others and the law.

I did so simply because I thought I could.

They say character is destiny, but so are our character flaws.

That same year the Watergate hearings led to the resignation of President Richard Nixon. The U.S. House of Representatives had initiated impeachment proceedings, charging him with obstruction of justice, abuse of power, and failure to comply with congressional subpoenas. On August 5, 1974, the president admitted that he had ordered the FBI to halt its investigation into the Watergate burglary. On August 9, Nixon resigned, becoming the first president in history to do so.

Nixon's vice president, Spiro Agnew, had resigned earlier, in 1973, after evidence was uncovered of political corruption. He eventually pleaded no contest to charges of income tax evasion. Speaker of the House Gerald Ford became vice president upon Agnew's resignation in 1973, and then president in 1974 when Nixon resigned. One of the first things President Ford did was grant a full pardon for Nixon, squashing any possibility of criminal proceedings against the former president.

As the Watergate scandal was being exposed, I was being honorably discharged from the Marine Corps. It seemed as if the corruption that had fueled my dad's run for political office was being exposed. Much of the corruption I had seen in Vietnam was finally being brought to light.

"Finally," I thought to myself, "integrity is being brought into the system. Maybe there *are* honest people in government."

When the non-elected President Gerald Ford pardoned former President Nixon, granting him immunity from all of his crimes, my faith in government and the political process was destroyed.

I was disillusioned.

I began to look for new answers to old questions, such as: *Am I powerless as an individual?*

I thought I had gone to school to gain some personal power. As a young man, I had heard former President and General Dwight D. Eisenhower warn the world about the power of the military industrial complex. In Vietnam, I had witnessed firsthand what President Eisenhower was concerned about. The military industrial complex *had* taken control. I had gone to school and trained to be a soldier and an employee of the military-industrial complex.

After watching a senseless war rage on, I wondered if anyone of us had any power to bring peace to the world.

Why do dishonest people win?

It seemed to me that might *did* make right. It seemed that if I was powerful, I would be above the law. I would not have to obey the rules. I could make and play by my own rules.

President Nixon got pardoned and President Kennedy was assassinated. I began to wonder if honesty *was* the best policy. It seemed to me that crime *did* pay. Questions begat questions. Why did bad things happen to good people?

Can I make a difference?

Mom and Dad had always worked hard to be of service. That was why they volunteered for the Red Cross, Civil Defense, and the Peace Corps, on top of working at full-time jobs. They believed their lives made a difference, even if in very small ways.

I had joined the Marine Corps to make a difference. I now had questions that needed new answers. I now wondered what *I* could do to make a difference, even if only in a small way.

Is there a god?

I wondered why god was not fair. I wondered why some people were rich and so many were poor. I wondered why some people were born with better health. I wondered why god seemed to be so cruel to some people, yet blessed others.

Why are more people killed in the name of god?

Why was I so average?

By the age of twenty-five, I realized that I did not have any special talents. I was pretty much an average person. I was not smart in school, nor was I a gifted athlete or especially talented. How could I be successful if I was average?

Did I need to find my own answers?

By 1974, I had done what my parents and society recommended. I had gone to school, attended church, served in the military, voted, and got a job. But I had not found the answers I was searching for in any of those institutions.

I flew in Vietnam from January of 1972 to January 1973. When my Vietnam tour ended I was assigned to the marine squadron at Kaneohe Bay, Hawaii.

In June of 1974, I was honorably discharged from the Marine Corps.

In 1975, the U.S. lost the war. Although the Vietnam War was over, *my* war continued on. At the time, I did not realize how deeply the war had disturbed me.

EMI: THE SWORD CUTS

At the time Robert left for New York to attend the U.S. Merchant Marine Academy in 1965, the stable family dynamic began changing. The protective bubble of family, overseen by Dad, was disintegrating.

In 1966, I graduated from high school, and it was my turn to leave the sleepy little town of Hilo. My destination was the dormitories at the University of Hawaii and the big city of Honolulu. Even the move to another island was a big change for me. Just the same, I adapted and made new friends there. I did not keep in touch with many of my friends from Hilo; we didn't have much in common, it seemed, after I moved away.

In 1967 Dad was nominated by the board of education to be the state superintendent of education for the State of Hawaii and so the rest of the family packed up and moved to Honolulu. It was a difficult move for Mom, who had to oversee everything. My grandmother, Dad's mother, was in failing health, and we flew to Maui several times to help her. I clearly remember Dad saying that he would take this superintendent's post for three years.

He accomplished so much during that time and was in the papers constantly, introducing new structures and trying new ideas for the schools, revitalizing old ways that had heretofore hindered a child's education. In Kona, schools started in December; child labor was utilized to pick coffee beans in the fall months. Dad convinced the local farmers to allow children to keep up and pushed the start date for the new school year back to September. He also took a boat to the private island of Niihau, encouraging the leaders there to allow the children to come to the Kamehameha School in Honolulu, furthering their education opportunities, helping to break tendencies of generations of family intermarriage that was leading to genetic weakness.

Honolulu was a city full of opportunities, and while in school there I attended theater productions and alternative film series and read books by intriguing authors and playwrights. It was as if a whole new world had opened up to me within the city. In my first year at the university, I met a guy from Long Island, New York. He came from a town not far from the academy where my brother was in school. Bob Murphy was a good-looking Irish Italian and had gorgeous eyes. He was fun and a great dancer, and we became friends. Over time, he went back to New York, and we exchanged letters during our freshman summer.

I found my passions and my awakenings through outside interests and friends, *not* the structured classroom of the university. And my grades showed it. By the end of my sophomore year, I was on academic probation. I decided I needed to take a break from school.

Of course, I was embarrassed to tell my parents about being on probation; after all, my dad was the state superintendent of education. But I broke the news to them, and, as expected, they weren't happy. But as always, they allowed me to find my own way.

The break gave me the opportunity to get away and do what I really *wanted* to do rather than what I felt was expected of me. The new hippie counterculture was calling, and so was San Francisco. And so, in the summer of 1968, I grasped my first opportunity to leave Hawaii and travel. In the fall and winter I stayed in Berkeley, California, and struggled with the cold weather.

One day I received a surprise call from Robert; he was on a stop in San Francisco on a ship, so I took a bus to meet him in the city. He wanted to take me to lunch and being the poor city hippie, I was ready to duck into the first diner or restaurant we passed. But

Robert, always appreciating good food, suggested that we keep on walking and find a good place. He was wearing his white U.S. Merchant Marine Academy uniform, and we headed to Fisherman's Wharf for lunch.

As we walked we approached three long-haired, bearded hippies. They pushed away from the wall and street lamp where they were lounging and moved to talk to Robert. The blatant visual contrast of the shorn military man and the peaceniks was striking. As he ended the conversation and we proceeded on our walk, Robert told me that two of them were graduates of the academy who had "dropped out" to live in San Francisco!

It was an amazing time to be on the West Coast. The Beatles had just returned from India, and they were popularizing Eastern music in Western culture. New ideas and openness were flourishing. And I was looking for the place and people that created an environment where I could study and learn.

The counterculture was blossoming, but so was an emerging culture of spirituality. And even though I was at the epicenter of free love and marijuana, I realized it would take more than just a relocation to break me out of my shy, island-girl mentality. I missed my friends in Honolulu; I was homesick and tired of the cold and the drab of the mainland. After a few months in San Francisco, I was out of cash and had lost my passion for being there. This wasn't my place, I realized.

So I moved back to the islands.

When I returned to Hawaii I continued to hang out with my friends from the university, but didn't go back to school. Bob Murphy and I reconnected when I moved back to Honolulu, and we began spending time together. Our friendship became romantic and in December of 1968, I learned I was pregnant. The prospect of dropping this bombshell on my parents made telling them I was on academic probation seem easy.

"Is he going to marry you?"

Those were the first words Dad said to me. In my parents' eyes, there was only one choice in the matter. But I was already in a dizzying swirl with the idea that I was going to be a mother, not to mention morning sickness and body changes. Slowly informing friends and families was hard, too. It was a tremendous leap to think of marrying the person whom I had known from school yet had only been dating for three weeks.

Yet my own choice, my own freedom, didn't appear to be options. I felt I had to do what was respectful for the family, so Bob and I got married in February of 1969. My daughter Erika was born later that same year. And while I loved Erika's father, I really didn't *want* to be married. Nevertheless, I did what was expected of me, as I had at other turning points in my life.

When Dad announced that he would run for lieutenant governor, I found myself nervous and uncertain. I did not understand the politics of the day. Because of this, and even though I loved Dad and respected his work and aspirations, I did not feel I could go out and campaign for him. I had an infant daughter to care for and was still adjusting to married life.

Erika was a beautiful and even-tempered child. Everyone loved her. I assumed total responsibility for raising her, and I wanted our relationship to be one of love and friendship, not of burdens or unhappiness. I had to look deeply into what I wanted to do in life and how I could do that as a young mother. While some aspects of my future were still to be determined, one aspect became very clear to me.

I could not remain in my marriage. Although I didn't know what I wanted to do, exactly, I *did* know marriage wasn't it. I was still searching for my place. For two years my husband and I both worked to "make a go" of our situation, but finally Erika's father and I separated and later divorced.

When I think back on my brief marriage, I recall it as a difficult and painful time because my reasons for marrying Bob had been from obligation and concern for Erika and doing things right, not because of happiness and love. I remember this time as one of confusion and uncertainty punctuated by several devastating months for Dad. At times it felt as if he were forced to endure more than any one person should have to bear.

He lost the election in November 1970, and in December Mom and Dad sent out lovely Christmas cards to everyone, thanking them for their support and looking ahead to the New Year. The months that followed were emotionally charged and changed Dad's world forever.

In January 1971, I returned to live at home as a single mom.

In February, Dad's father, who lived with us, passed away.

One month after that, in 1971, Mom died suddenly.

Three devastating losses, in rapid succession, coupled with two sons who were fighting the war in Vietnam, all took their toll. Dad was never the same again.

I have vivid memories of the day Mom died. She had been at home making tuna sandwiches for Erika, herself, and me. She said she felt her heart beating erratically and went to lie on the couch in the living room. She asked me to get a wet paper towel to wipe off her hands and to call my father.

Dad was working for the teachers' union at the time. He came home right away and Mom kept saying she didn't want to die. Dad tried to comfort her saying, "You're not going to die....Don't worry." He called the doctor, who told him to take her to Saint Francis Hospital because he was working there that day.

Mom died on the operating table, and Dad called me to come to the hospital. When I got there, he grabbed me to take me to see Mom. He was so overcome and emotionally drained he dropped his

The Kiyosaki family portrait taken after the unexpected death of our mother Marjorie, the day of her funeral. Dad wanted to have this photo taken, as Robert and Jon had to fly back to their military posts during the Vietnam War. The family put on a good face for the outside world, but inside there was much strife. This was four months after Dad lost the bid for lieutenant governor, and it must have been an unbelievably difficult time for him. Top row, left to right: Jon, Ralph, Robert. Bottom row: Emi, her daughter Erika, and Beth. You can see the stress on Dad's face.

arm on my shoulder like dead weight. Mom lay on a metal table in a white surgical gown, and there was already a white foam coming from her mouth. Dad seemed to know these signs of death. The whole event was dizzying because it happened so fast.

It took several days to retrieve Robert and Jon from Vietnam and Thailand for the funeral services, and Beth flew home from California. There must have been more than a thousand people at Mom's funeral, the result of the active role Ralph and Marjorie played in their community, the way Mom drew people to her with her kindness, and Dad's recent stint in the political spotlight. After a few days Robert,

Jon, and Beth had to return to their assignments. I can only imagine the kind of shock these men in war, my brothers, were facing.

All too soon they were gone again, and I was alone with Dad and Erika.

At the time I was too traumatized by my own life experiences to consider—and fear—the possible loss of my brothers. After the endless streams of people and mountains of mail, the absence of Mom and Grandpa echoed in the house. I could feel the tug of family obligations pull at me again.

Dad had lost so much in such a short time. Suddenly, Mom wasn't there to cook, run the errands, pay the bills, and Dad lost his post as superintendent of education.

There I was with Erika, living with Dad in a house full of memories and cluttered with Mom's and Grandpa's things. Dad had the huge and daunting task ahead of him that included taking over managing the household finances since that had been Mom's role, and he had never paid attention to them. I remember his remarking one day that he had, only a month prior, signed a new life insurance policy and paid one dollar more to cover Mom for an additional $1,000 death benefit when he became head of the teacher's union. He also shared his surprise to learn that Mom had charged all the credit cards to the maximum and made only minimum payments each month.

Sitting in the kitchen, Dad started pouring over mom's cookbooks and soon became a fantastic chef. He experimented a lot, just as he had with his artwork. Dad was a creative and talented artist who sketched and painted as well as crafted wood sculptures and mobiles.

Ralph Kiyosaki was a product of his time—"born into history," as Robert puts it. He and my mother, the World War II generation, lived at a time when the ethic extolled hard work, with employees often staying with one company for an entire life career, followed by a retirement enhanced by government support. My father was an extraordinary man. His moral bearing, service to others, his brilliance of mind in art, science, mathematics, nature, and literature, as well as his interest in and care for the peoples of Hawaii, are now part of Hawaii's history.

He was a futurist and contemplated the consequences of actions taken in the Education Department and how they would affect future generations. He was liberal in initiating new programs and redeveloping the city of Hilo after a disastrous tidal wave. My father was a generous man.

He also had a hot temper and could be impatient. When he saw the need for something, he didn't want to wait to see change initiated.

When those who had encouraged Dad to leave his post as Superintendent and run for political office abandoned him, the loss, the broken promises, and polarization impelled by the political machine caused a fracturing of old allies and familiar territory. Sometimes dad spoke of moving to the mainland and getting a fresh start, but he loved Hawaii and never left.

These were difficult times, and obviously Dad needed emotional support. Many people, family and friends alike, said, "Now you can take care of your father."

While it may have seemed logical, it wasn't an option for me. I could not just stay at home and assume the dutiful daughter role. Dad had his grieving to go through, but he was fifty-one and was still in his prime. I was coping with divorce, trying to be the best mother I could be for Erika, all the while searching for answers to the questions that haunted me.

During my short marriage and this period of living at home, I questioned the purpose of life. What was I destined for? In just a few years, I had gone through youth, education, marriage, motherhood, and divorce. What was left? Old age and death? I was in the midst of that, too, living in my dad's house.

The whole process seemed like a tragic reality with little freedom of choice. Perhaps because marriage and single motherhood had come unplanned, I felt as if circumstance had suddenly wrenched away from me my youth and my freedom. I needed to break away from family commitments. I am sure my physical presence—and Erika's—would have been of some comfort to Dad, but he had much to sort out about the world of the teachers' union, the department of education, the aftermath of politics and elections, and being a widower. These were things I could not share with him.

At this point in my early life, we didn't talk much or discuss things in depth, and I knew I had to move on. We became closer in his later years, and while I had a constant, fierce love and devotion for my father, even during those dark days, we both knew that it was time for me to grow and explore the new horizons that were calling.

From the time Erika was two, I regularly arranged one day a month for us to do things together as "friends" rather than as mother and daughter. We'd go to the movies or the beach or sit at a beautiful lookout and talk. During those days, I consciously put aside my parental disciplinary role, we would chat about anything under the sun, and simply enjoy each other's company. I got to know her as her own person rather than as my charge in those days. I resolved to create a relationship where we could talk about everything, and tried to give her unconditional love and support.

Observing death in our lives has had a profound impact on me, as a child and still today. It's that war and peace that we need to settle within ourselves, facing the fact that we all—one day—will die. So given that fact, I have pondered the question, "How do we live?"

Between 1971 and 1973, Erika and I were making our way through life together and the decisions I made about friends and relationships—even when to stay put and when to move on—were made with her in mind. Many of my choices may have appeared foolish to others at the time, but I was trying to balance the responsibilities of motherhood with my own search for answers to what this life was all about.

Erika's father tried very hard to be understanding and supportive, but my wanderings tried his patience. I spent what little money I had on attending seminars and talks, and few could understand why. At an event with Werner Erhard, founder of EST—Erhard Seminars Training—I couldn't quite believe how happy, friendly, and competent everyone seemed. I wondered if their lives were always like that, or if it was an act.

The two-weekend EST seminar actually helped me break out of my shyness and also helped me communicate with Erika.

In 1973, while Robert was landing on remote beaches and our country was trying to impeach President Nixon, Erika and I moved on and retreated into the lush landscapes of the Big Island of Hawaii. These were some of the new horizons I had been searching for, and there I found my kind of people; people living off the land, farming, learning and studying alternative technologies, and practicing spiritual disciplines, vegetarianism, fasting, meditation, and tai-chi.

I gravitated toward friends who lived near the Kilauea volcanoes and made geodesic dome houses designed by R. Buckminster Fuller. Living in these domes was fantastic. In temperate Hawaii, the domes were often constructed of clear plastic sheeting stapled onto plywood struts. Imagine living in an almost see-through house in a forest amid twenty-foot-high ferns. Sometimes the night sky would glow dark red due to the volcanic fountains spewing molten lava from earth fissures and recesses that came from Kilauea a few miles away.

One dome we lived in was a small, two-story house with the clear dome on top and a hexagonal room below. We had huge wooden barrels placed on the platform of the second floor that caught abundant rain, and gravity provided running water to a sink downstairs. My friend Joe made an umbrella top out of clear plastic, and it would swivel so that on rare sunny days we could open up the roof of the dome to the skies.

Three-year-old Erika loved living there. She had a sliding board outside that ran from the second floor of the dome to the ground floor. And on cold, rainy days, a gigantic iron wok seated into an old telephone cable spool gave off warm heat as our fireplace.

The Volcanoes National Park area where we lived was about four thousand feet in elevation, cold, wet, and continually enveloped in a bank of clouds. Ferns grew very high, and the vegetation was dense and wet and not easily penetrable. Occasionally, we would drive to the dormant but steaming volcanic craters nearby and climb down into some of the larger vents, strip down to our flip-flops and take steam baths.

Living the alternative life was great, and while there was a growing tendency toward asceticism, I had a strong need to incorporate more spiritual paths of practice into my life.

During one of our innocent adventures, several of us made an appointment to meet a Zen master. We were to meet his disciple, named Ananda, at a turnoff in the backwoods of a volcanic area in Puna. The altitude was lower, the weather dryer and hotter, and the vegetation very different. We met Ananda at the designated place, then traveled a few miles over dry backroads thick with grass, not knowing where he was leading us. As we followed, we could hear the sound of the dry grass sweeping underneath the car. As we traveled further into the unknown, one person declared, "This is your last chance to back out; it's now or never!"

We finally arrived at a clearing where there were two South Pacific–style buildings with a wood floor, thatched roof, four tree-trunk pillars, and no walls. The Zen master lived in the larger building, and Ananda and his wife lived a short distance away in the second building. The teacher had gone to town, so our wait was long, and when he finally arrived, Ananda went to speak with him. When he returned, he told us to come back next week, as his teacher was drunk!

We felt we were being tested and needed to persevere.

Finally we got to see him, and when we did he frequently spoke in parables. The most disconcerting thing, however, occurred when he stopped to call the cats to come to eat. His voice boomed out over the dry, grassy lands and from out of the underbrush, from under the trees, and from all directions, many dozens of cats came leaping into his shack, flooding the entire place.

He rescued cats wherever he found them. Many were sick and mutilated with oozing, open sores and cancerous growths. There were blind, fat, beat-up toms, skinny, mangy cats of every size and color. The shelter was dirty; it was disgusting to sit on any chair because of cat hair, refuse from their sores, and bits of food.

Yet we refused to give up on learning the Zen master's teachings. One time we met at a park in the mountains and started a fire in the shelter hearth since it was cold and rainy. The master spoke of strict training he'd experienced in his monastery in Japan and of the difficult, final test retreat for handpicked aspirants who strove for years to qualify. Every morning they had to break thick ice formed in the water barrels in which they bathed and then wash in freezing conditions before sitting in meditation for hours every day.

Just as we became engrossed, he pulled out a thick, bloody, dripping, two-inch steak from mounds of butcher paper and threw it right onto the open coals. That completely repulsed Joe, who was the strictest raw-food vegetarian. With that he couldn't listen to the teacher anymore.

In this way we jumped through mental hoops and embarked on adventures, seeking and finding gurus and teachers and living in spiritual traditions. I devoured books explaining many paths, chronicling the lives of fantastic yogis, practitioners, and teachers, and strove to find a spiritual community where I could meditate and develop a life inclined to spiritual practice.

During a visit to Honolulu to see my dad, I met Ward, a young man who had just returned home to visit after four years in India, Nepal, and Sikkim. His parents had given him a trip around the world as a high school graduation present, and he ended up living in India. I was fascinated by stories of his teacher, the Sixteenth Gyalwa Karmapa, of his studies with the Tibetan masters who were establishing their lives in exile in the Indian Himalayas after escaping from the Chinese Communist takeover in Tibet. I wanted to learn everything I could about their teachings, but there was little available in the United States in those early years.

When I left the dome life, I moved to Wood Valley Temple in Pahala, a small town also on the Big Island of Hawaii about fifty miles from Hilo. My parents had first met there after World War II while Dad was working as a teacher's supervisor and Mom as a nurse. I remember Mom and Dad taking me to the temple as a little girl and feeling scared because it was overgrown and had a reputation of being haunted.

Years later, I found myself living in this same temple, which was a little spooky. No sooner had I moved in than my friends left for a time, and I found myself alone in the eerie, isolated forest for two weeks. The place had no electricity, just dim kerosene lamps that barely penetrated the darkness.

It got worse.

The water, which was often polluted, made us sick, and we kept having to find ways to deal with it. This was during the energy crisis of the mid-seventies, which included gas rationing. So leaving the temple—which was situated five miles from town through the cane fields—wasn't an option because we had to minimize fuel consumption on the temple truck.

Once the others returned to the temple and we settled into the routine, things got better. During the gas shortage, on occasional designated fuel days, one of us would leave at 4 o'clock in the morning and spend most of the time in a gas line. It was these times of crisis for the environment and the economy that reinforced my desire for a simple lifestyle, in harmony with nature.

We had a regular schedule of repairing, preparing, and painting the temple. I attended classes held twice a day. There were only a few of us there, and it was clearly one of the best times in my life. The classes seemed to deliver everything I was searching for. The Tibetan Buddhist teachings were so rational, and the views of karma, consciousness, rebirth, and the nature of things suited me perfectly. Being isolated in a remote valley away from the city, I felt unencumbered, focused, and able to sustain a simple lifestyle without big-city distractions.

Erika was four at the time and didn't have to attend school. There was another couple living at the temple, and they had two young children, so Erika's days were filled with play, and we read many books together. We were all living in harmony with the earth, rising with the sun and going to sleep when darkness set in. It felt a bit like coming home.

Being raised in a Japanese culture, I was exposed to Buddhism as a young child. The life of the Buddha was familiar to me for that reason and because, coincidentally, my brother, Robert, was born on Buddha's birthday.

I remember going to a Japanese Buddhist service and asking my dad what the minister was chanting. He said it wasn't Japanese, so he had no idea. I later learned it was recitation in Sanskrit, common in Mahayana Buddhist traditions. Years later, in Wood Valley, the teachings were translated, so that they became tangible and clear. It was extraordinary.

I was finding my spiritual family, my home and my path.

In 1974, after living a year at the temple in Wood Valley, we heard that the Sixteenth Karmapa, Head of the Kagyupa Lineage of Tibetan Buddhism, was making a historic first trip to the United States. Many traveled to San Francisco to see him, and Erika and I were among them. After living in the isolated valley in Hawaii with our friends, attending the Black Crown ceremony with thousands of people was overwhelming. The event was regal, beautiful, and somewhat otherworldly.

The historical Black Crown was an ancient offering by celestial female beings to the Karmapa. During the ceremony, the hat is held up, and it's said that those persons who have a karmic connection with the Karmapa will be able to see the celestial female beings making this offering. In my innocence, I hoped that a full year of sincere study and helping repair a temple would merit me such a sight. But it didn't.

We followed the Karmapa, traveling north by car as far as Vancouver, Canada, attending the events all along the way. It was there that I first took my Refuge Vows to become a Buddhist, along with the five lay vows where I promised to not kill, steal, lie, commit sexual misconduct, or take intoxicants.

I took those Buddhist vows very seriously and wanted to keep them with heartfelt conviction. There were so many people there taking the Refuge Vows that we had to go in groups of about seventy-five people at a time. I asked my friends to watch Erika while I went in with my group, and when I came out I couldn't find her for a few minutes.

I was frantic, of course, but then a group emerged from their Refuge Ceremony and out walked little Erika, fresh from taking vows with the group! We had both taken our vows on the same day.

From Canada, Erika and I left our group of friends. I made arrangements to go to Boulder, Colorado, to study with Chogyam Trungpa Rinpoche. When I had met him briefly in San Francisco, he suggested that I move to Marpa House in Boulder, near the University of Colorado.

We settled in and I immediately signed up for a private interview with Trungpa Rinpoche to seek guidance, to discuss my direction and practice, and to have him advise me on my decisions for the future. I attended talks at Karma Dzong, the Buddhist center in town, and participated in the activities and daily meditation at Marpa House.

Trying to make a life there, I enrolled Erika in a preschool nearby and looked for work. That proved extremely difficult since Boulder—a college town—had ample talent, and I had few skills to offer. Plus I was on a short leash, juggling the care of Erika, dealing with the challenges of having no car, and owning few cold-weather clothes.

Overall, I found the community there confusing. I was a new Buddhist, having just taken my Refuge Vows and having lived most recently in a remote, austere forest temple. Suddenly I was dropped in the midst of a party atmosphere with all sorts of drinking and carousing. My responsibilities to Erika kept me out of too much trouble, as did my vows not to take intoxicants, but it wasn't the spiritual experience I had imagined.

Otherwise, in the Tibetan Buddhist tradition studying with a qualified teacher is important, and I finally had the access to real teachers, attending talks by Trungpa Rinpoche and Tibetan language classes with a Tibetan man who lived at Marpa House. After four months, I was finally granted a ten-minute personal interview with Trungpa Rinpoche, so Erika and I trudged off in the snow for the meeting.

I shared with him my indecision, my questions: Should I continue studying in Boulder, join friends to study in India, or travel to Alaska to make some money during the Alyeska Pipeline rush? He suggested that I go on a ten-day solitary retreat and do a shamatha meditation; sitting and focusing on my breath. That meditation period would help me make a decision.

I made arrangements to go to what was then called the Rocky Mountain Dharma Center, now Shambhala Mountain Center, and left Erika in the care of a friend at Marpa House. This was January 1975, and there was snow everywhere. Money was scarce, but I bought some brown rice and carrots and a snack or two, borrowed a friend's car, and wended my way up to the retreat site.

Two caretakers were the only other people there, and they escorted me up to one of the solitary cabins on the other side of Marpa Point, the highest point on the property. The isolated cabin was a very small single room with a wood stove that filled most of the space. The bed was a raised plank in one corner with windows on both sides, overlooking the valley below. It was breathtaking, vast, and quiet.

I saw no one for ten days. The caretakers checked in on me once, but that was it. There was a blizzard for three days, and with the shower room way down the hill I "bathed" one day by rolling in the snow.

Here was the opportunity to confront my own mind, stripped of all distractions. Of course, being good at following directions (and an excellent hider), it was not hard for me to keep my commitment to sit eight hours a day, read only one book, and stay in retreat. While I could sit for those hours, my untrained and unpracticed mind was all over the place. The decisions faced were huge because they would affect my future and Erika's, as well.

Robert mentions how the enemy was inside of him, and how he had honed his character flaws. My challenge was overcoming my own lies, too, to keep working on subtle inner and outer hatred, intolerance, and impatience. I had to learn to be more loving to myself and more sincere in my love for others. Though I could hide in my outer mask of sweet patience, this was my lesson, and it still is.

The book I read was Gampopa's *Jewel Ornament of Liberation*, which explains the stages of the path for a Buddhist practitioner. It helped me analyze the stages of my own path while holding in mind my principles, my promise to care for Erika, and my wish for enlightenment by studying with teachers who were further along the path.

Within the confines of my small room and in the vastness of my future, I realized I had to jump. I was going to keep my word to myself and to those around me. This clarity helped me see how difficult it would be in Boulder, struggling for meager employment while raising Erika at Marpa House. Weighing all my options, I chose to go on to Alaska and strike it rich. The money I'd earn would allow me travel later in the year with friends, to study in India.

It was a leap of faith, but I was ready and certain of my choice.

4

Heaven on Earth

In 1973 it was hard to see the positives, given the betrayals that had led to our dad's defeat, disillusionment over the war, and the corruption in Washington.

Vice President Agnew was forced to resign from office and was replaced by House Speaker Gerald R. Ford. In 1974, the U.S. House of Representatives initiated impeachment proceedings against President Richard M. Nixon. The Watergate scandal was on the news from morning until night.

Promises had been made to Dad by people who had to have known how difficult it was going to be for him to become lieutenant governor, and he had taken them at their word, yet those promises evaporated as soon as the election was over. This was unprecedented in his experience, and he learned a hard lesson about trust and honor.

While the Vietnam War left many soldiers physically wounded and emotionally scarred, it had the opposite effect on others, and left them emboldened. Having faced death in a war zone, some felt invincible, superhuman, overconfident in their abilities, and convinced they could get away with anything. In combat, the rules (as we had known them) often got thrown out the window. What counted in the heat of battle was your ability to get the job done—and live.

That cocky, invincible attitude left some out of control and, in their minds, bulletproof. Like President Nixon, they thought they were above the law. Then, when reality hit, they were left looking for answers elsewhere. Some looked to their churches.

The problem is that god can't be found in all churches. Although we understand the idea of being a good person, church was often about rules, about right and wrong, and about who was going to heaven and who was going to hell.

One particularly disturbing thing was when one church portrayed another church or another religion as wrong, claiming its members were following the teachings of the wrong god, the followers going to hell. One Sunday School teacher, when asked what the difference was between a Catholic and a Methodist, replied, "Methodists are going to heaven, and Catholics are not."

When asked why, her reply was simple.

"Because our cross does not have Jesus hanging on it. The Catholics still have Jesus on their cross, which means they do not believe in the resurrection, which means Catholics will not go to heaven."

ROBERT: FINDING HEAVEN

Church and religion were not a significant part of life in the Kiyosaki household, but the family spent a lot of time together. On weekends, we would pack a lunch and go explore our island home. There were deserted beaches where we could spend the day. There were also snowcapped mountains that the family hiked to for a day in the snow. A favorite place to visit was Volcano National Park, which was only about an hour away. There we would explore lava tubes, gaze into the craters of volcanoes along the Chain of Craters Road, or look at ancient Hawaiian footprints that were left in volcanic mud, hundreds of years earlier. When a volcano erupted, the family would drive to it and sit for hours in awe of nature's power.

In many ways, the wonders of nature served as a church for the family.

Money was always a problem, but we were never without the necessities. Items such as bicycles were always secondhand, always in need of repair. Clothes were patched and worn as long as possible. If they could be handed down, they were. We ate inexpensive, basic food, and there was always enough.

We spent a lot of time with three families who all had children around the same ages. In 1967, when Dad was promoted to superintendent of education for the State of Hawaii, it meant moving the family home from the Island of Hawaii to Honolulu, the state capital on the island of Oahu. At about the same time, we kids were leaving or had already left home, and the connection to a quiet small town, a simple life, close friends, and the raw power of nature was cut.

The family scattered and never really got back together again.

Leaving remote Hilo and going to school in New York changed my life. In 1965 I arrived there, a true country bumpkin. I still remember the clothes I wore for the trip: a black sports coat purchased from the used clothing section of our church, a white shirt, skinny red tie, khaki pants, and black leather shoes. I wanted to make sure I looked like a New Yorker when I arrived. I wanted to make sure I didn't stand out in the crowd.

And I didn't. I just looked strange.

If not for my aunt and uncle who lived in Manhattan, I might still be lost at baggage claim. My uncle, who was really my father's uncle and his mother's younger brother, was a commercial artist, and my aunt was recognized for her sculptures in wood, stone, and metals. Prior to becoming a sculptress, she had been the prima ballerina from

Paris during World War II. They met in New York after the war and lived an exciting life in the artist's scene.

My aunt, who was originally from Romania, could speak seven different languages fluently. She was beautiful, fun, dynamic, loving, and kind, and she became my role model for women.

After my bags appeared, their chauffeur took them to the limousine and drove us to their Upper East Side apartment. Hilo was a long way away.

It took me about two years to adjust to New York. There were many times I considered quitting school and going back to Hawaii. I missed my friends and the life I'd left behind. Then suddenly, at about the age of twenty, New York became my new home.

I fit. I was in-sync with the pace of the city.

At the same time, the school was sending me all over the world as a student on board merchant ships. Not only was I growing up in New York, I was also growing up in some of the great cities of the world. It wasn't long before I no longer fit in Hilo, Hawaii. I could not go home again.

Today, I continue to travel the world. I love this planet, its beauty, and its people. The world is my home. Today, I have businesses in a number of major cities of the world because business gives me an excuse to visit this incredible home known as planet earth.

Regardless of where I am, I carry with me the awe of a little boy, watching a volcano erupt or a wave pound a deserted, pristine white-sand beach. The view from the top of a snowcapped mountain or being alone in a forest—nature can be a kind of heaven. I believe growing up with nature deeply affected my thoughts about god and the possibilities of heaven on earth.

Even when running for a cab in New York, I carry the spirit of nature with me.

Occasionally I've felt the spirit of god in some churches. Every Christmas, when the choir my mom was in sang Handel's *Messiah*, I could feel the spirit of god fill the room. Later in my life, as I traveled the world, I often stood in awe of the spirit of god found in the architecture of great cathedrals such as Notre Dame and some of the ancient temples of Asian religions. I was deeply moved by the spirit of god when I visited the Vatican in Rome and the city of Jerusalem. Standing in both locations, it was obvious to me that, years ago, humans had been inspired by a power beyond this earth that allowed them to build such monuments.

Yet instead of finding god in my mom's church, I often found sermons filled with right-and-wrong dogma and the need to give more money. There wasn't much of the spirit of god. It was more the *fear* of god. And if war has taught me one thing about fear, it's this: fear of dying makes life a hollow and empty journey. Those who fear dying haven't yet found something worth dying for and, because of that, they fear death.

How could I reconcile this "fear of god" and blind faith with my belief that there are many ways to serve in this world?

Mom's friends were great people, as long as they weren't in church or talking about god, hell, and damnation. As long as they were just acting like moms, they were fine. They were kind, loving, and always had good food to eat. But the moment the name Jesus was mentioned, they changed. Every time one of the Church Ladies started talking about Jesus, I found a way to leave the room.

On the TV program *Saturday Night Live*, one of comedian Dana Carvey's characters was Church Lady. Every time Church Lady was on the air, I would howl with laughter. Carvey looked, acted, and sounded exactly like one of my mom's friends. His portrayal of Church Lady synthesized the very reason I did not find god in church.

Mom hung out with a *bunch* of Church Ladies.

There were a number of things a Church Lady and her friends would do that disturbed me. One was trying to *force* me to believe the stories about Jesus. For example, when I was old enough to know about the birds and the bees and where babies came from, and I questioned the idea that Jesus was born to a virgin, Church Lady had a fit, practically damning me for doubting.

Obviously, I had problems with some of the other stories, such as walking on water and rising from the dead. The stories did not bother me, though, as much as being persecuted for daring to question them.

I had a deal with my dad regarding church: I agreed that I would go to church till I was thirteen. He wanted me to have some religious education, but he did not require me to go to any one—or *just* one—church. I was free to attend services at different churches and with different denominations. In my youth, I went to Protestant, Lutheran, Catholic, Methodist, Buddhist, and Pentecostal services. I would have gone to the Jewish Temple or a Muslim mosque, but we did not have those religions in our little town in the 1960s, at least not as far as *I* knew.

In each of the different churches and religions, I found messages and meanings worth making a part of my life. I had a little trouble at the Buddhist Temple because the prayers were almost always in Japanese, and I do not speak Japanese. In Catholic Church I had a tough time with the Latin. The church I loved the most was the Pentecostal Church, because the services were alive, filled with singing, clapping of hands, and speaking in tongues. It was in this church that I felt the spirit of god moving through the room and learned the most about the Bible, the story of Jesus, and the importance of religion in a person's life.

But when I turned thirteen, I let my dad know that I had enough religious education and was going surfing on Sundays.

The problem I had with my mom's friends was who they became when I refused to drink the Kool-Aid. The moment I refused to believe the stories, they turned into Church Women. At one moment, they were sweet, kind mothers, but if a biblical story was questioned, a finger-shaking Church Lady appeared, insisting that I drink the Kool-Aid.

Now, I am not against drinking Kool-Aid. Life is filled with different flavors of Kool-Aid. For example, when I joined the Marine Corps, I had to drink the Marine Corps–flavored Kool-Aid. If I were to become a Republican, I would have to drink the Republican-flavored Kool-Aid. If I want to be accepted by the environmentalists, I have to drink the environmentalist-flavored Kool-Aid. So drinking Kool-Aid is a part of life. I just want to choose my own flavor—and I didn't want it forced down my throat.

Church Lady and I got into it once when I was about seventeen years old. It was a Sunday, and her son had gone surfing with me instead of attending church. It was winter, and the surf was spectacular. As soon as I got home, however, Church Lady called and told me to wait for her. She was so hot, the phone nearly melted. Within about ten minutes she was at our house, shaking her finger at me, spitting mad, and letting me know I was *not* to corrupt her son by taking him away from church and god.

"You will not go to heaven. But don't you ruin my son's chances. He goes to church on Sunday. Do you understand that?"

"I didn't call him," I replied. "He called me."

"I don't care," she snarled. "I want him to spend Sunday with god."

"We did," I replied quietly.

My relationship with Church Lady has remained tolerable. I see her son every now and then. She is a very sweet grandmother and great-grandmother today. We get along. We just do not discuss god. She finds god in church, and I find god everywhere—on a wave, in the woods, in church, flying across country, and even in New York City.

Robert (left) and his high school surfer friends cutting class at their favorite surf spot. To Emi it seemed as if the guys always seemed to have more fun.

Kool-Aid to me is symbolic for the dogma, the rules, the rituals, the beliefs, the mental structures around any group, such as religions, schools, the military, and various organizations. It is the mental glue that holds groups together. It is the element that keeps those outside the group apart.

For example, many vegetarians believe eating animal protein is bad for their health, even a sin. Steak lovers think a thick, juicy steak is a gift from god. Many religious people think drinking alcohol is a sin, yet in the Bible, there is mention of turning water into wine, and I love a great wine with my steak *and* my vegetables. To me, they are all gifts from god—bits of heaven on earth. At least that is my dogma, my Kool-Aid, when it comes to food and drink. My heart doctor thinks I should cut out the red meat and the wine, but he, too, drinks a different flavor of Kool-Aid.

One of the flavors of Kool-Aid I push back from is the idea that a person has to die to go to heaven. Church Lady often threatened me, saying I would not get to heaven if I did not go to church. One day, as I was passing through our living room, she was talking to my mom about going to heaven and sitting next to god.

Interrupting them I asked, "Why don't you sit next to god now?"

She took a moment to regain her composure before she answered. "Because when I die, I will go to heaven. Many people will not. When I go to heaven, I will be back with Jesus and god."

"And what about heaven on earth?" I asked. "Why do you have to die to go to heaven? Wasn't the Garden of Eden here on earth?"

My mom stood and told me to go do my homework. Pushing me through the swinging door out of the kitchen, she said, "You and I are going to have a talk with your father when he gets home."

In 1974, as I was being honorably discharged from the Marine Corps, I needed to find my own answers—new answers to old questions. As I've said earlier, I had not found the answers I was looking for in traditional schools, churches, corporations, or even the military. In 1974 I believed that many of our schools, churches, corporations, political organizations, banks, and the military had unwittingly become part of the powerful and virtually invisible multinational corporate machine behind the military-industrial complex that was controlling the world. I was very suspicious of what I had been taught and what I had been told.

I was disillusioned.

One of the good things about going to war was that I came in touch with the power of the human spirit. There were a number of times I witnessed friends who should have died, yet, miraculously, they lived. Two of my friends who fought with the army swear that they saw bullets go through a soldier without hurting him. They believe their friend was in a spiritual state beyond fear, that the bullets passed straight through him. I never saw anything that miraculous, but I have faith in my friends' accounts.

I do often wonder why I lived and two of my classmates from Hawaii, also marine pilots, did not. I crashed three times and lived. They crashed just once. After my crashes, I gave a lot of thought to the idea of the will to live. I wondered how much of a factor the human will plays in our lives.

In Vietnam, I saw a third world nation defeat the richest, most powerful nation on earth, the United States. Flying over a number of battles, it was obvious which side had the stronger will to live, and to win. One day, my aircraft was called to medevac a wounded soldier. When I saw his body being loaded onto my aircraft, I swore he had no chance of surviving. His body was in pieces—I could see right through him. Even though I thought he had no hope, I flew as fast as I could back to the aircraft carrier where the ship's medical team took him immediately to the operating room.

Three weeks later, very much alive, he was airlifted back to the States. His will to live was far stronger than my lack of faith.

By 1974, I'd had my faith tested, wondering if there was a god, wondering how god could allow such cruelty and corruption to exist on earth. At the same time, I had witnessed the power of god and the spiritual power each of us has in us . . . if we are called upon to use it.

I had seen too much. I had gone to school and I had gone to war. I no longer wanted to fight a quasi-holy war in the name of god. I did not want to "kill a commie for Christ." I no longer wanted to fight for oil, banks, multinational corporations, politics, greed, and power. I definitely didn't want to believe that I had to die or kill an infidel to go to heaven.

Instead, I decided to start working for and searching for heaven on earth, my own Garden of Eden. To me, this made more sense than drinking more organized Kool-Aid, living in fear of god, and waiting to die before I could live.

So I quietly cut my ties with traditional schools, religions, and politics. Today, if I go to church, I go much in the same way I vote. Instead of going to a church because of its denomination, I go to a church to listen to a pastor I respect, a pastor who I feel walks his or her walk and talks the talk. When I vote, I vote much the same way—I do not vote along party lines, I do not vote Republican or Democrat. I vote for the candidate I believe walks the walk and talks the talk.

I also stopped listening to my poor dad's advice of, "Go back to school, get your master's degree, your Ph.D., and get a job with the government or a big company." Instead, I went to visit my rich dad and let him know I wanted to follow in his footsteps to become an entrepreneur who invested in real estate. In my mind, my rich dad's path offered me the most freedom from the tyranny of being an employee of big business or government, and a better chance for me to find and define my own Garden Of Eden, my own heaven on earth.

I was twenty-seven years old. Before leaving the Marine Corps, I realized that I needed to define what heaven on earth meant to me, what my Garden of Eden would be like. This is when I began looking for new answers outside the traditional halls of traditional institutions. In defining my own garden, my own heaven, I realized that I needed to create and pour my own flavor of Kool-Aid—a flavor that tasted best to me. One of the first ingredients I wanted in my Kool-Aid was the idea that money is good. I was tired of the claim that the love of money was the root of evil.

Having been to school in New York, I got in touch with the spirit and the game of making money. My spirit came alive in the game of money and in the great cities of the world. Today, New York City is my Holy Land. When I tell my religious friends that I find the spirit of god in New York City, many of them bow their heads and pray for me. To many of my religious friends, New York City is the epicenter of sin, the modern Sodom and Gomorrah.

When thinking about heaven on earth, I also knew I wanted to find the woman of my dreams, my soul mate. My mom and dad had a very loving marriage. So did my uncle and aunt in New York. I wanted the same thing. Having seen many of my friends who were in bad marriages, I realized that being married to the wrong person could be hell on earth. I realized that if I were to find heaven on earth, I needed to find a soul mate who had the same definition of heaven.

For ten years, I had great fun dating as many women as I could. I met a number of women who were definitely *not* for me. It's not that they were bad people; it's just that we did not get along. It was bad chemistry. I'm glad I met them because I found out what I did *not* want in a relationship. At least I knew what a bad relationship was before I got married.

Overall, I'm happy to report that the world is filled with an abundance of fabulous women. Many helped me grow up, and god knows I needed to grow up. One or two, I could have married. Even though we did not marry, I cherish those relationships to this day. But when I met Kim, I knew I had met the woman of my dreams, my soul mate, my life's partner.

In 1984, after six months of my asking her out, she relented, and we went out on our first date. We have been together nearly every

The Best Book on the Future

Possibly, the best book I have read on the economic future is *The Sovereign Individual* by James Dale Davidson and Lord Rees-Mogg. I have been a student of theirs for years. They accurately predicted the 1987 stock market crash, the end of U.S.S.R., and the attack by Osama bin Laden. They say many of the same things as Dr. Fuller, especially about the end of nations as we know them. One of the interesting points they make about the end of any era is the increase in corruption as the end approaches.

They state that just before the Agrarian Age ended and the Industrial Age began, there was rampant corruption in the churches and religious orders. They point out that as the Industrial Age ends, there will be rampant corruption in government. We have all seen that.

Rees-Mogg and Davidson point out that the world changes every five hundred years. The changes have been:

500 B.C.	Greek Democracy emerged.
0	The Birth of Christ
500 A.D.	The Dark Ages began
1000 A.D.	The Advent of Feudalism
1500 A.D.	Renaissance and the Industrial Age
2000 A.D.	The Information Age

Like Fuller, Rees-Mogg and Davidson state that wealth generated from technology will no longer be controlled by just a few. The power of technology will be inexpensive enough for all of us, rich or poor to have access to it. This will bring good news and bad news.

The good news is that the Information Age will liberate individuals as never before. People will be able to educate themselves. They state, "Those who can educate themselves will be almost entirely free to invent their own work and realize the full benefits of their own productivity. Genius will be unleashed, freed from both the oppression of government and the drags of racial and ethnic prejudice. In the Information Society, no one who is truly able will be detained by the ill-formed opinions of others.

"Politicians will no longer be able to dominate, suppress, and regulate the greater part of commerce in this new deal." In other words, it will matter little if Republicans or Democrats are in power. In the Information Age, the power goes to you, the individual.

Dr. Fuller forecasted that we are entering the Age of Integrity. This is why our personal prophecy and vision for the future are important.

day since that date. In more than twenty years, we have been apart fewer than fifty days. She is my best friend, my business partner, and my wife.

Heaven on earth also applied to my work. I knew I wanted to be a rich entrepreneur who traveled the world. I wanted to be an entrepreneur whose business also matched the business of my soul. Most importantly, I wanted to feel confident that my work made a difference and made this world a better place to live.

As I prepared to leave the Marine Corps, I wanted to get my power back, power I felt had been crushed or sucked out of me in traditional schools, churches, and businesses. I didn't want to go back to school only to feel stupid again. I didn't want to go to church and be told I was a sinner and had to die before I could begin to live. I didn't want to be an employee of a company, allowing the business to tell me how much I made, whom I worked with, who was my boss, and whether or not I would be promoted.

I wanted to regain my power, the power to have my life on my terms, to find my heaven on earth.

In Sunday School I learned that Noah endured a rainstorm for forty days and forty nights. I also learned that Moses wandered in the desert for forty years before he was delivered to the Promised Land. In 1974, I was hoping to find heaven on earth in forty days, but I was also willing to wander for forty years.

EMI: TESTING THE WATERS

When we were in school, I was curious about the children who always ate fish on Fridays and who left school early to go to catechism. I so longed to join them, and was deeply curious about what they were studying.

Sometimes at the Methodist church and others we attended, there were really great teachers for the young people. I enjoyed their classes and looked forward to church camp in the summer. At camp, I realized what a shy person I was and how lacking I was in social skills. Yet I loved the interactions, discussions, bonfires, and sing-alongs that nudged me into meeting and getting to know new people. I admired young boys and girls who were outgoing, engaging, and who jumped in to participate and lead activities.

Growing up in Hawaii, like Robert, I attended services of many church denominations and temples with classmates and friends, and it was our Hawaiian way to appreciate all the different traditions. I did not question God or religious traditions as a child; I accepted and respected them. I did not have an inquisitive, challenging mind like Robert—at least not in childhood.

But in adulthood, my inquiries and study began in earnest. Alaska was a good place to earn money fast. I worked two jobs, one in an office supply company that was sending goods to the workers on the Alaskan pipeline and the other as a waitress. My goal was to earn the money I needed for my trip to India.

The trip to Alaska was grueling. My friend and I drove from Boulder, Colorado, to Fairbanks in a 1953 GMC truck with a passenger door that would fly open for no reason. With no seatbelts and no warning, the truck's crazy door had us on edge for much of the trip. The truck had no heat, so the January cold was brutal on us. At one point we slid off into a snow bank and without a snow shovel, we had to get creative to dig our way out. A frying pan did the job.

Work as a waitress meant serving lots of tourists in the summer and, in the colder months, pipeline workers and a few locals who knew how to brave the winter. It was a transient place: everyone wanted to get out on the pipeline as quickly as they could to make their fortune in this twentieth-century oil rush. Most were bad tippers.

Even though I was working so much, it was freeing in a way. I had made an arrangement with Erika's father for him to take care of her in Hawaii during the time I was in Alaska and India, and I dedicated myself toward my goal of making it to India. I was with friends from Hawaii and Colorado, and we lived our simple life in the middle of what was a modern-day Wild West. Everyone's dream was to get out on the pipeline with a union job because it meant a lot more money. Overtime paid time-and-a-half or better. One friend of mine got a job as part of the carpenters' union, and through her good wages and lots of overtime funded her master's degree in no time.

For me, I wanted to get in and out of Alaska as quickly as I could so I could travel to India by the coming fall. I never joined the union. Many saw Alaska as the land of milk and honey, a place where riches came easy. My goal was to get to India, study there with authentic Tibetan teachers. I saw Alaska as a means to that end.

I knew Robert had spent time in Valdez, Alaska, in 1969 as a ship's officer. He was making $48,000 a year working seven out of twelve months. He had no expenses and was able to make and save far more than me. This seemed to be a pattern in our lives.

By contrast, my nine months in Alaska, socking away nearly every dollar I made, amounted to about $4,000. That was enough to buy me two trips back to Hawaii to see Erika, passage to India, and the money to live there, frugally, for six months.

My friends and I left for India in September 1975. My heart soared with the opportunity to study with Venerable Geshe Ngawang Dhargyey, and the town of Dharamsala was amazing. It was like little Tibet in the mountains of India. His Holiness the Dalai Lama had set up the Tibetan Government in Exile, and all the important offices had been reestablished. The Tibetan community was very poor then; sometimes I saw people walking in the snow with no socks and terrible, ill-fitting shoes. Those same people were incredibly happy, unified, supportive, and helpful to each other, and always willing to lend a hand to us. They lived their teachings and were happy to be alive and near His Holiness the Dalai Lama.

It was at this time that Venerable Geshe Dhargyey stunned me by suggesting that I become a nun. I was flabbergasted. Becoming a nun was the farthest thing from my mind. Erika was now living with her father, so it was understandable that those around me would not know of my family or my life in Hawaii. We left it at that, but I couldn't get the idea out of my head. I wondered how I would live in the West, as a nun with a young daughter.

"It might be difficult," I blurted out. "I have a young daughter." He seemed undeterred, and we let it go at that.

During the six-week break, my friends and I went on pilgrimage to the four major Buddhist holy places: Lumbini in Nepal, where the Buddha was born; Sarnath where he first taught; Kushinagar where he passed away; and Bodhgaya where the Buddha attained enlightenment. We also made it to Rajgir, called Vulture's Peak, where the Buddha taught the Heart Sutra.

Travel was difficult. The coal trains were sooty and very crowded. We took bicycle rickshaws to Lumbini because there were no buses. It was an improvement over the rickshaws in Calcutta, however, where they were drawn by emaciated men who pulled us well-fed Americans to our destinations over terrible, potholed roads.

In Bodhgaya, I spent weeks in a tent shared with five Tibetans to attend some teachings by His Holiness Ling Rinpoche, the Dalai Lama's senior tutor. All the while, I considered what Geshe Dhargyey had said to me about becoming a nun. And though I did not know what becoming a nun *meant* at that point, it began to appeal to me. When we resumed classes in spring of 1976, I asked Geshe Dhargyey about becoming a nun. He parroted my earlier response saying, "It might be quite difficult; you have a young daughter." His reply surprised me, and I laughed nervously. But then he said, "It would be wonderful if you did that."

It took me ten years to finally take my vows to become a monastic. After returning to Hawaii yet again, moving to Los Angeles and studying with another wonderful teacher, Venerable Geshe Tsultim Gyeltsen, I had the opportunity to go back to India and was ordained by His Holiness the Dalai Lama in 1985. For the most part, I have never looked back.

There have, of course, been times of struggle and questioning, but being a nun and making the study and practice of Buddhism my life focus has been thoroughly rewarding. What drew me to the teachings is that I wanted suffering to stop, and I wanted answers. I felt as if there was so much unfinished business, and my mother and grandparents had passed on before I could appreciate them and the heritage and history they carried.

As people passed away, refuge in family became unstable; I learned that they would *not* always be there. Even the earth beneath my feet was unstable, especially on the Big Island, which was still going through growing pains. Isolated there in the middle of the Pacific Ocean, it was forming new surface area, yet it is said that Hawaii will eventually disappear because of rising waters and barely perceptible sinking of the land.

Death propelled me to seek understanding of both life and death. Given the fact that we will all die, I wanted to learn how to live, and

Emi (center), with two inspiring translator friends in Hawaii in 1983, before taking the leap of faith to become a Buddhist nun.

to deal with my many questions. Why do people we love experience such tragedies in their lives? And why do we die?

Where does everyone go at death?

Must we die?

Why are people cruel and deceptive with others, and then remorseful and filled with self-loathing when they lose their friends, loved ones, reputation, and position?

Why do people think they can get away with lies, destroying others' lives, stealing, and cheating?

Why did Dad, who was such a good person, have to experience such upheaval and deception in his life?

Weren't there consequences, both obvious and subtle, to our actions? Were there no consequences if we weren't caught? Do consequences not matter then and after—if there is an after?

My Buddhist studies offered answers to those questions. I found an excellent path and excellent spiritual community—my spiritual family. But while my study and practice of the Buddhist teachings fulfilled my spiritual needs, I found that some of my Buddhist friends still struggled with keeping their own promises, just as people did in other faiths. And I've struggled, too.

There are ten basic non-virtues to be avoided—killing, stealing, engaging in sexual misconduct, lying, gossiping, slandering, using harsh words, engaging in covetousness, harmful intent, and wrong view—and these are straightforward, but sometimes hard to observe. It is difficult to follow through and hold our vows when attachment, anger, jealousy, or competitiveness creep in.

Friends I admired, who had professional or lowly positions, who appeared to be diligent, brilliant practitioners of Buddhism, sometimes fell into wrong actions. I was trying so hard to practice well myself, but I still made people upset and angry. I still found myself gossiping and speaking covertly about others.

Even when I felt I was being so good, becoming a better person for the benefit of all beings, conflicts arose. My daughter wanted me around more, my ex-husband felt I was a flake, I needed to get a job, my friends established their careers while I worked just enough to pay the rent and to feed us.

Nevertheless, the lifestyle suited me for decades. I managed to continue my studies, make trips to live in India, finish two degrees, to converse in Tibetan, and spend a lot of my time in attending teachings and being in retreat. Yet two strong patterns crept into my life that were hindering my practice. One was seeking the approval of people I deemed worthy, and my life often revolved around this. First I sought approval from my father, later my teachers.

The second pattern was hiding in my shyness, always hanging back, never speaking up. In doing so, I avoided having to expose myself or reveal what I considered my faults—lack of knowledge, anger, confusion, jealousy, and fear, although they probably showed in other ways.

Sometimes in cultivating a spiritual path, one can have the appearance of being diligent, serene, devoted, and knowledgeable. But in fact, a subtle habit of seeking approval through such appearances was creating misery in my life. Hiding kept me from learning or growing. While I was seeking personal peace, I was uncovering in myself subtle warfare of deceptive delusions that were battling for power.

In his first teaching after his enlightenment, Buddha taught the Four Noble Truths. Basically they are:

- The truth of suffering
- The truth of the cause of suffering
- The truth of the cessation of suffering
- The truth of the path to attain cessation from suffering

It is for the practitioner to purify the obscurations and delusions that block one from understanding that their true nature is empty of inherent existence. Because we misunderstand the nature of reality, we develop mistaken views to everything in our world. We understand the importance of being kind, following sound ethical principles, not harming others, and learning to extend this view beyond only our friends and loved ones. But when delusions of clinging attachment or aversion set in, we engage in unwholesome, unkind acts of body, speech, and mind.

In my old pattern of seeking approval, especially from my teachers, I found myself caught up in pleasing, doing things that handicapped me, and falling into subtle misdirected action. As a nun, I could embed this tendency in trying to be so good, helping others at the cost of losing myself; it was a subtle delusion that threw me off balance. This was my suffering.

Perhaps it is inevitable that because my view and actions were overextended, like the pendulum of a clock, I swung the other way: wanted, needed, and had to stop. My medical condition was a physical sign of inner imbalance. Ever since then, I've had to be watchful of how I continually set myself up. Because of the ingrained patterns, when some situations arise, I can easily go on "automatic," volunteering for the next project, handling new affairs or whatever happens to be falling apart at the moment. The "savior" part of my Samurai myth kicks in, and I swoop in to save the day.

It is easy to become overextended again. Meditation practice, watching my actions and words, catching my tongue, all help me to pause and think about what's happening, watch the old pattern, and be careful to choose what I engage in so that I do not get locked into yet another "urgent" project. For my well-being and practice, I have to conscientiously work to create physical and mental ease and mindful balance regarding habitual seeking of approval. Cutting through old, unhealthy patterns is a process of purifying delusions and misperceptions, and this gives us greater clarity to progress on the path.

It's become a personal internal engagement to bring attention, love, right action, and wisdom to this old, deep tendency and to bring right balance and right livelihood into my life and actions. This is beneficial war, challenging unhealthy habits and views.

The Buddha said:

"Be a light unto yourself."

"After my death, the teachings will be your teacher."

"Hatred does not end by hatred. Hatred ends by love."

Such are every person's challenges. In contrast with Robert's story, I call this struggle a war, but in fact the work requires love and kind attention, not battling ourselves in harsh, unforgiving ways. With skillful care and interest we can relieve painful, enduring, insidious patterns. Confusion, misperception, and erroneous habits often start because we did not experience love, wisdom, appropriate attention, or guidance and fell into imbalance.

We all respond to love. We compensate and hide when there is unpleasant force. It is remarkable that as beings who need and respond to love, we engage in so much war, so much strife at home and in the office, games of deceptiveness, unhealthy competition, jealousy, greed, withholding, and refusal to lend a hand.

Robert's comment that, "Even though we all want peace, war would always be a part of the human condition," is as sobering as Will Durant's analysis that in all of human history there have been only twenty-nine years when man was not at war somewhere. Where are we headed? Is this the only outcome and possibility?

The Buddha spoke of the three poisons:

- Desire/attachment
- Hatred/anger
- Ignorance/delusion

Until we overcome these conditions, we succumb to the inequities of these poisons. Teachings say it is possible to gain freedom from these delusions, but we must do the work. There isn't someone outside of ourselves who can wash away our delusions or remove them. Even though I was "being a good nun," in fact, I was living my neuroses. Something had to change. In contemplating old questions, I found myself looking for new answers.

Am I powerless as an individual? As a nun?

I joined a greater community than I could have imagined when I became a nun. I have studied with the Tibetan masters, and there are Buddhist monastic communities in India, Sri Lanka, Thailand, China, Burma, Cambodia, Japan, Mongolia, Taiwan, Singapore, Malaysia, Korea, and historically from Indonesia, Greece, Afghanistan, and other countries. Today there are Buddhist monastics in many countries who work to cultivate inner peace.

In seeking the power to bring peace to the world, I have held my sights on our human potential in the person of His Holiness the Dalai Lama. Yet even he often says, "I am just a simple monk," which reminds us not to view him as separate and different, but it inspires us to develop our best potential.

His capacity to warm the hearts of people around the world, to bring people together from so many traditions and views, shows me the possibility of living the high ideal, of being an excellent human being. While there are countless numbers of persons who quietly live their lives as excellent human beings, it is remarkable that the world has recognized the Dalai Lama and his efforts to bring a peaceful resolution to the displacement of the Tibetan people and the loss of their country.

I feel powerless regarding war and conflict—globally and locally, and it speaks of my concern and sadness, my questions related to reasons for not taking action, or confusion as to what to do. But since the power of the pen is mighty, and the power of speech can benefit countless people, I teach and write about cooling the three poisons—hatred, greed, and ignorance—so we can stop outer and inner aggression and conflict.

Why do aggressors win?

The Chinese government and its people currently occupy Tibet. They call the Dalai Lama a "splittist" of the people and the Motherland, say he should be quiet and stay out of political issues, and claim they have freed the Tibetans from serfdom and brought them greater economy and prosperity. But they have taken Tibet for their own advantage, claiming it for natural resources, moving Chinese people in to settle Tibetan lands, giving jobs to the Chinese, and holding back the native Tibetans from education, employment, and other opportunities.

We must acknowledge that the United States did this to the Native Americans as well.

In 1986 I made a trip by bus with some Tibetan travelers from Dharamsala to Katmandu, Nepal. I was asked by a friend to help keep an eye out for them in our travels. We passed four border checkpoints, and I realized that the Tibetans were being segregated and taken to separate areas at the checkpoints. Though every border check was free to the few Westerners and numerous Nepalis, border guards were taking huge sums of money from the Tibetans, unbeknownst to other passengers. This unkind treatment was small compared to what they face inside Tibet and when they try to escape Tibet by crossing over the borders to enter Nepal and India by foot. So many have been imprisoned, tortured, and returned to the Chinese for bribe money. They have endured frostbite and starvation to come into freedom and to escape from Chinese oppression in Tibet.

As Robert said of politics in the United States, as well, "It seemed to me that crime *did* pay." And, "Why did bad things happen to good people?"

Can I make a difference?

Early on in life I made a strong prayer to make progress, to be used well, and used up, as in Dylan Thomas's poem, "Do not go gently into the night./Rage, rage against the dying of the light." I do not interpret this to be angry or abusive, but to take the very heart of our lives and use it up, learn from life, and not leave any stone unturned.

Is it possible to live an ethical, powerful, beneficial life, helping ourselves and others without compromising strong prayer or ethics? Can we rise above oppression and hatred, disturbing mental attitudes and depression, distractions and useless endeavors, and still tremendously enjoy life?

This is the challenge of life.

Can we live in diversity?

With some dedicated years of study, interfaith events and work with ministers and practitioners of other faiths, the question for me is: How in a shrinking world can we live harmoniously with all the different faith groups?

Having the wonderful opportunity to regularly engage with people of other faiths, including practitioners of different Buddhist traditions, I've grown to appreciate people's faith in their chosen traditions, the effort they make to practice and study and to be good disciples. We have a long way to go in deepening tolerance and kindness for people of faiths other than our own. When we look down upon others or belittle them, it shows our intolerance and narrow perspectives. This quote from Dave Barry is sobering and sometimes true: "People who want to share their religious views with you almost never want you to share yours with them."

Many cities and communities have diverse cultures and faiths living together. We should learn about each other just as we enjoy delicious foods, drink, clothing, and songs from other countries. Isn't there intelligence, even wisdom, in the ability to entertain and appreciate different, even opposing, points of view?

Can an average person like me be successful?

Here I have more questions and answers. How can I be successful if I am average? If I am a spiritual aspirant? I don't have any special talents. What can I do? The answer is *yes*, we can be successful! That's what our intelligence is for! Groom good qualities.

Did I need to find my own answers?

Getting married and having a family was not the answer for me. I marvel when I see people who are happily married to each other for decades. Today, it is often the exception rather than the rule. When we as individuals go through so many changes over the years, it is commendable, remarkable, and wonderful that two people together can grow and change in harmony and shared vision. I had to search in my own way.

The Buddha showed us a path to enlightenment. But we have to tread the path and find our own way. Answers and lessons are for in-dividual understanding.

People can speak to us until they are blue in the face but we must experience and uncover our own lessons. Sometimes I have to learn things again and again; sometimes I get it right away. We do what we want anyway, and sometimes the answer doesn't come through clearly because we aren't paying attention. The universe does show us the result of our efforts.

5

Transforming Paths

Sometimes you get what you ask for in life.

The problem is you may not like the way the answer comes to you. You may not like the package it comes in. You may not even recognize that you are being offered what you are asking for.

Our searches took us in radically different directions, yet parallels were already beginning to emerge. And for one of us, the key would be to stay out of prison.

ROBERT: A CHANGED LIFE

While my sister was looking for spirituality in the wilds of the Big Island, I was looking for sex in the wilds of Waikiki. Now that my helicopter had been taken away, keeping up with the island-hopping party life wasn't as easy as it had been.

Nevertheless, early in 1974, I met a beautiful young woman in a bar. Her name was Jennifer, and she was kind of a fringe hippie. I didn't know if it was my short Marine Corps haircut that turned her off, or if it was just me in general, but every time I asked her out she found an excuse to say "No."

Finally, my persistence paid off, and she said, "Yes, but on one condition."

I had to go to a free seminar with her, attending as a guest. Desperate for any time with her, I agreed.

The free seminar was an EST Seminar—Erhard Seminars Training like my sister Emi had attended years earlier. The event was held in a lavish ballroom at a big hotel in Waikiki, and the room was filled with about five hundred people. I had never heard of EST, but I was impressed with the number of beautiful young women at the event. Having so many attractive women in one place, all smiling at me, was something I had never experienced before. I had been locked away at an all-male military school and in the military since high school.

I thought I had found heaven in Waikiki.

Soon after I took my seat next to Jennifer, the lights dimmed and this stunning young woman dressed in a spectacular white dress stepped onto the stage. She said a few words and then introduced Werner Erhard. The people in the room sprang from their chairs and erupted with applause.

Werner was also dressed in white. He was in fantastic physical condition with sharp, handsome features, and was extremely confident. He was a great speaker, but the more he talked, the less I understood. All I got was something about needing to have my life work better.

It didn't take long before I was bored stiff and ready to leave. I had no intention of enrolling in this training, especially since it cost $200 and took up two full weekends. There was a break, and I turned to Jennifer, asking if she wanted to go get a drink. Shaking her head at my denseness, she asked me a question I wasn't expecting: "Well, are you ready to enroll in the EST training?"

"No," I said emphatically. "I don't need this stuff. This crap is for losers. Come on, let's go to the bar and get a drink."

Jennifer just shook her head silently, giving me a look of disgust.

"What?" I asked. "You think I need this junk?" That caused her to smirk.

"Of all the people in this room, you need the EST training the most."

"Me?" I asked indignantly, feeling as if I had been verbally slapped across the face. "Why me?"

"Why do you think I don't go out with you?" Jennifer countered.

"I don't know," I replied toughly. "Tell me."

With that response, I guess I had asked for the pounding she delivered next. "The reason I don't go out with you," she said, "is because you're so needy. You lack confidence around women. You're embarrassed and terrified of being rejected. On top of that, you're so horny you're desperate. I can tell there is only one thing you want. But why would I want to go to bed with such a needy man?"

"What?" I yelped like a kicked dog.

"On top of that," Jennifer continued, "you pretend to be so macho, but I can see right through you. All you are is one big, tough marine pilot act. You drive around in your Corvette looking like 'high school Harry' made good."

"Okay," I said, now feeling hurt. "If that is what you think, then I'll leave."

"Look" she said, softening her approach. "Listen to me. I don't like telling you this. I like you. You have good qualities. But you asked."

The break area of the room was filled with people, some talking, some signing up for the training, and others were nervously hiding by the refreshment table. The good thing was that the din of the crowd was loud enough that no one had heard Jennifer's comments. And even if they had heard, they didn't care.

Touching my shoulder she smiled and spoke, gently now.

"That's why I invited you to this guest event. I took the training myself and found my entire life changed for the better."

At that she led me over to the registration table. I was still sting-ing from her comments. My gut was churning and my mind was rac-ing. I didn't know what to do, so I slowly reached for a pen and began to fill in the blanks. I was still on the edge of bolting. I really didn't know if I should run or stay. I had no idea what I was getting into.

Eventually, I put down a $35 deposit to hold my space in the train-ing, and I left the ballroom, heading for the bar in the hotel.

Jennifer stayed to listen to the second half of the event.

In March of 1974, I walked into the EST training, and two weeks later, as she had promised, my life changed.

A great deal of the training was about agreements. In other words, do you keep your word? Notice the word *word* again. Agreements are about keeping your word. When someone says, "He is a man of his word," it is a very high compliment.

During the training, it became glaringly clear that most of our personal problems begin with our not keeping our agreements, not being true to our words, saying one thing and doing another. That first full day on the simple class agreements was painfully enlight-ening. It became obvious that much of human misery is a function of broken agreements—not keeping your word, or someone else not keeping theirs.

At last I realized that my misery was caused by my lack of integrity and not keeping my word. I stayed with the EST programs for about two more years and learned a lot about myself. Soon after I stopped attending the seminars, the organization went through its trials and tribulations and today is known as Landmark. I do not necessarily recommend the program; I only report that for me, it was a life-changing experience.

On the Monday following the completion of the two-weekend training, I worked up enough nerve to call my squadron commander to ask for an appointment. Practically frozen with fear, I walked stiffly into his office, saluted, and was asked to take a seat. I began by saying, "Sir, before I leave the military, I want to let you know about the agreements I have broken with your squadron."

The colonel sat there and listened while I told him about taking a helicopter on a Friday, landing on a remote site near the base, picking up a bunch of women, coolers of beer, and flying to a remote beach on a remote outer island, where we spent the weekend. I also admitted to transporting scuba equipment—which is strictly forbidden because the altitude could cause the pressurized tanks to explode—and flying drunk.

Shaking his head, he sat silently. Finally he spoke.

"Thank you for telling me. Are other pilots doing the same thing?"

"I'd rather not say," I replied. "I am only here to tell you what I have done."

"I understand," said the colonel. "I will do my own investigation. Are you prepared to stand trial if charges are brought against you?"

"Yes," I answered.

"Do you realize how serious these charges are, and that you might go to jail?"

"Yes," I said.

"Okay," said the colonel. "The military authorities will be in touch with you."

About two weeks later, a military lawyer—a marine captain—called and asked me to come to his office on base. Once in his office, he informed me of my rights and asked if I wanted an attorney.

"No," I replied. "I am here to tell you everything and face the consequences of my actions, even if it means going to jail."

The captain then called in a court reporter, and we began a three-hour deposition on all my activities that broke the rules. At the end of the deposition, I was exhausted, limp, drained. I had told him everything, every little detail and how many times I cheated the system. I hid nothing.

Sitting in silence, I watched as the captain dismissed the court reporter and began putting his notes away.

"Am I going to jail?" I asked, expecting to be led away in handcuffs.

The captain kept fumbling through his briefcase for a while longer before finally looking up and saying, "No. You're free to go. You're getting out in a month, and I'll make sure you receive your honorable discharge. Thank you for your service to our country."

The weeks of pressure and the surprise of the decision got to me. I could not stand it any longer. Bursting into tears I said, "I don't understand."

"Take the gift, lieutenant," the captain said. "Thank you for telling the truth. Now get out of here before I change my mind."

Standing there confused, I did not move. I could not move. Finally the captain smiled and said, "We've known about you and your fellow pilots. I heard about giant lobsters you were catching and the naked parties. Hell, I wanted to be invited. It sounded like great fun."

"You heard about it?" I asked.

"Of course. News of a good time always gets out. There were a number of you pilots doing the same thing. I was invited once, but I didn't go. I knew you guys would get caught sooner or later, so I'm glad I didn't."

"Who else was doing it?" I asked.

"There are a number of pilots who have been misusing government property. Some of them outrank you and me. I'm just glad you had the courage to come forward and tell the truth. I'm not after you. I'm after the other guys who do not have the courage to come forth. Flying women to deserted beaches and drinking while flying is pretty bad. But lacking the courage to come forward and lying are even worse crimes. It shows a lack of character, a tragic character flaw.

"We all make mistakes," he continued. "We have all broken the rules. We all do stupid things and think we can get away with it. So making a mistake and being stupid is not a crime. Being foolish is not a crime. Lying is."

With that, I left.

He kept his promise. In June of 1974, I drove off the base a free man.

Freedom for me was more than avoiding a court-martial. And my "changed life" went well beyond the two weekends I spent in the EST seminar. I realized I had the power to create the best destiny for my life, or the worst. It was my choice.

I had to stop thinking I was on the "right" side of things all the time. I had to embrace my dark side and bring it into the light. The enemy was inside of me, not "out there" somewhere. In developing my strength of character, I had come to realize that I had also honed my character flaws.

At this point, I decided that my lifetime work would be to focus on myself and develop a higher ethical, legal, and moral character. Those lofty words, "commandments" muttered by Sunday school teachers and my mother's Church Lady friends, were coming back to me in a language that was understandable and my own. I knew it would be a lifelong mission; I had a lot of work to do on myself.

The life lessons I had been taught in church were valuable. They were simple and made a lot of sense. And because they were simple, I began to wonder why people had a hard time following them. Why go to church if you weren't going to make the lessons a part of your life?

At that I became very cynical—not about church, but about the people who went to church. I often wondered why a person who attended church regularly and appeared to be a devout follower of god and the rituals of their religion did not put the lessons into practice.

Mom and Dad had done their best to shelter us kids from the cruel realities of the real world. And as hard as they tried, life's dark side often got through to us. For example, when we kids were all under the age of six, our family learned that one of Dad's friends from work was getting a divorce. The kids didn't know what divorce meant, or why a mother and father would split up. Mom and Dad did their best to explain the reasons without getting into explaining what adultery was, but we soon found out anyway.

A few years later, a classmate's father was arrested for embezzlement and sent to jail. This also took a bit of delicate explanation. Another friend—also a family man—was an alcoholic. He spent a lot of time hiding his secret. One day, while in a drunken stupor, he hit a pedestrian in a crosswalk and was sent to jail. The family broke up, and the wife remarried.

The tough part in the explanations was that the families were religious, church-going people. The question that baffled us kids was, "Why go to church if you are not going to obey the laws of god?"

This isn't to say I am above sin and folly. I assure you that almost everything I was told not to do in church, I did my best to accomplish. My defense is that I have never pretended to be a good Christian who followed the rules. What bothered me was the number of people who acted like followers of god, went to church, talked about a loving god, claimed they followed the rules, yet in private they weren't what they pretended to be.

As time went on, I began to wonder why so many people pretended to be saints but were really sinners. If the rules for a good life were so easy to follow, why did so many people not follow them? Some specific examples that have disturbed me are:

We all know we should not lie.

We all know we should tell the truth. So my question is, if this is such a simple lesson to live life by, why do so many people lie? I was especially amused when President Nixon, the most powerful leader in the world, was caught lying. He went to church. He was a good Christian.

Why did he lie?

We all know we should not commit adultery.

Yet, why do so many people cheat on their spouses? A picture I love is the picture of President Clinton posing for a photo opportunity as he left church with the Bible in his hand, and later we found out that he was on his way to meet Monica.

We know we should not kill.

Yet governments spend so much time, technology, and money in the pursuit of building weapons to kill people. Why does the United States—supposedly a godlike nation—spend so much of its gross domestic product on weapons? Why is the Holy Land one of the most violent places on earth?

We know we should "love thy neighbor."

We all understand that we should be kind to our fellow man, yet why do so many people gossip behind their neighbor's back, stabbing them in the back with words? Why do so many people spend so much time, creativity, and effort on the Internet to smear someone else?

Once again in my life I found myself looking for new answers to old questions. It seemed to me that if we just followed the Golden Rule—"Do unto others as you would have them do unto you"—life would be a lot better. So while the rules seemed simple, following them seemed difficult. I wondered why.

I also noticed that humans struggled a lot within themselves. It seemed as if many people went to church to genuinely pray for a better life, yet a better life eluded many of them. For example:

- Many people want to be rich, yet millions of the spiritually rich remain financially poor.
- Millions would like to be thinner and healthier, yet millions pray to lose weight only to gain more weight.
- Millions pray for more love and happiness with their spouse or partner, yet some of the most vicious fights are with those you love the most.
- Millions of families go to church to set a moral example for their kids, yet some of the kids from religious families turn out to be the worst kids of all.

I just wondered *why. . . .*

EMI: TRYING IT ON FOR SIZE

All of us kids were born in Saint Francis Hospital in Honolulu, Hawaii. When I was young, Mom was a nurse there, and on rare visits to her workplace we would see the nuns rushing about caring for people. Small children weren't allowed in the hospital, so this was an infrequent sight for us.

I tend to be a faithful type of person. I have a great love of the teachers and saints of different traditions, and when I've traveled to different places for work or family events, I've gone to visit holy places of all traditions.

Perhaps because of the early associations with Saint Francis, I was always drawn to his amazing life and work, and in 1999 when I attended a Buddhist teacher training conference in Pomaia, Italy, I took the opportunity to visit Assisi, where Saint Francis had lived. It was wonderful to be on the very ground where he and Saint Clare had been and where their monastic traditions started. Even though some people call it "touristy," Assisi feels empowered by all the heartfelt prayers of the faithful who have made pilgrimages there over the centuries. I almost cried when I realized that the people have kept Saint Francis's body at the cathedral. They showed determination, protection, and faith in keeping the holy site and the relic of his body safe over many centuries, through strife, modernity, famine, war, and times of zealousness and disregard.

Another place I visited was Lourdes in France. I went to Toulouse to assist my daughter Erika and her husband Frederic during the time of the birth of their second son. The day before I left France, I took a break and traveled two hours by train to Lourdes, arriving about lunchtime, so I got a bite to eat before exploring the area. At the café, I noticed a Catholic monk who was also dining. After lunch, as I wended my way down to the cathedral and grotto area, I ran into him again. He was very engaging and pointed out the holy sites to me but then asked, "What are you doing here?"

I answered that I loved the stories of the saints, and when I had a chance I would visit holy places.

"But for what reason are you in Southern France?"

I explained that I came because my daughter just had a child. He was shocked and asked, "You mean you monastics can marry?"

Tenzin and her grown-up daughter Erika in December 1994 at Los Angeles International Airport. Tenzin was on her way to India again.

"No," I said. "That was a very long time ago."

"But what happened to your husband?" he asked.

"We separated many years ago," I said.

"What! You mean you Buddhists can divorce?" he asked.

"It was before I was a Buddhist," I answered.

"Well," he said, "you know you cannot get any blessings here unless you've been baptized."

"But I was baptized when I was a child," I responded.

"What! You mean you gave it all up?" he asked incredulously.

"It's not that I gave it up, but I found my path in Buddhism," I said. I explained that I didn't feel as if one has to reject one faith when embracing another.

After that, he kindly walked me down to where people were filling bottles of spring water, and we sat outside the grotto where Bernadette Soubirous had the vision of Our Lady of Lourdes and prayed for a while. Then I went to the women's tents where people receive the blessing by the spring water. Not speaking French, I didn't realize until the last moment that we had to strip down completely to be immersed in the water.

Meetings between monastics of other traditions and people of other faiths is important because it develops friendships and harmony. We no longer live in an insular world where we can remain untouched by modernity, different cultures, and views. In centuries past, we were isolated due to technological and travel limitations. It is always important to study deeply in our chosen traditions and communities, but today we need to have more dialogue and develop more tolerance and appreciation of different faith groups. This will lead to greater friendship, peace, and harmony.

In 1998 I accepted a post in Colorado to be the resident teacher for a small Buddhist group. One year after I arrived in Colorado Springs, one of the chaplains at the U.S. Air Force Academy asked me to meet with cadets who were interested in Buddhism, and I ended up serving as the Buddhist chaplain for six years. During those years I also completed my master's degree on a scholarship fund, volunteered in hospice, and participated in interfaith groups.

In 2005 and 2006, I went through Level One Hospital Chaplaincy training at UCLA Santa Monica Hospital in California. After my years in Colorado Springs—which is known for being a center for conservative, fundamentalist Christian groups—I was looking forward to what I thought would be greater ease and friendship in the chaplaincy training where I could let down my hair, so to speak, in trendy and liberal Santa Monica. Our group was composed of Christians of different denominations and me, the Buddhist. Our supervisor shared with us that she preferred to have faith diversity in the training sessions as the process of learning together became more interesting and gave us more interfaith experience.

I was surprised during the training to find that some of the chaplains expressed more conservative views than anything I had experienced in Colorado Springs. In fact, seven years in Colorado Springs had been a refreshing surprise—people were very friendly, and strangers would always say hello when we passed on the street.

In chaplaincy training, we had to compose and share a personal mission statement as to what we expected to gain out of the training, and why. In my statement, I started one paragraph with the words, "In the ecumenical spirit I hope to work and learn together with the other chaplains."

One chaplain confronted me hotly saying, "Why are you using the word ecumenical? That is only for Christians. And why are you using the word 'spirit'? That represents the holy spirit of Christ."

Another chaplain diffused the tension by saying that "spirit" has more diverse meaning, such as when we say "the spirit of kindness" or "the spirit of joy." I went home that night and looked up "ecumenical" in the dictionary, and discovered that we both were right.

One definition was the meeting of various Christian traditions, but the first definition—as listed by Merriam-Webster—is "worldwide or general in extent, influence, or application."

I changed the phrase to "interfaith spirit" so that it would work better in the broader sense and wouldn't offend others. However, as Buddhism is studied and practiced in the West, we need to be aware of the words we are using and remember that English is Judeo-Christian based. Culturally, we will bump up against bias and tradition and will need to exercise tolerance and kindness as we find common ground.

There is a sticking point I find when people from another culture convert to a different faith. Sometimes they are more adamant, more strict, and more fundamentalist in their attitude than families that have spent generations in their faith. They can also be less tolerant of a faith different than their adopted one. A wonderful outcome, however, when someone converts or adopts a new faith different from their cultural tradition, is their tendency toward great practice, sincere study, inquiry, and love in cleaving to their new beliefs.

His Holiness the Dalai Lama says that it is generally better for one who is studying Buddhism to remain in their own faith tradition while they do so. Then if they find anything of interest or worthwhile in their study of Buddhism—or other faiths, for that matter—they should utilize it but not feel as if it is necessary to convert. One important thing to consider is that Buddhist philosophy does not profess a divine, independent, creator god. Thus, when one comes to an important juncture in life—particularly when one nears death or has a near-death experience—their early upbringing and deep beliefs may yield more solace in the belief that there is a creator god who oversees their life.

In the tradition of Buddhism, a person is responsible for his or her own actions, and what happens at death and after is based upon their accumulated merit and karma. This is a huge but subtle point not often examined by the faithful. Many Buddhists, in fact, tend to deify the Buddha or Buddhist saints, praying for salvation and relief from suffering and thinking they will set them free. While our teachers are indispensable to guide and teach us, we must through our own effort and understanding accomplish the stages to enlightenment, accumulating merit and virtue and purifying negativities and delusions.

Because I am part of an established faith, I have opportunities to attend many faith-based events and interfaith gatherings. I attend and sometimes organize annual Western Buddhist Monastic Conferences in the United States. Since we are a small population scattered across the continent, more often than not Western monastics are alone or associated with Buddhist centers that are predominantly lay communities, so we provide occasion for Buddhist monastics to get together.

In this materialistic age, monasticism will be rare, appealing to few. Monastics often work long hours in operational, management, or teaching duties. Our gatherings have become an event we anticipate, enabling us to take a break from our duties, and discuss and share our practices, traditions, and concerns. At one of our earlier conferences we had a "robes of the world" presentation to allow us to understand the history and meaning of different robes from China, Japan, Tibet, and Thailand, all of which were very different.

As Westerners practicing in the Buddhist tradition and culture, there is some adaptation and sorting that occurs where we question what effective practice and what cultural expression is, what is essential to keep, and what can be viably put aside. Though the vows have mostly remained the same, our ways of monastic practice evolved uniquely through the different cultures. Now as we meet together in the West, the cultures and traditions converge. While we learn a lot from each other, we need to have a more tolerant, open mind in accepting difference as well. In the Tibetan tradition in which I have been trained, the monastics often eat three meals a day, eat meat, prepare their own food, wear leather shoes, and won't kill a fly or mosquito. Our temples are also filled with vibrant colors and magnificent images.

Contrast this to the Chinese, Korean, and Vietnamese traditions in which the monastics are vegetarian, sometimes eat only once a day, and won't wear leather items. Japanese Zen temples are calm, more monotone in color, and sparse. In Theravada traditions, monks won't touch money, don't operate a vehicle, don't prepare meals, and will only eat what is offered, including meat. Some traditions adhere to principles of having only a handful of possessions, while in the West, many monastics fend for themselves, some work, live on their own, and have a car and a houseful of possessions.

Think about it. Many Tibetan temples were established in very high altitudes; my teacher's monastery of Gaden, for instance, is on a solitary, distant hill about fourteen thousand feet above sea level. It is above the tree line on bare, rocky land. There is little possibility of having a thriving vegetable garden to feed thousands of monks. There, the monks thrived on a diet of roasted barley flour and butter tea and sometimes a little bit of dried meat. (Many of the monasteries reestablished in India serve vegetarian meals now.) Entering the temple, the practitioner can enjoy the warmth of color and representations of Buddha images.

In the lush landscapes of countries of lower elevation, disciples and friends of the monasteries can cultivate land and bring fresh vegetables and other food for the monastics. A diverse, balanced vegetarian diet can be sustained. Zen temples provide a serene, unencumbered contrast to the outside world.

These are just some of the external differences! And then there are many philosophical and interpretive differences, just as there are in other faiths.

In some traditions women hold powerful positions, and can take higher ordinations; in others these opportunities are not available.

Many of these differences are due to their culture. Economic, and political shifts within each country over the millennia and climate and vegetation add to this factor as well. Even in the Buddhist monastic traditions, we must continue to engage in dialogue and come to appreciate and learn of others' traditions while deepening our own wisdom, conviction, and faith in our own traditions.

While I was in Colorado Springs, I had the good fortune to hear a talk given by Bishop John Spong, who takes a frank look at some of the assumptions and views in his own Christian tradition. While he has been criticized for being radical in his stance, what he does is analyze and question with a deep love of his faith. In the Buddhist teachings, the Buddha himself said we should not just blindly accept the teachings but test them as we would test gold—by burning, rubbing, and pounding them—to check their authenticity and quality before accepting things as true.

Bishop Spong speaks with humor and love when he says that if heaven is somewhere just beyond the sky, and Jesus rose into the sky and went to heaven, then according to what we know now about space, Jesus would have gone into orbit. According to the views of science and Christians in the first century, Mary had the immaculate conception of Jesus, and her womb was borrowed to nurture and bring forth the Christ child. But Bishop Spong says, and I paraphrase, "Taking what we know now of genetics and human reproduction, a woman contributes an egg to create a child, so it wouldn't be that it was only Mary's womb that was borrowed to produce Jesus. Does that mean that Jesus is then half human and half divine?"

The Christian monk David Stendl-Rast also questions how we can reach that joyous heart in our spiritual practice and break through dogmatic beliefs and encrusted, boring rituals that don't make sense. He writes that when someone has an ecstatic spiritual experience, it is recollected through writings, teachings, and moral purity, and celebrated in ritual. But over time, writings become dogmatic and may be disconnected from that joy. Ethical requirements become unchangeable and restrictive, and the celebrations become formalized and empty. Gratefulness is forgotten. To tap back into that joy often requires that the "fire of mysticism" breaks through the crust of formality, that there are men and women who can "distinguish between faithfulness to life and faithfulness to the structures that life created in the past and get their priorities right."

He says that what may appear as betrayal to the structure actually turns into faith, and is a courageous journey where the hero finds that joyous heart at a higher level.

Good ethics, right livelihood, and right thought lead to one's Garden of Eden.

Yet I had been hiding so long, seeking approval, doing what others requested rather than exploring what I could, would, or want to do, that I lost myself. Even as a Buddhist, I had run my life fulfilling other's wishes and suggestion. I lost my power and my life energy. It had been poured into my work as I focused on aligning myself with the center's activities.

When I lived at the nunnery in India, I tried to be a "good nun," helpful, teaching, setting a positive example for the younger nuns. All of this had been fulfilling for years. Even so, I always took the path of least resistance to avoid conflict; that allowed me to conserve my strength and gave me new opportunities, but it also subtly enhanced my skill in hiding, of not having to show up. In most situations, it was a beneficial action, but there are lessons to be learned in standing up and facing conflict to regain power and take charge of my life.

We must tackle our own demons, and sometimes they are subtle, appearing as skill, support, or a friend. The antidotes need to be more skilled, too. I had been drinking my own concoction of Kool-Aid, specializing in seeking approval at almost all costs. I had hidden myself in the warp and weft of a person of the cloth.

That is not what spiritual enlightenment is about.

While we deeply immerse ourselves in prayer, practice, study, conduct, and discipline, we must be authentic in our personal journey. In my walks on the path, subtle deception of erroneous views shut me down. My smiling outer form held a sad frown inside. But as long as seeking approval held the upper hand over speaking up, a part of me would be forced into mental exile. The result is that my work and life appeared worthy and good, but there was a subtle corruption in my practice, and it was hurting me. We sometimes live a long time, compromised and captive to our flavor of delusion. External structures of religion, discipline, and work ethic provide guidelines for us, meant to enhance our relationships and ability to live in harmony with others. These we take up, and choose to abide by to help reflect and direct our inner motivations and directions.

But we need vigilance to correct and redirect ourselves when we go off course. The course may be valid, but our interpretations and conduct may be flawed. We need skillful teachers and kind spiritual friends.

Buddhist teachings say we should check our teachers and the teachings carefully before we accept them, for even up to twelve years before one accepts them. But I think we need to always check, always be responsible to ourselves and others, and not fall into passive acceptance. We are so easily influenced by the times, by others, by our delusions. Our aspirations and guides need to be clear, true, beneficial, and lead to the results of benefiting oneself and others. While engaging in everyday activities, can we sustain the aspiration of enlightenment?

My life as a nun has been a surprising adventure. I wouldn't call it "heaven on earth," but it certainly has been more than I could have asked for or expected in ordinary life expression and opportunities.

I spent one year traveling with Tibetan monks all over the United States and South America, and doors opened for us everywhere. It was a goodwill tour, sharing the traditions from Tibet and the monasteries while raising funds to build a new hall for Gaden Monastery—a huge monastery reestablished in exile in South India. We were able to meet and enjoy the company of so many enthusiastic people who were interested in the monks' lives and eager to discover how they could help the Tibetan people.

We stayed in every kind of facility from modest homes to mansions. We even stayed in a mortuary called Nirvana in El Salvador and performed the healing ceremonies amid empty coffins with a large crucifix leaning over us. The people of El Salvador had just emerged from a twelve-year civil war, and the country was getting back on its feet. We couldn't believe the endless crowds in Caracas, Venezuela, who came to see the monks.

In Santiago, Chile, we stayed in a beautiful, new building complex with bricks made from the earth right where it stood, and even the glass panes were poured and made there. It was a site of an ancient battle and the owners wanted to build a center of healing for the people. In Buenos Aires, we met in a brick complex that was an urban tennis club with the courts built on top of the old buildings. We were invited to meet the governor and mayor of Medellin, Colombia, and enjoyed the view of the beautiful city and valley from the lofty office windows. One of our Spanish translators commented that, only a year before, the streets had been a blood bath of fighting drug cartels and police. Still, the people invited us in, welcoming the monks and their prayers for healing and peace.

Some might call this heaven on earth. Seeing and meeting people at heart level—in trust, interest, and goodwill—this is an expression of "the Garden." Being with the Buddhist monastics at our conferences, going to retreats with excellent and skilled teachers in beautiful urban and country settings, meeting remarkable people who are living and sharing their talents is most rewarding. Going to the U.S. Air Force Academy and meeting the cadets who took time for their spiritual practice and discussion. Living in the Himalayan foothills and studying with His Holiness the Dalai Lama and my teachers, living with the Tibetan people. It is a rich world.

6

Broken Promises

Between the EST seminars and the Buddhist studies, many of our friends and family—perhaps our Christian friends in particular—didn't understand the paths we were taking. They called EST, in particular, a new age cult program. But in many ways, it was an age-old program, a blend of ancient East and West teachings, with timeless principles worth living for.

It also was a new form of education that went far beyond traditional education. The program had been powerful enough to change both of us, and offered a world we had never seen before. It wasn't about being a prisoner of right and wrong, traditional versus new, and what is acceptable and what is not. And it showed that taking a broader view—seeing something from multiple points of view—could be valuable.

Buddhism offered new ideas and opened the mind up to new concepts, as well. But there, again, what people took away from the lessons depended a great deal on the degree to which they were committed to becoming better persons.

In both cases, not everyone was interested.

ROBERT: TAPPING A SPIRITUAL POWER

I invited my dad to the EST guest event. The moment he saw the room, he stormed out and went to the bar.

Like father like son.

I wasn't able to talk to him again about the event without having him lose his temper. The event remained a sullen wall of silence between us. Both of my sisters went through the program, and it brought us closer together as siblings. While we still had our differences, we were at least better able to understand each other. We were growing closer together, years after being torn apart over the war.

Over the years, as I pursued other avenues of nontraditional education, I realized that I had heard many of the same ageless words of wisdom at home, in church, in school, and in the Marine Corps. At home, I was strongly punished if I lied or stole. I heard similar words in church, in school, and in the Corps. The problem was that I heard the words—I just didn't get the message.

In March of 1974, the first full day of my EST training was about the class agreements. The seminar leader would go over each of ten or twelve agreements, slowly and deliberately. He would then ask each person in the room, "Do you agree? Are you willing to keep this agreement?"

Just when I thought the entire room of three hundred participants had agreed on a point, someone would raise their hand and argue, or want to be an exception to the rule, or want more details about the agreement. An hour later, the room would still be all churned up over the same topic—a discussion which had seemed to have been closed.

I had never seen such human psychoses show themselves around keeping one's word. After eleven hours, we finally were granted our first bathroom break, and I was ready to wet the floor. By that time I believe we were only on agreement number five, on the first day of the training, and I still had three full days to go.

I wanted to run.

But first I had to get to the men's room.

As I've said, I had *heard* the words before, but I never got the message. I knew about the importance of keeping my agreements. I knew I should not lie, not cheat, that I should follow the rules and keep my word. I knew the words. I had heard them in the Marine Corps, and there I got the message with a swift boot in the butt or a knee to the groin.

In the EST training, I was experiencing the message by sitting in a room filled with hundreds of people, arguing with the message. I cannot say that I got the message—not in its entirety—and that today my life is perfect. I *can* say that I keep hearing the same message, again and again. Each time, I gain a little deeper understanding of the meaning, incorporate it a little more into my life, and my life gets better.

After four full days of the training, I fully got that I was a liar, a cheat, a con man, a phony, a dreamer, a blamer, a loafer, a sex fiend, a thief, and whatever else I was pretending not to be. Worst of all, by pretending that I was *not* any of those people, I was only deceiving myself.

Jennifer—and many other people—had seen right through me.

Now that I was back stateside, I was very disappointed in the quality of our government leaders. And I also realized I was behaving no better than they were. Everything I had learned in Sunday School had gone by the wayside, starting with "thou shalt not kill." I had faced death in Vietnam, repeatedly, and come out alive. After making it through that, what kinds of other consequences could possibly scare me?

My war experience helped me develop a knack for using my dark side—along with issuing the license to use it—in the name of bravery and patriotism. My dark side was of value; it kept me alive. But off the battlefield, those tendencies had no place, yet turning them off was impossible. I had continued to use my dark side at will, always for my own gain, rather than harnessing and reordering it.

The marines gave me strength of character, but what was considered bravery in Vietnam was deemed recklessness back at home. As noted earlier, my character had become my character flaw. My personal checks and balances were gone, and I lived my life with complete disregard for others and the law.

Again, they say character is destiny, but so are our character flaws.

I didn't quite make the connection at the time, but today I see many political leaders—from Richard Nixon to Bill Clinton to Elliot Spitzer—fall by the same sword of perceived invincibility. They, like me, gave their life to a higher purpose, and their world changed. They, like me, developed strong character traits, but their character traits also came with character flaws. It's the flip side of the same coin, and they allowed their dark sides to surface . . . because they could.

In fact, that's what Bill Clinton's response was to a reporter who asked why he'd had relations with Monica Lewinsky. He humbly said, "Because I could."

He went on to say that it was no excuse.

I was living the reckless life I was living because I thought I could.

Today, I better understand why my father's friend broke up a great family for a younger woman, or how another family friend could go to jail for embezzlement. They probably had heard the words, but it took one man losing a family and the other going to jail for them to get the message—*if* they got it.

And the alcoholic who pretended not to be one—his failure was deceiving himself and not asking for help. He may not yet have gotten the message. He may still be lying to himself.

I better understand how Nixon could lie about a burglary or Clinton could think he could get away with sex with Monica. Two very smart men who knew the words, knew the rules, but it took being impeached or threatened to be impeached before they got the message, though I doubt they got the message.

"I am not a crook." Nixon is infamous for that line, and Clinton is famous for saying, "I did not have sex with that woman." He then tried to defend what he said by getting into the definition of sex, and trying to explain that what he and Monica had done was not sex. I wonder if he has gotten the message. It's not the definition of sex that is the sin, but the failure to keep his agreement as a married man, breaking his wedding vows, and then lying to the world. Breaking a promise—especially a vow made before god—and lying about it reflect tragic flaws in a person's character.

After four days of EST training, I realized I shared the same flaws. I better understood the thief and the con man. They know the words, too, yet our jails are filled with "innocent" crooks and con men who still don't get the message. I feel for the religious leaders who condemn others and are then caught in sexual acts. Or the politicians and ministers who bash gays and are then forced to admit they have been seeking gay sex from young interns in the halls of Congress.

Again, they know the words, but fail to understand the message.

I also better understood why so many people are poor when they want to be wealthy. They, too, know the words. They *say* they want to be rich, but when you look at their financials, you know they fail to get the message.

The same goes for people who are overweight or are suffering from illnesses when they want to be healthy; they know the words, but each time they step on the scale or receive a health warning from their doctors, the bathroom scale or the medical tests carry the message. Oftentimes it is a message they do not hear.

The world is filled with people who are looking for love. We all know the words "I love you," but being alone, hurt, or angry is the message. In our search for our spiritual families, it is the combination of the message and the *actions* that draws us together and binds us—not just the words.

When I passed through the gate of the Marine Corps Air Station at Kaneohe Bay, Hawaii, in 1974, I entered a new life. I left with a better appreciation for the lessons I learned at home, in church, in school, and in the marines. The words were the same, but I was finally getting the message.

I left the Marine Corps with a far better understanding of ethics, morals, legality, love, courage, and integrity, realizing that I had a lot more understanding to go. I knew I had to develop further, bringing a higher personal standard of ethics, morals, legality, love, courage, and integrity into my life. I knew that if I worked diligently at being better at living these values—not just saying the words—I would be heading in a direction closer to god, tapping into a spiritual power that is available to all of us, if we want it.

But I had a few things to take care of first. That's why in 1974, right after the completion of the EST training, I decided it was best to come clean myself and begin by cleaning up my broken agreements. I decided to start with the biggest ones and then work my way down to the tiny ones.

My most egregious issue involved the many rules I had broken as a marine pilot. Even though I was about to be discharged, I knew I couldn't leave without cleaning up my mess. Which I did.

The result was that I left the marines with a better understanding of the words, "And the truth shall set you free." I had heard the words before, but this time I was getting the message. I confessed everything I had done, and a month later I received my honorable discharge and left the Marine Corps. The captain had kept his word.

One of the reasons for my lifelong search and my hunger for personal development training and tools was that for most of my life I had been told the same thing.

"You have so much potential, but you don't use it."

The entire time I was looking for education and for ideas that would help me find my gift and use it in the best way possible. I wanted to tap into the potential I knew I had. Little did I know that one of the most important lessons would be one of the simplest, as would the tools it would reveal to me.

Words. All my life, words had shaped me. When I lied and lied again, to try to avoid prosecution, it was my words that reflected who I was. And when I told the truth, it was the words that revealed who I was becoming. In EST, my search had taught me the value of following through on my agreements, of keeping my word.

In my search, I began tapping more and more into spirituality and, inadvertently, coming closer to god.

EMI: TESTING THE WATERS

One Sunday, when I was six or seven years old—I remember because we lived at the Lono Street house—I woke up, looked around, and everyone was sound asleep. The funny thing was that the table was set, and breakfast was already on the table. That was Mom's job, but she was still sleeping.

Then I realized that Robert was not there. He had gotten up early, cooked scrambled eggs with chives grown from a little patch of garden outside the back door, made toast, and laid out a beautiful table for all of us. Then he had caught the rickety little bus to church.

That seemed so grown up and courageous to me! At most he was eight years old. It would still be a few years before I could steadily crack open an egg, let alone decide to catch the bus and go to church by myself.

It's true that Mom and Dad tried hard to hide the dark, sad sides of life from us. This resulted in my naïve, Pollyanna-ish view of people and life. With Dad as head of the department of education and Mom being a nurse, they must have encountered every form of human suffering—and happiness too. But we kids definitely were shielded from the difficulties of life that our parents and other Japanese Americans may have encountered.

As we grew older and could understand more, news would filter through to us, of domestic violence, alcohol abuse, or teachers fired for propositioning students. The few young girls who got pregnant just seemed to disappear from school, and it was taboo to speak about it. I don't know if it's better these days or not to have young girls bringing their children to school. It makes it difficult to stay focused on subjects of study when you have a child to watch.

I think it is definitely better to have discussions on sex education, both in school and at home. Mom and Dad didn't approach me— or probably any of us—on this subject.

World religions uphold strong ethical standards as guidelines for us to live in harmony. Church and other religious gatherings are meant to help us meet likeminded people and maintain good ethical standards in our relationships, in addition to learning and abiding by the philosophies and prayers of the respective traditions. Yet it is when we follow our delusions, or are influenced by negative people and ideas, that we succumb to wrong or harmful behavior.

In the Buddhist tradition, there are the ten non-virtues to abandon, and then ten virtues to cultivate. As a monastic, I have many more vows to keep, but the basics for everyone are these foundational premises. There are three non-virtues regarding the body:

- killing
- stealing
- sexual misconduct

There are four of the speech:

- lying
- slandering
- harsh words
- gossip

And there are three of the mind:

- covetousness
- ill will
- wrong view

The ten virtues contrast these non-virtues, beginning with three of the body:

- to protect life
- to respect the things belonging to others
- to use our sexuality wisely and kindly. (As a nun, I have a vow of complete celibacy.)

There are four virtues of the speech:

- to speak truthfully
- to reconcile others
- to use gentle speech
- to speak of things worthwhile

The three virtues of the mind are:

- to be content
- to have an attitude to benefit others
- to give up wrong views

These may seem self-evident, but when we check carefully and observe the realities of daily life, we see how we act in the heat of anger or out of jealousy, hatred, lust, and greed. These delusions override our better judgment and get us into hot water. Our rational mind may be good at seeing the reasoning for abstaining from non-virtue, but when our deceptive, delusory mind arises, that is when we have to apply every antidote we can.

During my time as a Buddhist chaplain at the U.S. Air Force Academy, there was a cadet I worked with for a few years who asked exceptionally good questions about ethics, particularly concerning deception and lying. I appreciated his questions because they helped all of us dig deeper into the way we operate.

He stopped attending our group after a while, and I later found out that the Academy had dismissed him for cheating!

Another cadet, who also was let go from the Academy, railed against the sexual misconduct issue because she felt it was fine to engage in extramarital affairs, as long as others did not know about it. She was sure the wife of the policeman she had been seeing didn't know a thing, and so she felt her actions would hurt no one.

When we want something badly we rationalize, justify, and perpetuate our actions. One teacher said this condition is like showing the good things—the things you are proud of—in bright spotlights, but the disturbing, harmful acts are like drinking poison while hidden behind a darkened staircase. While no one sees it, it's still going to catch up with you.

Even when there is study, discussion, and meditation on aspects of ethical conduct, the power of our delusions, our grasping attachment and aversion, can take over. Even if we want good things, and desire to be good people, our cravings for forbidden fruit can challenge us. When we indulge, we feel the surge of excitement, living on the edge and being alive. We crave at least an occasional thrill, seek this in our lives and want the honeymoon blush forever.

When we fall into the same old, predictable days in our work, home, and family, we sometimes fall into discontent and boredom, craving diversion.

Ethics and toeing the line of practice exist on one level. Working deeper, to clear away more subtle misperceptions and misunderstandings, exists on a deeper level. It is there, at the more subtle level, that we begin to peel away the more ingrained views, revealing our motivations, biases, views, and the way we operate in life.

Like Robert, I was always attracted to the opposite sex. But being so shy, I never dated or even kissed anyone right up through high school. I was terrified of being alone with a guy, to even go out for a soda.

Actually, I did go to a school dinner once with someone from the football team, but I was too shy and too nervous to engage in any conversation of consequence. Another friend invited me to a school dance, but I changed my mind several times and finally showed up to the dance alone. I didn't mean to confuse him. I loved to dance but preferred to go stag, to enjoy dancing with friends and not be obliged to anyone.

Still, I had that inherent attraction.

As Robert says, "Sometimes you get what you ask for in life." My rude awakening came in the summer of 1968. I had just turned twenty and I was ready to explore sex. More than ready, but still shy. It took me getting away from Hawaii and being away from my roots to finally indulge. I was with friends, and one of the girls gave me her leftover birth-control pills. Having had no education about any of this, I didn't realize that having unprotected sex after going off these pills made me even more fertile. I quickly learned the realities of life, and was pregnant three months later.

The results of my actions—as they have manifested in my life—have yielded very powerful messages. The present reflects past actions, ripening and bearing fruit. The answers to my own questions came in choosing to take responsibility for my actions, and raise Erika. As I said, it was a rough road for several reasons: The pregnancy was unplanned, I was unprepared for motherhood and marriage, and I was seeking answers to inner questions.

The day of Mom's funeral service was the day Dad revealed to us that she had had an abortion. I never asked him what happened, but I do recall that, as kids, we experienced her emotions and pain that she must have felt but hid from us in her life. And sometimes, with a brunt of anger we didn't always understand, we heard the emotions she *didn't* hide.

"Do you know the doctor said I never should have had you kids?" She would hurl her pain at us in ways to which we could not respond.

We knew she had suffered from rheumatic heart disease, but we never were encouraged to treat her differently. We didn't have tools to understand or to cope with what seemed like her hypochondriac focus on sickness.

For Dad to bring up the abortion on the day of her funeral tells me that it must have been something that weighed heavily on their minds during their lives together. It was another secret that festered into a wedge between people who loved each other. It made me wonder if that influenced why we did not have discussions about sexuality, or why they gave me no other options when I was pregnant with Erika.

I cringe to even think that I might have chosen differently back then because today Erika is one of the most important people in my life. Taking responsibility for her—amid my confusion and ambivalence—ultimately gave me strength and direction. Life choices and directions were made with her in mind, as were decisions about friends and relationships. Those decisions might have appeared confusing or even foolish to others at the time, as I found myself faced with challenges and was desperately seeking answers to what this life was all about.

It didn't seem fair—let alone sufficient or reasonable—that suddenly, with such finality, my lot in life was to settle down with a husband and child. Bob, Erika's father, tried really hard. For both of us, our lives were changed forever. We didn't stay together long, and during the years I raised Erika alone, my wanderings and travels to India and elsewhere were difficult for him to accept; he did not think highly of my peripatetic life.

Like Robert, I was also invited to attend an EST guest seminar, and couldn't quite believe the happy, confident, friendly, and competent presence of the volunteers. I wondered if their lives were always like that or if they were faking it.

I took the training in 1972—the first weekend led by Werner Erhard and the second one by Randy McNamara—and for several years I attended EST seminars. Before I did so, I was caught in a web of shyness, and the program allowed me to break through, clearing my mind. I learned that I could speak up, and more directly address each situation. The sessions helped me break out of my shell and the insular world in which I lived. Learning to think more effectively and see clearly through all the layers of concepts and presumptions helped me greatly. Erika later took the EST children's training, and we were able to communicate in better ways.

The EST training really hammered home the importance of keeping agreements. In many ways, I found it was easy to keep those agreements. I could almost always be at my seat on time, keep myself from missing a seminar, and make the number of calls I had committed to make.

But I could still hide. By keeping my agreements and showing up, I could disappear, more from myself than others because externally everything was in place. I could sit there and listen to people complain about the agreements and be very patient. I thrived on being calm and cool that way, so I could be a model graduate. I wasn't a colorful graduate, just an obedient one. I followed directions, I didn't make waves; I was playing the role of the "good" one.

What a bore. And it perpetuated my tendency to hide.

Still, I knew that change was in my future, and I was committed to it. I began to learn that as people change, it challenges those around them who have become comfortable in knowing their place, and are suddenly threatened by unexpected actions and new resolve.

At the core of the EST sessions were the agreements, the commitment to keep our word. Our word—our *words*—convey the strength of our heart and mind, of our convictions. In my case, I've developed the vocabulary of a monastic. Couched in this life, I felt I was doing great things for a long time, decades even. Yet we can subtly hide from our life lessons and its messages, recoiling from the opportunity to break out of our safety zones. When the safety zones become inadequate, discomfort increases, pushing us to grow.

When I think of breaking our agreements, of not living up to our word, I think of broken promises, and I'm reminded of those that were made to Dad when he made his run for lieutenant governor. People he trusted assured him he would land on his feet, should his election bid fail. He was told that a well-paid job would materialize, but it never did.

A man like my father took people at their word. He learned a hard lesson about trust, and honor, and broken promises. Witnessing the toll it took on him . . . that lesson was not lost on me or any of the Kiyosaki children.

7

Visions for the Future

Back in high school, when both of us were struggling as students, we couldn't have imagined what the future held for us—that one of us would become an author and educator, and the other would become a nun.

In our own fashion, and thanks in part to our parents, each of us started out naïve, even idealistic, with a touch of rebellion. Life's events tempered each of those things, and in doing so made us free in more ways than one.

Our paths took unexpected turns, whether into the traditions of Buddhism or the world of business. We seemed to be following radically different roads, yet as we looked to the future, we had more in common than we suspected.

ROBERT: FLASH OF REALIZATION

The irony of it all was that I was a far better marine on the day I left the Marine Corps Air Station at Kaneohe Bay than I had been when I was on active duty in the corps. As I drove away, I had a deeper appreciation for the Marine Corps and the Marine Code of Honor. I better understood the words duty, courage, and valor. I better appreciated the words "The truth shall set you free," and why lying was for cowards.

I finally recognized that truth took courage.

It became very clear to me why so many people were not free, even though they lived in the "land of the free." And why so many people lacked courage, even though they lived in the "home of the brave."

I remember taking my last salute. Returning the salute to the young marine guard, I reflected on how much of my life had been put into the receiving and the returning of that gesture. Watching the marine base grow smaller in my rearview mirror, a sense of loss overcame me as I headed over the mountain range to enter a new world in Honolulu.

That new world was the world of business.

As much as I missed the military, I realized that leaving gave me the opportunity to redesign my life. I was older and far more experienced. I was in a position to make wiser choices about my future. I remembered grownups always asking me when I was a kid, "What do you want to be when you grow up?" Now, at the age of twenty-seven, I felt I had a chance to ask myself that question.

What *was* my vision for the future?

With the benefit of my experience, I felt as if I could respond with different answers. With age, I felt I knew myself a little better. And as I entered the tunnel that goes through the mountains—separating the military base from Honolulu—my mind drifted back to when I was just ten years old, the age that I decided I wanted to go to sea to be a ship's officer. I also thought about when, as a twenty-one-year-old, I decided to go to flight school to become a marine pilot.

At the age of twenty-seven, I no longer wanted to be a ship's officer, and I did not want to be a pilot. At the age of twenty-seven,

I thought that sailing ships and flying planes seemed like the dreams of a boy.

Seeing the city of Honolulu unfolding before me, as I exited the tunnel, I was grateful to have this opportunity to once again choose my own path.

As soon as I got home to my condominium in Waikiki, I took off my military uniform and put on civilian clothes. I realized that I had been wearing a military uniform for more than nine years, and I took it and the other uniforms in my closet and packed them away, never to be worn again. I had invested so much of my life into what the uniform stood for, so much of my life and who I had become was represented by those uniforms.

About a week later, I drove to the Xerox Corporation's office in Honolulu, wearing a blue business suit, a white shirt, and a tie. I was about to see the world and become a new person behind a new uniform. It's the uniform I still wear today.

From 1965 to 1974, I didn't really know what my sister was going through. We rarely talked to each other during that time—since she was seeking peace, and I was fighting a war.

Over the next decade, her life was still a mystery to me. I heard she was living in a mountain commune with her daughter on the Big Island. My dad often complained to me about her lifestyle. He felt a need to protect his granddaughter. I didn't pay much attention to his grumbling, though; I was going through my own changes. My sister's world and my dad's world weren't the same worlds I was living in.

The years between 1974 and 1985 brought many changes.

IN RELATION TO WOMEN

During this time there were not many women in my life. Being in the military had offered few opportunities because the men greatly outnumbered the women. At least that was my excuse. Most women in my life then were war girls and prostitutes, and I enjoyed these relationships.

By 1974, I was ready to make up for lost time. I met many wonderful women at work, in church, in bars, and at seminars. Entering the world of business in 1974, I thought I had died and gone to heaven when it came to women.

IN RELATION TO EDUCATION

My poor dad suggested that I go back to school and get my master's or law degree. I went to the Law School at the University of Hawaii and quickly realized that I had neither the aptitude nor the desire to become a lawyer. I applied for the MBA program and was informed that I needed additional business courses before I would be accepted into the program.

My attempt at taking those additional undergraduate courses lasted about two months, and soon I knew that I did not want to remain in traditional education.

After attending the EST seminar, I had discovered that I was more interested in personal development seminars than I was in traditional education. I liked attending classes to expand my mind and spirit,

Playing Games with Money

At an event conducted by Dr. R. Buckminster Fuller, he stated, "The government is playing games with money."

Up to this point in his talk, I was not very interested in what he had to say. Up to this point, he was talking about the true coordinates of science and math. But when he went into his explanation of how the rich manipulated the money system via government officials, fundamentally stealing from honest people who worked for money, I became interested.

He wasn't the first person I had heard say this. My rich dad ranted and fumed about the financial deceptions the rich used in order to steal from working people. President Kennedy often spoke about how people used senators and congressmen to pass laws to make the rich richer. Kennedy emphasized the role of the president was to represent the people, not the rich. And now Dr. Fuller was saying the same things, saying that greed had taken over the world.

My ears perked up when I heard him say, "The rich use the government, via elected politicians, their lawyers, and accountants to legally put their hands in your pockets to take your money and put your money into their pockets."

Sometimes we need to hear things more than once and from more than one person for the message to sink in. When Dr. Fuller said the same things that my rich and poor dads and presidents Eisenhower and Kennedy had said, the message carried more impact. It was like finally finding a piece of my life's puzzle—that piece helped my life make more sense and take on greater meaning.

Fuller talked about each of us having a purpose to be here on earth— a job to do. He talked about each of us having a special god-given gift and that it was our job to develop our gifts and give our gifts to the world. He was adamant that we weren't here just to make money. He was certain humans were here on earth to create a world that worked for everyone, not just the rich or those born in Western countries.

He thought it ludicrous that our economic systems were based upon the economic philosophies of a preacher named Thomas Malthus, preaching a philosophy of scarcity rather than an economy of abundance. Fuller often punctuated his talks by reminding us that god or the Great Spirit was abundant and gave abundantly to us all. It disturbed him that a few men would claim god's abundance as theirs, and sell god's gift back to us . . . as did oil companies.

rather than compete for grades with my other classmates. I spent most weekends attending different seminars on a variety of subjects. I went to seminars on whole-brain learning, tantric sex, rebirthing, neurolinguistic programming (NLP), and past-life regressions. I even attended a class on communicating with the dead.

No one returned my call, not even my mom.

In many of these classes I came across the notion that our souls had a life's purpose—a purpose higher than being an employee or a soldier for the government. The idea of possibly having a higher purpose for my life intrigued me.

In relation to finance, I attended investment classes and business skills classes, not for the grades but to become a better investor and entrepreneur.

IN RELATION TO LIFESTYLE

I knew in my soul I wanted to be wealthy. I knew I wanted a rich lifestyle, not the middle-class existence of my parents. I wasn't sure exactly how I was going to go about becoming rich, but I just knew in my soul I wanted to get there.

Spiritually, I did not want to worship or be a slave to money. That point was crystal clear because my parents had had friends who saved, saved, and saved. They had tons of money, yet they lived frugally, below their means, claiming that money was the root of all evil. To me, this attitude was making money the god they worshiped—or feared.

I simply wanted to be rich, which meant being rich mentally, physically, emotionally, and spiritually. I wanted to develop a Midas touch, so that everything I would touch would turn to riches. I was willing to study, work hard, and develop my spirit so that one day I could truly be a rich person, rather than a middle-class person with a lot of money.

IN RELATION TO VISION

Observing Dad later in his life gave me a vision of the future. There he was, a highly educated, hard-working, socially responsible man, struggling in his final years working at odd jobs with very little in savings or investments to his name. He was completely dependent upon the government for financial and medical support.

Sadly, in him I saw the future for my entire generation—the baby-boom generation.

Little did I know that observing my dad's struggle would one day be the catalyst for my life's work. Today I wonder if my dad's struggle led me closer to my life's purpose; if it was the reason for writing *Rich Dad Poor Dad*, for creating the CASHFLOW® board game, and for my efforts to provide financial education throughout the world. Could my vision of the future lead me to my future mission?

IN RELATION TO LUST VERSUS LOVE

Over the years I had met many wonderful women because of lust, and I fell in love with some of them. Between 1974 and '84, I learned the hard way that I was not ready or mature enough for love. My relationships never seemed to work out. I met great women, but I was not yet a man worthy of a great woman.

Now married to Kim, I am grateful that I know the difference between lust and love. I would not have a strong marriage today if I hadn't learned this important distinction.

IN RELATION TO MONEY

In some of the churches I attended, I knew people who prayed to god to solve their financial problems. Many seemed to think that god should provide; just as many people think the government should provide. In some of the self-development seminars I attended, many people believed that positive thinking—or writing your goal on a piece of paper and looking at it daily—was all it would take to become rich.

I don't believe in wishing for money. Thanks to my rich dad, I believed that financial education, experience, skills, work, and dedication were required to solve money problems. It seemed that many people, regardless of whether they went to church or not, believed that "god will provide" and conveniently seemed to forget the second half of the message, which is "Give and you shall receive."

In one church, I heard the preacher say, "It is important to have faith that god will provide, but you must still do some work. Faith without work is dead." Many churches stress the importance of tithing, which means giving back to god. Once again, it seems that many people want money, but when it comes to *giving* money, they'd rather be on the receiving end.

My rich dad often said, "Give what you want. If you want a smile, smile. If you want a punch in the mouth, throw a punch. If you want money, give money." He also said, "Poor people are often poor because they do not give enough. They often say, 'I'll give money when I have money.' That is why they don't have much money. If you want money, give money. If you want more, give more."

IN RELATION TO FINDING YOUR LIFE'S PURPOSE AND GIVING YOUR GIFT

In some of the churches and some of the seminars I attended over the years, I learned that god or a higher power had given each of us a gift. Our job as human beings was to discover and give our gift to humanity. Even though I did not know if I had a gift at the time, I kept an open mind to the possibility that I had something to give, and focused on giving rather than praying that god would provide. I focused on generosity and service as paths to manifesting my dream.

Today, I realize that many people do not give their gift for two reasons. One is that they do not recognize it. And two, if they *do* recognize their gift, they do not work at giving it. Many people seem to think that a gift should come easily. For example, Tiger Woods is a gifted golfer. Although gifted, he still works very hard at developing and giving his gift to the world. Many golfers may be just as gifted, but they fail to work as hard as Tiger does at developing and giving their gift.

IN RELATION TO CHARACTER AND
CHARACTER FLAWS

In churches and seminars, I also learned that personal character is essential to giving your gift. Since your gift is a gift from god or a higher power, it is essential to deliver it with the highest degree of personal integrity and character. Over the years, I have personally experienced my gift being diminished when I allowed my character flaws to overpower my character. I found that if I wanted to improve the returns on my life, I needed to improve my personal character by not letting my character flaws cancel out my character strengths.

As I said earlier, character strength and character flaws are two sides of the same coin.

In one seminar, I had the blink of cognition and realized that many people fail to fully develop their character strengths because they *are* aware of the power of their character flaws, their dark side. In that seminar the leader skillfully demonstrated that our flaws reveal themselves under times of pressure or strength. For example under stress a person who does their best to be honest suddenly becomes a thief, or an outwardly sweet person reveals the vicious character hiding behind the façade.

Stress and challenges have a way of bringing out the very best, or the very worst, in people. During that seminar, I realized that if I was to develop my full potential, I had to find a way to allow my dark side into the light. Today I believe I am a more forthright person because I am more comfortable with the shy, good boy of my youth and the cold, blunt marine from my young adulthood, using both characters interchangeably.

IN RELATION TO LIFE'S MISSION

Again in churches and seminars, I learned that our life's purpose or mission is to take the gift we have been given, develop it, and give it.

My reason for working at the Xerox Corporation was to overcome my shyness and fear of rejection, as well as to learn the business skills of selling. Rich dad said that selling is an essential skill of the entrepreneur. After four years at Xerox, I eventually achieved my goal and became one of the top sales persons, with an income to match.

The problem was I found it hard to stay motivated. After so many different seminars, I knew my life's mission wasn't to get promoted, make more money, and climb the corporate ladder. Selling the latest model of Xerox copier didn't excite me, even if I did make a lot of money doing it.

Also, even though I was naturally competitive, I couldn't get fired up about beating IBM, our main competitor at that time. I discovered that a job, profession, or career is very different from a life's purpose, a calling, and a life's mission. My spirit was getting stronger, bolder, and I wanted the latter, not the ladder.

IN RELATION TO DEDICATION, DETERMINATION, AND DISCIPLINE

From my rich dad I learned that there are four types of people in the world of business. They are defined by the CASHFLOW Quadrant illustrated here:

Our school system does a respectable job training people for jobs as E's or S's. The problem is that the richest people on earth are B's and I's. From my rich dad, from personal development seminars, and

E stands for employee
S stands for self-employed, small business owner, or specialist
B stands for big business owners
I stands for investor

from church, I learned that being successful in any of the four quadrants required sacrifice.

In 1974, I decided not to follow in my poor dad's footsteps, which was to become an E with a safe government job, or listen to my mom who wanted me to become a medical doctor, at best an S. In 1974, I decided that when I grew up, I wanted to become a B and an I, a big business owner and investor. With that goal, I started to create my vision for the future.

When I told my rich dad that I was going to be an entrepreneur, he asked me if I was willing to wander in the wilderness for forty years. When I asked him "Why forty years?" He replied, "Because that is how long Moses wandered in the desert before god delivered him and his tribe to the Promised Land." He added, "Most people are not willing to wander for forty years because they find it easier to get a job and settle for a paycheck.

"They never find the Promised Land, that land of abundance, milk and honey, the Garden of Eden, heaven on earth." They give up the search for what they were born to do and never find their spiritual family.

For my sister, her test of faith was in Buddhism. My test of faith was in capitalism. For the second time in my life I wanted to find out if I had the right stuff.

The year 2014 will mark forty years of wandering in the B and I quadrants and finding my way to my own promised land. In 2014, I'll find out if my test of faith was strong enough.

By 1981, despite all my wisdom and good intentions, I found myself broke and divorced. I had built and lost my first business, and I had married and split from my first wife. I had tasted success, having built the first company to invent and bring to market nylon and Velcro® surfer wallets. The business had morphed into a company that manufactured goods for rock bands like The Police, Van Halen, Boy George, Duran Duran, Iron Maiden, and others. For about a year I was a millionaire. And I had fallen in love and married a great woman.

But I let wealth, success, lust, and love go to my head. I got cocky and arrogant, bought fast cars, and started cheating on my wife. My character strengths had turned back into character flaws and self-destruction. Instead of keeping my word to work on myself, my "self" took over.

I had repeated the same pattern that had gotten me in trouble in the Marine Corps. It became obvious to me that I needed to do some deeper soul-searching if I wanted to gain the strength I needed to go forward in my life. We have all seen people fall from grace due to flaws in character, and I had fallen hard . . . for the second time.

The sad part was, I knew the power of words and the importance of keeping my word; I had heard this again and again in the many seminars I attended over the years, as well as in Sunday School as a kid.

"And the word became flesh," was the line, though it never really related to my life at the time. But in 1981, in my vulnerable state, the realization of the meaning of those words blasted through my head like an electric shock.

Could it be that something as simple as words could pack so much power? Could it be that something as simple as words could determine the quality our lives? Could it be that our lives are simply a reflection of our words?

Could it be that simple?

In a stunned state, I began to wonder if the difference between a rich person and a poor person was simply their words? Could the difference between a happy person and a depressed person simply be the words they chanted to themselves? Is the difference between a crook and an honest person a choice of words? Is the difference between a millionaire and a billionaire their words?

As I thought about it in more practical terms, I realized that the difference between a dentist and a lawyer—both smart and trained people—was the words they used in their professions. The more I thought about it, the more I realized how powerful words are, and that we *do* become our words.

The flash of realization lasted about a minute. After that, I was back to normal thinking. The impact of the flash subsided, but I never forgot the message. In simple terms, it seemed that our brain was like an engine in a car, and words were the fuel. If we put bad fuel in the engine, the engine performed badly. Could it be the same with our minds' relationship to words?

I realized that my word—my ability to carry out an agreement, or the lack of it—along with the words I spoke, had become flesh. I was the product of my words, and I had lost everything. Now my own self-talk, the words inside my head were telling me that my life was a shambles, and it was.

I was calling myself a loser, and I was becoming one.

With a clear realization that I needed to change—and that I'd need some help doing it—I went in search of a new teacher and new answers. That year, 1981, I met and began studying with Dr. R. Buckminister Fuller.

After my poor dad and my rich dad, Dr. Fuller was the third major influence on my life. People have called him one of the most original minds of the twentieth century. He was a futurist, author, inventor, and philosopher. Many of his predictions are coming true in our age. Dr. Fuller also had an opinion on words.

He said that words are the most powerful tools created by man.

EMI: CHOICES

Robert speaks of people knowing the words but not getting the message, and of the Christian saying the "word becoming flesh." He asks, "Could it be that something as simple as words could determine the quality of our lives? Could it be that our lives are simply a reflection of our words?" He reflects on the words we use in our professions.

Likewise, I think words are a reflection of our mind and a key to our beliefs.

He asks if the difference between a rich and poor person is their vocabulary. Vocabulary is a reflection of our mind and mental states. While we use the vocabulary of our professions, we also embody the characteristics of mental attitudes about our station in life, our social relationships, our relationship to wealth. In every profession there are some who are wildly—or quietly—successful, prosperous and famous, as well as those who are obscure, poor, and challenged in their work. It's true for politicians and businesspeople, for farmers and monastics.

If anyone had told me in high school that I would be a nun when I grew up, I would have crumbled. Becoming a monastic was never a thought that entered my mind. When I was in college, I chose psychology and teaching as my course of study, but I was a wanderer; searching was a part of my life.

My brother, on the other hand, was far more focused.

Whenever I thought about my future, I was always attracted to social sciences, but my dad discouraged me and, at the time, it was easier for me to just acquiesce, rather than to defend my position. He suggested that I go into more exacting sciences rather than the "pseudo-sciences," which was what he used to call psychology. Robert was the opposite. When Dad questioned him, asking, "Why do you want to be a marine?" Robert just went ahead and did it. He didn't concern himself with approvals or permissions.

We were both rebelling in our own way. Robert just went on and did what he wanted, while I searched quietly, exploring new lifestyles and paths and learning about life. That was a big difference between us. Until 1968, that is—the year I got pregnant.

Once Erika was born and I began raising her, I had many new lessons to figure out, like how to take care of my daughter and support ourselves. And I had to do so while I continued trying to figure out life.

About the time Erika and I moved to the mountains of Hawaii, I went on welfare, which would have violated every bone in Robert's body if he had known. It rankles me now to recollect it. My dad always thought the government should take care of us, although welfare wasn't what he had in mind. At the time he knew I was getting assistance, but we never talked about it. His question would have been, "Why don't you get a good government job with a good pension?" just as he'd tell Robert, "Stay in the Marine Corps and get a good retirement."

Those were acceptable ways for the government to take care of us; welfare was not.

The way I justified being on welfare was by telling myself I was doing "good work" for others. I was studying spirituality; I was helping others with the money that I received from the government; we were making dome homes, wooden hot tubs, and working with whomever wanted to join us. A lot of unusual people passed our way.

I was part of a community, and searching for a perfect utopia— my heaven on earth—with a group of likeminded people. We had a great deal in common, and unfortunately, one of those commonalities was that we were welfare recipients. We justified our behavior together, and looking back, I can see how I bought into the pattern of government welfare assistance because it was so accepted by the people around me.

My feelings about being on welfare began to change when I ran into a woman who had been a sorority sister of mine. She told me that since the government gives money to single moms with kids, her plan was to just keep having kids.

That disturbed me.

Deep down I knew this wasn't right. Another wake-up call came several months later when I went to apply for food stamps in Honolulu at the government office. It was a crowded hall, and as fate would have it, my caseworker was another sorority sister. It was her job to validate my need for food stamps. I was so embarrassed. She said, in a matter-of-fact way, "We all go through changes in life." It was a loaded statement. And at the time, it just was one more signal for me to make a change, take control, and get out of the welfare mentality.

When Erika was four, I got off welfare and resolved never to get into that situation again. It was hard because my studies were important to me, so most of the money I earned was going to sitters and spiritual and personal development seminars. It was a struggle financially, but those classes were something I knew I had to do. But I discovered that to be congruent with my spiritual path, I had to be ethical and get off welfare—for myself and my child.

Welfare was killing my spirit.

In addition, my welfare attitude conflicted directly with my desire for spiritual freedom. Buddha teaches us that we have the potential to be free and that we need to work at it. Even the term Buddha means "awake." A Buddha is someone who has purified all "veils and delusions" and accomplished excellent virtuous qualities. It was time for me to work at removing my own veils and delusions and become a better person.

Buddhism appealed to me because of the excellent teachings and the clarity of the teachers who were explaining how to apply them. Another reason for my attraction to the Buddhist path was that most of the teachers I met were kind, happy, had a great sense of humor, and embraced life. Those were qualities I wanted to cultivate in myself as well.

I had to learn to trust my spiritual leanings and follow the deep, ethical principles that our parents infused in me, rather than rely on the government. I believed that following my spiritual path would provide for me. But I also had to make sure that I wasn't trading one institution for another. This time, my path had to be my own, and I had to walk it with my eyes wide open.

Upon my decision to work in Alaska—so I could earn enough money to travel and study in India—I asked my ex-husband to care for Erika for a year. He agreed, so she returned to Hawaii from Colorado, and he enrolled her in a Japanese Buddhist school in Honolulu. The decision to leave her went against everything I knew to be right as a mother. She desperately wanted to go to India with me. Unfortunately, I knew I wouldn't have the money for both of us to make the journey, let alone providing for her while we were there.

I was also concerned about health and the possibility that she might be exposed to disease there; after all, she was just a little girl. Yet despite it all, the truth was that I wanted nothing more than to take her with me. My wish was for us to experience India for the first time together. But it simply wasn't financially possible, and I saw that as part of the sacrifice.

My decisions—leaving Colorado, going to work in Alaska, and then traveling to India—made no sense to the people around me. My ex-husband thought my idea of leaving was irresponsible; he thought I was a flake. My dad was very concerned, my mom wanted me to be a "good girl," and my actions often baffled them. Mom and

Dad wanted a life of security and guarantees. But I was on my own path, and even though I realized I might not find what I was searching for, I was willing to take the risk.

In me, there was a compelling need to go, and for one of the first times in my life I wasn't going to let disapproval stop me. I was moving forward with or without permission. I knew what I wanted; there was no question in my mind or heart. Going to India to study was what I had to do, even though it meant putting aside my role as a mother for more than a year.

Today, I realize that this was "my calling," and I was seeking spiritual wholeness. Back then, it felt like an undercurrent within me, telling me I had to go. A call, a pull so strong that I knew I was choosing the right path. Sometimes callings involve sacrifices and challenges, and that was certainly true then. It was tremendously fulfilling on one level, but there was a part that was out of balance. Erika, as every child always would, wanted to be with her mother, but my financial limitations and my drive to study in India and elsewhere caused separations. In looking back, I missed some precious growing times when more nurturing and being present would have been good for both of us.

8

Food for the Journey

Dr. R. Buckminster Fuller considered himself an ordinary man. By rep-utation, however, he was considered one of the most accomplished men in United States history.

His life touched upon ours in many ways, both directly and indirectly. He was the one who designed the geodesic domes near the Kilauea volca-noes, and in 1979 and '80 he shared a lecture tour across America with Werner Erhard, the developer of the EST seminars that we both embraced.

He devoted his life to determining what the individual could do that larger organizations and even governments could not, and in his own words, "applying the principles of science to solving the problems of hu-manity." He was known as "The Planet's Friendly Genius."

ROBERT: SEEKING STRESS

When I was a kid, I realized I had two handicaps in life.

One: I'm inherently lazy. That laziness caused me to flunk out of school and has cost me millions of dollars over the years.

Two: I have no particular talents. There wasn't anything I was good at. I had no specialty. I was average.

Knowing I was inherently lazy, I realized that if I wanted to do anything in life I'd have to find environments where laziness wasn't tolerated. Surfing was good for me. If I was lazy, the waves pounded me. One of my friends actually died at Sunset Beach where we surfed. He took off on a large wave and was a little late on the turn. He wiped out, and they didn't find his body until a few days later when searchers discovered what remained of him after the sharks had finished with him.

Dr. Fuller was not a surfer, but he was a sailor, and he often said that men of the land were different from men of the sea because men of the sea respected the powers of nature. Having spent so much time in the ocean, I learned to respect the forces of nature early in life.

Football was another environment that worked for me. I didn't particularly like football, but I needed the discipline of the sport. Playing football wasn't for lazy people. The training was intense, and the constant fear of bodily harm meant that I couldn't allow myself the luxury of what the coach called "pussy-footing." Even during practice, being lazy got you "two more laps." Laziness in a game meant someone else played while I sat on the bench.

I went to Kings Point for much the same reason. I knew that a strict military and academic environment was the best way for me to graduate. The discipline was extreme, twenty-four hours a day, seven days a week. If I had gone to the University of Hawaii, I would have flunked out. A party school wouldn't have been a good environment for me.

Even at the Academy, I sought out more disciplined environments. I joined the rowing team because I had to find a sport that was more painful, more disciplined than school itself. The pain of rowing on freezing Long Island Sound in the winter was so grueling that my hands and butt were always bleeding. But the pain gave me the escape I needed from the misery of school.

At the Merchant Marine Academy at Kings Point, New York, the rowing team provided the most intense activity of any sport. Robert is the team member at the top right with his oar in the air.

After the Academy, I joined the Marine Corps where laziness was defined as dishonor. It meant that you let your fellow marines down, and it was not tolerated. In Vietnam, laziness meant death.

This may be why I am an entrepreneur today. For entrepreneurs, laziness means going broke. There's no job security. Many countries—like France and Australia—make it very hard to fire an employee for laziness. But entrepreneurs are fired every day—by the market. Again, it's an environment that does not tolerate laziness.

By finding the environments where I was pushed mentally, emotionally, physically, and spiritually, beyond my reality of what was possible, I would find myself being pushed into an altered state of consciousness. Today, it's called the "zone." I experienced it so many times. In football, I'd catch a pass that no one could catch or make a tackle that seemed impossible. The pressure caused me to play beyond my self-defined limits. I was playing outside of myself.

Some therapists call this "forced meditation."

Rowing races are ten minutes long. After the first four minutes, you are running on empty, and for the next six minutes your body is acting on pure willpower. The pain is so excruciating that there's no energy left, only a spiritual synchronicity that exists above the pain and settles into the boat. The entire team of eight rowers taps into an altered state of power. It's the eight-man crew that can run on sheer willpower that wins.

In Vietnam, there were times when my crew and I should have died but didn't. Something else took over. Often, after such an incident, we asked ourselves, "Why are we still alive? Why are those guys dead? How did *we* get out of that situation?" Many times we went beyond life and death.

My sister meditates. I never meditate. I tap into my zone through stress. Ilya Prigogine won the Noble Prize in Chemistry in 1977 for the Theory of Dissipative Structures. He believed that stress was the way intelligence grows. By putting myself into intense situations that pushed me beyond the limits of what I think I'm capable of achieving, I grew. And I discovered all this because of my inherent laziness.

Most of my life has been about taking myself to the breaking point, which, as Prigogine said, causes the stress that causes things to reorder. Most people go the other way; they take the easy way. Like the people in my neighborhood who walk slowly around the loop, thinking they are exercising but never shed a pound. They are moving, but not stressing, so their bodies never reorder. High-performance athletes know they must take themselves to the breaking point and beyond if they want to get stronger, better, faster. Improvement happens by going beyond the limits.

When I was fifteen years old, and I went out for football, I weighed 240 pounds. By the end of the season, I was 195 pounds and stronger, thanks to the stress of exercise. To make steel stronger, the metal is often heated to red hot then dropped into cold water, and it's the stress between hot and cold that strengthens the metal. This is what Prigogine was talking about. Just like steel, humans are capable of becoming stronger through stress.

Many of us have experienced the feeling of going beyond what we think is possible and not giving in to reality. It's beyond an adrenaline rush. The zone is an out-of-body experience.

I found that I actually need stressful situations in order to relax. Golf is relaxing for many people, but it doesn't get me into a state where I can let everything go. I end up thinking about everything else *except* golf when I play. So I relax by going extreme. This is why I enjoy sports that are extreme. When I play rugby, I think of nothing else but the game.

From 1974 to 1980, my full-time focus was on increasing my brain power. Working at Xerox, my job was to educate my brain to become an entrepreneur. My part-time job was to increase my willpower. While my fellow Xerox sales people were at home watching football or in the bars chasing women, I was constantly at seminars or workshops, chasing women, and searching for answers.

The idea was to win financially by increasing both my mind power and my willpower. My dad thought I was wasting my time and money doing these seminars. To him, the only real education was found in prestigious universities such as Stanford and the University of Chicago—schools he had attended. Although he never graduated from these schools, he was very proud to say that he studied there. Dad always wondered why I attended courses that did not count toward an advanced degree, a promotion, or a bigger paycheck.

My rich dad understood what I was doing. He hadn't graduated from high school, nor did he have a college degree, yet he regularly attended seminars such as the Dale Carnegie courses. He was into personal development. When my poor dad found out that rich dad would fly from our sleepy little town of Hilo to Honolulu just to attend sales courses or listen to motivational speakers, he thought my rich dad was wasting both time and money.

I wasn't able to discuss what I was learning with my poor dad. He didn't want to hear about anything that didn't come from an accredited school. On the other hand, rich dad and I would spend hours talking about what I was learning. He knew that success was more psychological than academic. He was more interested in personal power than advanced degrees.

Rich dad knew that the subconscious mind was more powerful than the conscious mind. He knew that the subconscious mind could be our best friend—as well as our worst enemy. He knew the importance of educating both the subconscious mind and the conscious mind.

My biological dad—my poor dad—focused on educating his conscious mind.

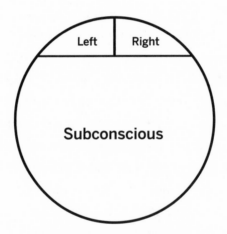

**This is an over-simplified view
of the human brain.**

Having attended both traditional educational courses and personal development courses, I understood the value found in both forms of education. A traditional education is important, especially if you want to be a doctor or lawyer or climb the corporate or government ladder. A personal development education is important, as well, especially if you want to develop personally, emotionally, and spiritually. I believe personal development is especially valuable if you are very ambitious and want to accomplish as much as you can in your life.

There are a number of philosophical differences between the two types of education. Traditional education focuses primarily on the conscious mind and on being smart, having the right answers, and avoiding making mistakes. Personal development, on the other hand, focuses on your spirit. These programs focus on motivation, expanding one's reality on life, taking risks, and being willing to fail and stand up again after you fail. These courses focus on the sub-conscious mind and how to have your subconscious mind work *with* you, not against you.

I invited my poor dad to attend seminars with me because I thought he needed to learn how to stand up again. He had always been an A student. Until he lost the election, he had never failed in his life. After he lost the election and then his wife, he could not stand up. His heart was broken, and he was grieving. He still had his brain power, but he had lost his willpower. His spirit was broken.

By 1980, I had lost my first business and my first million. If not for my training in personal development courses, I too might not have stood up again. I lost two more businesses before I made another million dollars and finally hung on to it. As most of us know, it's not how many times you fall down, it's how many times you can pick yourself up.

One of the greatest motivational speakers and best-selling authors is Zig Ziglar, a devout Christian who was able to reach a wider audience with his message of personal empowerment. His book *See You at the Top* is filled with religious principles put into everyday language. I have personally met Zig, and he is one of the finest men I have ever known. He is a real Christian who practices what he preaches and writes about.

Today Oprah Winfrey is the most prominent female name in personal development. She inspires millions of people all over the world by touching their hearts and their minds, inspiring them to stand up and take charge of their lives.

A blessing from on of the most powerful woman in the world

Alcoholic Anonymous (AA) has its roots in Christian religion. And when the Beatles went to India, they popularized Eastern music—much of it religious—introducing it to the West. John Denver is famous for country and folk-rock music that has deep religious influence. So it's true that many of the greatest influences in personal development are based in religion.

Many network marketing and direct sales companies have extensive personal development components in their programs. This is a major reason I endorse that industry. It does a lot of good: first building up people, and then teaching them how to build up a business. I support those businesses that teach people to survive in the real world.

Personal development has taught me that we can and do, indeed, create our own reality. Let me give you a personal example. When

I failed English because I could not write, and flunked out of high school at the age of fifteen, I was emotionally hurt. The pain was a scar on my soul. I felt as if I had let my family down. I was ashamed, embarrassed, and teased by my classmates. The emotional pain was then glued to the thoughts "I am stupid. I will always be stupid. I will never be smart."

These thoughts, fused with emotions of sadness and anger, became real when I *believed* I was stupid, and continued to struggle and fail in school. If not for sheer willpower, I would not have graduated from college. I had to *face* my thoughts—thoughts that had become flesh, thoughts that I was stupid—every day of school.

In my science classes, I learned that two objects cannot occupy the same space at the same time. For example, you cannot fit three large cars in a one-car garage. In some of my later personal development courses, I discovered that two thoughts cannot occupy the same space at the same time, either. In my example, I could not embody the thought "I am smart" as long as the thought "I am stupid" was already in that space. It was only after the emotions of sadness and anger were melted away that the thought "I am stupid" was set free and the new thought, "I am smart," could occupy that space.

Once the emotional thought "I am stupid" was dissolved, my thirst for learning was renewed, brought back to life. In 1974, at the age of twenty-seven, I became a student again—a student with a hunger to learn.

This is an example of one of the transformations I went through as a result of my personal development classes. I was able to heal a mental and emotional scar that went back to high school. It's ironic that today I am best known as a writer and yet, when I was fifteen, I flunked out of school because I could not write. If not for a personal development class, today I might still be an intellectual cripple, and you would not be reading this book.

Concentric Circles

Many personal development courses have their roots in Eastern and Western religions, tapping into spiritual power. I have studied concentric circles, which are credited to Eastern educator Confucius. When you look at Confucius's's Concentric Circles of Life, the first five rings are:

Spirit   Mind   Body   Family   Human Kind

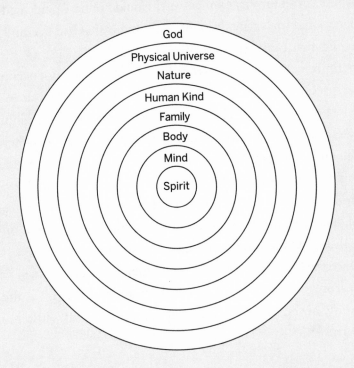

As I studied, I found out that our spirits are like sawdust, floating around in the first circle. When we add the mind—circle number two—our thoughts can act as the glue for our spirits, making them whole. Once our spirits and our minds become whole, they then manifest in our bodies—circle number three. When this happens, our thoughts become flesh. Our thoughts become us. We then create our reality.

When you go to a chiropractor, the chiropractor checks for vertebrae that are out of alignment. If a vertebra is out of alignment, your life forces have trouble getting to the different parts of the body. If life forces are blocked, the body begins to degenerate.

The circles of life are much like the human spine. Many people have blocks emotionally, mentally, and physically. If these blockages are severe, then the life forces between a person's spirit and god are diminished. If the line between god and a person's soul is blocked, their personal power—their ability to do and create—is diminished. Many personal development courses, therapies, self-help programs, and religious courses are designed to reconnect a person's spirit to god. It's up to the individual to come to terms with *wanting* to increase personal power and then seek the appropriate assistance to regain their power.

Today, almost anyone who is anyone has a personal coach. Many coaches are using human potential technology that comes out of East-West religions, modern psychology, and indigenous cultures. My rich dad was one of my first coaches. Today, I have a number of coaches for different aspects of my life. A coach is there to help you tap your power and support you in strengthening your spirit so it will shine through the downs as well as the ups of your life.

One of the definitions for the word *power* is "the ability to do or create." My reason for attending these seminars was simply to get my power back. I felt as if my personal power had been beaten down at home, at church, at work, and at school. Yet I knew I had potential. I knew I had more power. I knew something was holding me back.

Another lesson taught in a seminar I attended was that we are not our minds.

The concept was that our minds could be our enemy as well as our friend, actually sabotaging our dreams. Until that seminar, I had always thought my mind was my friend. After the seminar, I began to realize how much my mind could prevent me from achieving what I wanted in life. Understanding this helped me better understand why poor people who want to become richer nevertheless remain poor, fat people who want to become thinner get fatter, lonely people remain lonely, and success eludes many people with talent.

The point the seminar made was that our minds often cause us to do things we know we should not do. It is our mind that causes us to sometimes lie when we know we should tell the truth. It is our mind that causes us to sometimes cheat instead of play by the rules. It is our mind that sometimes causes us to do things we know we should not do, especially if our willpower is less than our brain power.

The point the seminar leader was making was that every time we are morally or ethically out of integrity and lie about it—especially to ourselves—we sacrifice a little bit of our personal power. If we want to *regain* our personal and spiritual power, we have to come clean, tell the truth, and face the consequences, just as I did when I told my commanding officer the truth about drinking and flying women to deserted beaches. Simply put, we hold the ability to increase our personal and spiritual power, if we have the courage to tell the truth.

This seminar also reminded me of church. In church, I heard similar messages about the power of truth, although phrased in different ways. In the seminar I was hearing the same message expressed in much more blunt and often confrontational ways. I also found it interesting how many people, myself included, had trouble coming clean and telling the truth. It seems that our desire to be perfect—that person who does no wrong, makes no mistakes—can cause us to cling to our little secrets.

As the years went on, the same lesson, the same message on the power of words, kept appearing and reappearing in many of the courses I took.

In 1981, I attended a course entitled "The Future of Business" at a ski resort near Lake Tahoe, on the border of California and Nevada. It was a week-long event with Dr. R. Buckminister Fuller as the featured speaker. It was a horrible, boring event, and many times I thought about leaving. Yet, for some reason I stayed, and I'm glad I stuck it out to the end because on the last day I went through one of the most powerful transformations in my life. I would not be writing this book, and you would not be reading it, if I had left the seminar early.

Twice during my time with Dr. Fuller I attained a different state of being. I believe I entered a dimension parallel to the current reality. Those two events, although very different from the states of consciousness I achieved through stress or danger, were just as powerful. They arrived through compassion rather than pain. Every organization I was part of—football, rowing, the military—required toughness.

When I was around Dr. Fuller, my zone wasn't a state of toughness but a state of compassion.

Ultimately, I am thankful for my handicap of laziness. It put me into places where the laziness or karma of my past could not drag me down. I don't allow myself the luxury of saying I "can't do" something or "can't afford" something. That's laziness, and I won't allow my laziness to dictate my future.

My future is today.

That's karma.

Today I have two "zone" states, and I use them both. One is the tough state, and the other is the compassionate state. Each takes me to a similar spot, and it's a kind of euphoria where the things that I worry about are of no consequence.

When I hear of or talk to people who are stressed out about paying bills and keeping their jobs, I can't help but feel that the reason they are in such a state is that they have not stressed themselves *enough*. They have not pushed themselves beyond the limits of their pain. On one of the morning news programs, I recall seeing a woman lament about being four months behind in her house payments and on the brink of foreclosure. The reporter asked her what she was going to do. Her reply was astonishing: "Well, I'm just going to hope for the best." It reminded me of a sermon my minister gave when I was a kid. It was titled "Hope is for the Hopeless."

When I heard Dr. Fuller say that he considered himself an ordinary person with no special talents, I felt a connection. Just as I had had my challenges with conduct in the marines, he was thrown out of

---

Vision and Prophecy

There are lines from *Have You Ever Seen the Rain?* by Credence Clearwater Revival that go:

> *Someone told me long ago,*
> *There's a calm before the storm.*
> *I know . . . I know*
> *It's been coming for some time . . .*
> *I want to know,*
> *Have you ever seen rain?*
> *Coming down on a sunny day?*

When Noah was building his ark, he was building his ark on a sunny day. He was doing so in response to a message and vision from God. I would say that most people, throughout history—people who have done extraordinary things—are motivated by some vision, some prophecy, an urgency to change the future. For example, Albert Nobel created the Nobel Prize for Peace once he saw the power inherent in his creation—dynamite—and how dynamite's power could be used for construction and *destruction*.

Harvard twice for conduct issues and finally finished his degree at the U.S. Naval Academy. He claimed to have no special talents, but he accomplished so much. The American Institute of Architects gave him their Gold Medal award, yet he has no degree in architecture. Harvard recognizes his as one of their most noted graduates, yet he never actually graduated from Harvard. He authored twenty-five books and held more than two thousand patents, even though he was a specialist at nothing.

Dr. Fuller said that a life of specialization could easily become a life of obsolescence. And the more specialized you are, the fewer

At the time I met Dr. Fuller in 1980, I, too, had a vision and a prophecy for the future. It was the same vision my rich dad saw and my poor dad was living. It was the problem many of us are aware of now—the tremendous economic gap between the rich and poor and the dependence of millions of people in Western nations, becoming dependent on government financial and medical life support.

The problem was, at that time, I was working only to save myself from the vision and prophecy I could see coming. I could see the brewing financial storms and was working as hard as I could not to be a victim of what I saw.

When I met Dr. Fuller, I was working only for my own personal salvation. After my meeting with him, I realized I needed to work for more than my own personal needs.

Seeing my father sitting at home, dependent upon government programs such as a teacher's pension, Social Security, and Medicare to keep him alive, I saw my own future as well, especially if I did not take immediate steps to change it. Looking into the future, I could see growing numbers of people just like my dad.

people you can serve. He thought it was better to be a generalist than a specialist. Specialists look at the world from a narrow point of view, while generalists see life in the big picture.

Our traditional schools actually train us to be specialists, not generalists. Entrepreneurs are often generalists, and they usually are the richest because they have served the most people. This theory has played out in my life. As a generalist, I can assemble great teams of people who are more expert than I am to make things happen. In the process, we all learn together and grow together, make money, and serve others.

Dr. Fuller provided me much inspiration for just about everything I do. He said that god is not scarce, god is abundant. He revealed that economics defined conventionally as "the allocation of scarce resources" is a myth. Resources aren't scarce. Everyone can participate in abundance, and in fact that is what god wants us to do.

He helped me realize that anyone can be wealthy if they are taught. It is everyone's right to have the opportunity to learn. By combining my poor dad's sense of service, my rich dad's sense of money, and Dr. Fuller's generalized principles, I was able to live a somewhat experimental life of my own—removing myself from the rat race, then seeking and doing god's work.

Fuller also had a lot to say about the state of the planet. He said that humans are in what he called "the final examination," and if we don't take care of this planet, we will perish. He thought it insane that we kill each other over oil and invest so little in limitless renewable energy, such as solar power. All the energy we need is at our disposal, yet we fight over a vanishing resource that when burned contaminates our planet and harms us all.

I make a point of reallocating the money from my oil investments into solar energy development. Earth, Dr. Fuller said, is a little "dirtball planet where nature is allowing us to create heaven on earth." He didn't think god really cared one way or the other, but be believed that *we* should care. After all, our home, the earth, is a living organism, and we are killing it. If we believe that change emerges only through emergency (*emerge* is the root of *emergency*), then we are hitting that emergency now. Think about the business of energy; it's not science but greed that has caused such slow progress. Business hasn't figured out how to put a meter between us and the sun.

Dr. Fuller also had his view on the power of words. He said, "Words are the most powerful tools created by man." Although he believed in a god—a supreme being not of human form—he was not a religious man. He often mentioned how nonmilitary religious and educational leaders used words to counter military leaders' use of weapons. (Being a person who spent four years in military school and served nearly six years in the Marine Corps, with one year on the front line of a war, I found the idea that words could be used to counter the power of weapons a novel idea.) He also cautioned us that words could be used as weapons—used to destroy and cripple people. Most of us have had our feelings hurt or had someone spread rumors about us that are not true. We see words used as weapons all the time.

These are not my rules, and they are not Dr. Fuller's rules. As he stated in a class I attended in August of 1981, "You did not create this universe, and certainly you are not running it." The universe will proceed upon its path with or without us. But I believe it is up to this generation to solve our problems in order to survive and to experience what God intended, which is heaven on earth.

EMI: MORSELS TO DIGEST

My handicaps have been with me all my life. Since I can remember, I have avoided conflict and sought the approval of authority figures.

While I was seeking my path, I was hiding from my own self-image and the embarrassment of my past actions. In school I never was considered smart; now as an adult I think what I really had was undiagnosed ADD (attention deficit disorder) that made me feel disorganized and have poor concentration. Because of that, I didn't consider myself smart, either.

Since my dad served as the superintendent of schools, it put added pressure on me and made me afraid to speak up in class because people would realize how much I *didn't* know. I loved my dad, and I wanted to please him, so rather than embarrass myself and disappoint him, I chose to keep quiet. Withdrawing to avoid difficult situations became an early pattern in life.

Perhaps if my classes had allowed more opportunities for exploration, inquiry, and discovery, I would not have retreated. In school there wasn't much chance for teachers to offer personal attention or for me to build my self-esteem. I was too afraid of being wrong to risk exploring and discovering what was "right." Nevertheless, exploration and discovery became important to me.

I didn't want the same old life. And in a way, my handicap of hiding from conflict became a blessing, for it led me toward a path of study that became my life's work, and toward study with excellent teachers like His Holiness the Dalai Lama. That's not to say that even today I have overcome my handicap and can face conflict head on, but I continue to work on it.

My second handicap of quietly seeking approval dovetailed with my first one so perfectly that together they formed an elegant system that has governed my life since childhood. Today I have awareness of my handicaps, and I still have to watch that they don't hold me back. I work to recognize them when they arise and then use them as tools to help me move forward into more constructive action.

From the time he was a teenager, Robert put himself in situations that forced him to overcome his handicaps. Unlike him, I put myself in situations that *perpetuated* mine. In fact, looking back on it, the everyday choices I made to avoid conflict and seek approval were reflexive, not even conscious. Nearly everything I did in my life reinforced my negative tendencies, while Robert pushed himself in ways that would eventually conquer or repurpose his handicaps.

From an early age, he had his rich dad as a mentor and teacher.

One time, I do recall sticking my neck out. It happened through our local 4-H chapter when I was fourteen years old. My sister and I attended meetings, and at one meeting I was assigned the task of setting up the booth for the annual Market Day, to sell sushi. This project included rounding up donations of all the ingredients, recruiting all the volunteers, and preparing hundreds of rolls. It was a big community event for our town and a huge fund-raiser. I had agreed to take on a massive job, one that as a fourteen-year-old, I could not fully comprehend.

When I got home and told my mom what I had been assigned, she asked why I would choose to take on such a huge responsibility, implying that I couldn't do it. I immediately felt a sense of conflict—while I was worried that I couldn't do the job, failure would let down my 4-H leader, who was counting on me. I had taken a big risk, yet in the process I had set myself up to lose the approval of my mother.

The event actually turned out to be a success, and tons of sushi showed up. I helped, but it was the 4-H leader who did most all the work, not me. Even though things ended well, I felt terrible about the whole experience and never forgot it.

Looking back, I have to ask myself, how much could have been expected from a young girl who was handed such a huge task with no training, no support, and no encouragement? Hindsight offers the luxuries of objectivity and clarity. At the time, however, the whole episode just reinforced the grip my handicaps had on me.

I wish I had known then this simple Buddhist practice:

In all my actions I will examine my mind, and the moment a disturbing attitude arises, I will firmly confront and avert it.

These are the words of an eleventh-century Tibetan master named Geshe Langri Tangpa as found in the *Eight Verses of Thought Transformation.* Over the years, I have been drawn to verses such as these, which combine contemplation and practice while deepening my understanding. I take a verse like this, and through what's known as "analytical meditation," I weigh it in relation to my own life experiences.

Here is another powerful verse that has helped me through times when I've encountered difficult people: "When someone I have benefited and in whom I have placed great trust hurts me very badly, I will practice seeing that person as my supreme teacher." We have all experienced co-workers, family, friends, or neighbors who have let us down, who say one thing and do another. This teaching removes the blame, reflects our expectations, and helps us develop greater tolerance for those around us. It helps us develop compassion, rather than anger and justification.

His Holiness the Dalai Lama mentions that Chairman Mao Tsetung was his great teacher. It was under Mao's reign that the Tibetans lost their country and faced famine and the destruction of more than six thousand monasteries and the deaths of more than one hundred thousand people. The Dalai Lama says that the situation helped him be "unencumbered, and almost a simple monk."

I study and I teach these meditations and must put them into practice every day. No one is perfect, and certainly I am not. The years of my own imbalance of overextending myself took its toll on my health.

In 1998 during a routine examination, I was told that I had cancer. I was scared, first because the diagnosis was cancer, and second because I had no idea how I would take care of my medical expenses. I had spent my life trying to develop skills I could use to benefit others with little regard for myself or for money.

Thankfully, the spiritual community I was visiting in Seattle took care of everything, and I very much appreciated their support. But it was also their support that perpetuated my erroneous view about money. There is a historical tradition of laypeople supporting monastics with food and medicine, in exchange for teachings, prayers, and blessings. But this can be a precarious situation, especially if the expenses overburden the support system. Providing daily rice and aspirin is one thing; expecting laypeople to pay for MRI scans and surgery is something much different. It also becomes precarious because people don't learn to take care of themselves, or it makes them more dependent.

Unfortunately, my cancer was only a momentary wake-up call. I saw the need, but felt I had overcome my financial problem. Shortly after my illness, I accepted a post in Boulder to lead a small Buddhist group. I earned a stipend that started at $200 per month plus a small apartment and peaked at $600 a month toward the end of my stay. This stipend, typical for Buddhist monastics, was the way I was attending—or not attending—to the basic human necessities. There was a conflict between my need for money and my belief that being a monastic meant I should live a spartan existence.

A year later, one of the chaplains at the U.S. Air Force Academy asked me to meet with cadets who were interested in Buddhism, and I ended up serving as the Buddhist Chaplain there for six years. I then received another small stipend as a "defense contractor."

The Dalai Lama says, "Money is good. It is important. Without money, daily survival, not to mention further development, is impossible. ... In fact, Buddhist texts mention the fruition of eight qualities—including health, wealth, and fame—that define a fortunate existence." He also says, "Worldly happiness is based on the four excellences, which are the spiritual teachings (the Dharma), wealth, nirvana, and satisfaction."

Living a life of simplicity, as I had defined it, worked when life was relatively uncomplicated by things such as cancer. But when life became more challenging and medical bills, health insurance, and ongoing care became realities, I had to expand my definition of "simple" if I wanted to survive. I had to find a way to integrate my monastic life with my own health.

9

Leaps of Faith

Taking a leap of faith implies that you won't have all the answers, and some people are afraid of that. Even more frightening are the people who believe they actually have all the answers.

ROBERT: PROOF OF GOD

In December of 1984, ten years into my commitment to work on myself, I found myself asking the same question I asked as a child: "Is there really a God?" To be honest, the reason I questioned it as a child was because I couldn't get beyond the dogma of the church to find the spirituality. I couldn't have stated it that way then, but the truth was that I couldn't understand how people who were so religious on Sundays could be so sinful every other day.

I knew why *I* did bad things. They were fun. But I was a kid. Surely adults should be able to keep their word and be more true to their faith than a kid could be. As a child, I wondered why so many people publicly professed to believe in God, yet did terrible things in private. It was as if they had secret lives.

As an adult, with the question of "Is there a God?" left unanswered from my past, I searched for a way both to answer the question and to *prove* that answer's validity.

Though I wanted something more than someone else's opinions, much of my impetus came from that week-long seminar hosted by Bucky Fuller. For five days he talked about the future of business and that the greatest economic changes were over the horizon. He spoke of the end of the Industrial Age and the dawn of the Information Age. He spoke of the cruelty of excessive greed, and how the coming Information Age would be the dawn of generosity and abundance.

Even though I did my best to pay attention, I missed much of what he was saying. His talk was way over my head. I can see now that he was speaking of changes we are undergoing today. And he said one thing that really connected with me. He talked about the proof of God. He mentioned something about there being "no secondhand God." In other words, he did not need a preacher to come between him and the Great Spirit to act as an interpreter. (He preferred to use the term "the Great Spirit," a term the Native Americans used. Or he would refer to *nature* rather than God. He felt the term God implied a man.)

Dr. Fuller revealed that in 1927 he had begun a project he named Guinea Pig B, which stood for Guinea Pig Bucky. He considered himself and his life as a huge experiment. And at the age of thirty-two, penniless, married, and with a young daughter, he set out to prove or disprove the existence of God. Finally, I was hearing something new and interesting! During a talk that was supposed to be about the future of business, he was addressing the proof of God.

He had my ear.

As the seminar continued, Dr. Fuller explained that he had once been a minor real estate developer who lost everything. He'd realized that he didn't have what it took to be successful as a businessman. His friends reminded him that he had a wife and children and told him he should get a job. Yet every time he was employed, the money and security diminished his ability and mental acumen to learn. He learned that money and security made him dim. So he would leave the security of his job, jump off the deep end, and either sink or swim.

He said he got smarter every time he took that leap without any security or means of financial support. I could not have been more intrigued.

He also put forth the concept of committing your life to the highest advantage of others. That made me pause. You mean it wasn't just about me getting rich? Now he was sounding like my poor dad. The difference was that my dad was all about job security, and Dr. Fuller wasn't. He was about taking a leap. There was so much conflict going on in my mind—between Fuller's ideas and the ideas and beliefs expressed by my two dads. But I was fascinated and eager to hear more.

At the seminar I received a copy of Fuller's book *Critical Path*. It includes this passage:

> *I assumed that nature would "evaluate" my work as I went along. If I was doing what nature wanted done, and if I was doing it in promising ways, permitted by nature's principles, I would find my work being economically sustained—and vice-versa, in which latter negative case I must quickly cease doing what I was doing and seek logically alternative courses until I found the new course that nature signified her approval of by providing for its physical support.*

The passage held the key for proving or disproving the existence of God. What it meant to me was that if I were doing what God wanted done—solving a problem that God wanted solved—money or some form of life support would show up. If money *didn't* show up, it meant that I should change directions quickly or starve to death.

This idea was exciting and actionable. It was about taking a leap of faith and trusting in God. If money showed up, it meant God was approving of what I was doing. Also it meant that I was using my intuition to do what God wanted done, not doing what *I* wanted to do.

So much for the idea of doing what you love.

As if this concept wasn't enough, Dr. Fuller also shook me to the core when he said that most businesses produced what he called "*obnoxico*." That was his term for products that did not create a better world. The only purpose for companies classified as *obnoxico* was to make money. Today these products are called "*bling*" or "*chatchkies*." In my heart, I knew that my rock 'n' roll business was a classic *obnoxico* company, and I spent days and weeks in denial, mentally rationalizing how nylon wallets and hats with silk-screened rock band logos added value to the world.

Just as Emi spent her days wrestling with being on welfare, I was wrestling with the idea that my business and its products—the things I was spending my life producing—had very little real impact. I was making money, but I wasn't doing much good. This realization was a major upset and marked complete collapse of the very foundation of my business, my work, and my value as an entrepreneur.

It challenged just about every belief I had.

I was a different person, changed forever by the notion that I was doing well financially but not doing much good for the world. Today, through Dr. Fuller, I realize that *two* financial statements paint a picture of our lives. One is a personal financial statement that tells us how we're doing in terms of our finances. And the second one—

our social accounting—measures how much good we have done for the world. Bucky called this "cosmic accounting." I was rich on the first financial statement and bankrupt on the second.

That needed to change, and I had to figure out how. I wouldn't feel good being rich, no matter how wonderful my lifestyle, if I got that way by owning, say, a tobacco company, especially since my dad died of lung cancer. My personal financial statement might look good, but I wouldn't be happy with my *social* statement.

Of course, there are people who have done a lot of good for planet earth and are very strong in social accounting terms, but their personal financial statements are weak. My sister fell into that group, and that's what brought us back together—the belief that *both* our financial statements, the social and the personal, can be strong.

Many people of faith believe that monastics should always be poor, but in my sister's order there is no vow of poverty, just an expectation that they will live a simple life. This was my opportunity to share with Emi what I know about money so her personal financial statement could look as good as her social one. That way, she could look after herself while she helped others.

Helping is what big brothers are for.

This reminds me of the story of Indian guru Bhagawan Shri Rashneesh, a rather colorful and controversial character. In the 1980s, he and his religious order took over a ranch near the remote town of Antelope, Oregon, and upset the forty or so people who already lived in the town. He drew thousands of followers and a good bit of attention. During one interview, a reporter asked him, "Why do you have ninety-three Rolls Royces?" His reply was unexpected.

"That is not the question. The question is, Why don't *you* have ninety-three Rolls Royces?"

The number of Rolls Royces may get embellished every time this story is told, but the guru's comment is still funny and, to me, filled with some truth. Personally, I don't think being poor makes me any more spiritual. In fact, when I was poor, the circumstance actually robbed me of my spirit; it didn't make it stronger. After the Fuller seminar, I realized that I wanted two financial statements, and I wanted both of them to be strong.

And I knew that dream was impossible as long as I was producing *obnoxico*.

What I haven't yet revealed is my own personal "last straw." After attending *The Future of Business* seminar with Dr. Fuller, I took a trip to my overseas factories in Korea and Taiwan. What I saw there horrified me: children laboring in terrible conditions to put silk-screened rock band logos on my company's products. Kids were squatting in cramped conditions and inhaling noxious fumes in unbearable heat with no ventilation. I was getting rich but using their lives to produce *obnoxico*, a product with no long-term value.

Once again my life changed.

Don't get me wrong, I liked my *obnoxico*. I'm not saying that it had no value whatsoever. I love the nice things in life, and I have the ability to pay for them. I'm just glad I don't produce them any more.

After returning from my factories, I spent time reading more from Fuller's book *Critical Path*. For me it was a tough book to comprehend. So I called a few friends and asked them if they wanted to start a Bucky Fuller study group. Surprisingly, about six people said they would invest one night a week to study as a group. Working cooperatively—rather than competitively, as we do in school—was a profound experience.

There are ten chapters in *Critical Path*, so each week we all agreed to read the same chapter. Then, on Wednesday night, we would get together at my apartment for four hours in the evening and discuss what we had learned. It was always interesting to note how each person picked up points the others had missed. Once we had a uniform and comprehensive view of the chapter, we would take one large sheet of flip-chart paper and, using colored pens, produce what was known as a *"mind map."*

A mind map was a right-brain, creative way of using as many images and drawings as possible (and as few words) to explain the messages found in each chapter. There were no *right* or *wrong* answers. If there was a question on what Dr. Fuller meant, we would all turn to the passage in the book and do our best to understand what he was trying to say, rather than inject our personal opinions.

By the end of the ten weeks, all of us had evolved into different people, people who saw the world from a different, broader point of view.

I studied Dr. Fuller during all of 1981 and '82, then decided to start my next career as a teacher. It was a profession I had sworn I would never pursue since school and teachers had never ranked high on my likeability scale. But I vowed to learn to become the kind of teacher I wished *I'd* had when I was in school. My idea was to teach through games and actions, rather than words, rote memorization, random lectures, and meaningless tests.

In one of the workshops I attended, I came across the following information. According to the instructor, there are four types of people in the world. They are:

• People who must be liked
• People who must be comfortable
• People who must be right
• People who must win

While each of us has all of these four traits within us, one of the four traits will be dominant. I fall into the "must win" category. This is why I needed to increase my willpower and my brain power.

People who must win are found in sports, entrepreneurship, and sales.

People who must be right generally need only brain power. These people are often found in universities, medicine, and in law. People who must be liked and those who must be comfortable probably seek peace, harmony, friendships, and balance in their lives. These people seek secure jobs, work for the government, in religion, with charities, and in public service. They probably find pleasure in quiet meditation, praying, or seeking more tranquility in their lives.

Truthfully, I know I should be seeking more peace, balance, and harmony in my life, but my need to win is my priority. I thrive on action. I love my work. I suffer on vacation. I've retired twice and hated it. Even my doctor said I'm one of the few people he has found whose health is better under stress. I will revel in the beauty of nature, a kind of meditation, but only after I have climbed to the top of a mountain. I prayed often in school, especially at test time. And I talk to God and Jesus a lot, especially on the golf course.

This is my way of saying that my path to God was discovered via my need to win. I really did not discover God by doing my best to be a good person. I came across God because I wanted to maximize my personal power so I could win. Obviously, other people have different motivations for seeking God.

In another program, I came across the following three words. They are:

Be   Do   Have

In this course, the instructor said, "When a person sets goals, they are focusing on the have." He went on to say, "For example, many people want to have a million dollars. What is more important than the goal is what you have to *do* to have the million dollars, and then who you would have to *be* in order to do what it takes to have the million dollars."

My rich dad would say, "There are millions of things you can do to have a million dollars. Your job is to find that one-in-a-million thing you are willing to be your best at."

And once I found that one-in-a-million thing, I knew it would take a leap of faith to forsake all else and follow that path. The instructor would have agreed with my rich dad, and he finished by saying, "The bigger your goal, the bigger your spirit."

Rich dad explained that the goal, especially when it comes to money, is measured by the personal financial statement. He said, "When I look at a person's financial statement, I can clearly see what this person has in their life. When I look at their *social* financial statement, I can see what they do and—more importantly—how big their spirit is."

"Poor people are often poor because they lack willpower," he continued. "They may be good, honest, and fine people. The problem is they probably find it easy to make excuses, to say they can't afford something, or they blame other people or personal circumstances for their problems." He went on to say, "If they pray, they ask God to give them something, rather than focus on what *they* have to give in order to get what they want."

"If you want to receive a lot," he said, "you have to give a lot."

In late 1983 I met a beautiful young woman named Kim and began asking her out. It took six months for me to get her to agree to go on a date with me, and in February of 1984, on our first date, we talked until dawn about life's purpose, business, and my impending Fuller-inspired leap of faith.

In early 1984, I began selling off my business and factories to do the work God wanted me to do, and to prove God's existence. My plan was to teach—outside of the school system—the important lessons that were not being taught within it. In many ways I wanted to save others from what my dad was facing due to his own lack of financial education. He was still struggling with his finances. I wanted to save him, too.

In December of 1984 I sold my Mercedes, left my luxury apartment in the Colony Surf Hotel on Diamondhead, and gave up the finer things in life. Kim left her advertising job, sold her car, and said good-bye to her friends. We held each other's hand and took the leap together.

For Kim and me, the year 1985 was the worst year of our lives. We left Honolulu and moved to San Diego to pursue our next careers as teachers, business people, and investors. Sometimes we had less than five dollars a week for food. Thank God there was a little taco stand down the street, which we could walk to and get a quesadilla for ninety-nine cents. But each quesadilla had to last for more than one meal.

Things got worse than that. We eventually became homeless, slept in people's basements, and studied with what the Bible calls "false prophets," much like Emi's Zen master in Hawaii who showed up drunk.

Bobby McKelvey (center) is the friend who helped Kim and Robert in 1985 when they were homeless. She opened her heart and her home to them.

We probably encountered as many as fifteen false prophets, some of whom were geniuses. Despite their intelligence, they always had a flaw that wiped out their strength of character. For example, one teacher made a habit of sleeping with his attractive young seminar participants. It's hard to have spiritual power when you are unethical or amoral.

Regardless of how long we studied with any of these teachers, though, we learned from every one of them, took the best of what they had to offer, and moved on.

Kim and I changed direction again and again. As Dr. Fuller had taught, money or life support would show up if we were doing what God wanted to have done. So if money didn't show up, we'd trust our intuition, change direction, learn our lessons, and keep going.

For almost a year we found that companies didn't want to send their employees to learn about living a more fulfilling life; they wanted seminars that taught them how to be better employees. Finally in December of 1985, one seminar we performed actually showed a small profit, and we made $1,500. We took it as a sign that we were doing what God wanted done.

It was a joyous Christmas.

As with Emi, even though we had no money, I was the happiest I had ever been because I was finally doing something I was *supposed* to do and studying things I *wanted* to learn rather than things I *had* to learn to pass a test. For the first time in my life, I had become a student because I had found one of my life's teachers in Dr. Buckminster Fuller.

Dr. Fuller died on July 1, 1983. All I had after that were his books and his tapes to further my learning. Ironically, the last time I studied with Dr. Fuller was in Pahala, Hawaii, in May of 1983, the same town where my mom and dad first met in 1945 and the same place where Emi lived in the Buddhist temple in 1973. If you ever see how small this town is, you'll wonder why *anyone* would be there, let alone all of us.

EMI: BECOMING TENZIN

During the years when Robert and I were searching, each in our own way, for the paths we would follow, I hardly knew him. We were so far removed from each other that it was only much later that we discovered we were both taking leaps of faith.

After my adventures earning money in Alaska, in September 1975 my friends and I flew to India, landed in Calcutta, and took trains to New Delhi. From there we traveled further into the Himalayan foothills on sooty and crowded coal trains. Even the "direct" trains stopped en route, so we stayed in different towns, and it took several days to cross the continent.

I arrived in Dharamsala, the place where His Holiness the Dalai Lama lives in exile. The small mountain village was still very poor, with only wood, coal "cow patties," or kerosene for heat and cooking. There were almost no toilets and little running water. People would line up to wash their dishes at the two village taps and use ashes from the fire as an abrasive to clean their pots and pans. Life there was like nothing I had ever experienced.

Most people don't think of India as cold, but in the Himalayas it was. I arrived there with a good goose down jacket, but with snow on the ground and frigid cement houses, it was still very uncomfortable. I didn't care, though. I had found my heaven on earth. I was where I was supposed to be.

It didn't take long to find a place to stay. Rent for a very small room, barely larger than my sleeping bag, was thirty-five rupees per month, which then was about four dollars. It was fine; I didn't need much. I was simply happy to be there.

The Tibetan people are incredibly warm and welcoming. Here is an entire civilization of people who have lost their country, their homes, and their temples. They were exiled to India with only what they could carry over the Himalayan Mountains. Many live a very meager life. Fortified by many excellent teachers and practitioners, these people have great strength and direction. Rather than be defeated, they are buoyant in their determination to live in freedom, help themselves, and build their communities.

This strength is observed in people across cultures who do not let obstacles or troubles in their lives stop them, who have great conviction in their faiths or ethical practices, and who are strengthened with determination and endurance to accomplish their goals.

Attending the courses at the Tibetan Library was amazing. They were taught by Venerable Geshe Ngawang Dhargyey, a senior Tibetan monk, and then translated into English. The class was for visitors, and there were people who had come from all over the world. I could hear translators murmuring in French, Spanish, Italian, Japanese, and other languages. The teachers were highly trained and educated scholars who took so much joy in teaching. They didn't just teach; they infused their understanding and experience into each lesson.

For example, they spoke of the suffering of human life—those times when we work so hard to attain what we want but don't make it. Or when we strive so hard to attain what we want, get it, and then decide that we don't want it anymore. Or when we strive so hard to attain what we want, only to have it ripped away from us.

They posed the question that, if there were, in fact, no release from suffering in life, then why study suffering at all? Yet if there were the potential to attain freedom from suffering, then we should find a way to do so and leave no stone unturned.

This is one of the many topics in Lam Rim, the "graduated path to enlightenment," and what I went to India to study. I was drawn to a path that inspired striving for our greatest potential as human beings; the possibility of attaining enlightenment by removing all the misperceptions and delusions of life and to attain all excellent virtuous qualities. I wanted to find the courage to take up the path to enlightenment, and to find the joyful spirit the Tibetans lived—even with such hardship.

Now that I was at the feet of my teacher, I had found what I wanted to spend the rest of my life pursuing, and I took the leap—no meditative retreat required for that decision.

Some people find their calling early in life; they know that they want to go to medical school or study music. Some find it very late in life, and others never find it at all. That calling is your spiritual family beckoning you to the life you were born to live. Many times other people in our lives—parents and teachers and friends—tell us what our calling should be. Sometimes we may believe that we have found our gift and know our calling, and even then it may require a leap of faith, as it did for Robert and me. I never could have guessed I would find my calling at the foothills of the Himalayas.

It was on this first trip that I met His Holiness the Fourteenth Dalai Lama. We were granted two private interviews with him to discuss questions Westerners have about Buddhism. When we were before him, he focused entirely on us and the discussion at hand; his presence was commanding.

We were shocked when he remarked that most Tibetans were not Buddhist.

"I would say 90 percent, 90 percent are not Buddhist," he said. We later felt that he was speaking of people in general; people who may claim to be practitioners but who still cling to reputation, greed, and grasping at possessions and seeking pleasures that lead to the sacrificing of ethics, marriage vows, and sometimes even health in an effort to imbibe in selfish, fleeting happiness.

Receiving an early warning about the pitfalls of tainting our spiritual practice from one of the greatest Buddhist masters of our time gave us a lot to think about.

I recall the time we went to visit the "Rainmaker"—a meditation adept who lived in a little shack up the mountainside. He was called the Rainmaker because of his ability to start or stop the rain through prayer and ceremony. The walls of the his building were nothing more than flimsy, wood slats rummaged from orange crates. Streams of sunlight shone through the spaces between the slats, and wind whistled through them.

Once inside, we sat on grimy mats atop the pounded earth and made an effort to read a Tibetan text placed on an overturned box. Someone quickly intervened and placed a crumpled, charcoal-smeared rag under the pages. It was all he had, but even in these poor conditions, out of respect for the Teachings, we did not place the prayers on bare surfaces.

Toward the end of our stay, we wanted the Rainmaker to journey with us to New Delhi so we could have his poor eyes and ears checked. He said he couldn't go on the date we chose because he may have to stop the rain for the celebrations on New Year's Day. We changed our plans to go after that date. Sure enough it snowed for a few days before the New Year, and then on New Year's Day the sky was bright and the weather beautiful; a perfect day to celebrate.

My return from India and reentry into Western life and parenthood was not easy. I had to find a job and become a parent again. In fact, it was a rough time.

I worked as a bookkeeper, eking out a living in Honolulu and Los Angeles and raising Erika. It was the clash of lifestyles that hit me. The luxury of being able to study with my teacher all day was gone. It had been replaced with working full time, struggling to continue my studies, and being the mother of a pre-teen.

In 1984 I wrote the Dalai Lama, requesting ordination as a nun.

By this time I had been considering ordination for almost ten years and had received an endorsement from my teacher in Los Angeles to move forward with my aspiration. It took several months to hear back from the Dalai Lama's office, and I was nervous, wondering whether I would be accepted or turned down. When I got the letter, I experienced a full spectrum of emotions: excitement, fear, relief, and more.

I was accepted. Life was changing once again. I began preparing for my return to India.

I had requested ordination with the Dalai Lama because I looked up to him as an excellent guide. I was honored to have been accepted. I felt that by taking my vows with him, I'd be able to keep them for a long time.

Ordination in Dharamsala was truly an experience of entering a different world. Before ordination, they gave me my robes, which felt very different because I felt as if I were wearing my promises, which were precious. Before I went into the temple, monks shaved my head, leaving a little tuft of hair to be clipped by the ordaining master during the ceremony.

I had never before been in a room with only monastics, and here I was before His Holiness the Dalai Lama and dozens of monks in colorful, golden robes. A monk receiving a higher level of ordination sat with me, and he translated the entire ceremony. It was very solemn, with monks chanting and reciting the vows I was to keep.

During the ceremony, the Dalai Lama gave me my ordination name, Tenzin Kacho. *Tenzin* means wisdom, and *Kacho* means skygoer.

I became Tenzin Kacho on October 5, 1985.

I had come full circle, returning to India and to my studies, and now going even further. It was like being a caterpillar wrapped in a cocoon and emerging as a Buddhist monastic.

After ordination, I had spent another six months in India so I could gain some experience and understand my new role. The time there was supportive and encouraging, but I was nervous about returning and facing my duties. Would I be worthy of wearing the robes? How would I cope in the Western world as a Buddhist nun and a mother? I was confident in my leap of faith and knew that I would rise to the challenges I faced.

Yet when I returned to Los Angeles, I found myself struggling again with the same life pattern of wanting the simple life but not having adequate finances, even in the most rudimentary sense.

In 1986, Robert was participating in a Tony Robbins seminar in Hollywood, teaching students to walk across fire. The prospect of seeing him after all these years made me both excited and apprehensive. It had been such a long time, and I was a different person. How different would *he* be?

I went to Hollywood, and Kim was the first to speak. When she saw me in my robes she said, "You really must be committed to this."

"Do you think I'd be walking around the streets of LA in robes and with a shaved head if I wasn't committed?" I replied. That was the awkward beginning to a wonderful and long-overdue visit with my brother and his new wife.

He, too, had changed.

10

Enlightenment
and a Fuller Life

"Everyone wants to go to heaven, but no one wants to die."

This is a telling statement because it's as true figuratively as it is literally. This is the precise reason why many people don't take leaps of faith. They fear dying—even when they believe the leap is what has the potential to take them to proverbial heaven.

A leap of faith is both a death and a birth; it is a transition in life, and we all have taken leaps of faith many times. That first day of school is a leap of faith for many little kids. Getting married is a leap of faith between two people in love. Some leaps of faith are not voluntary, such as suddenly being fired, or having the person you love suddenly say, "I'm leaving you." Those leaps of faith are thrust upon us, forcing us to make drastic changes.

Despite the fact that they can be traumatic, leaps of faith shouldn't be a big deal; they are simply transitions in life, pivotal moments that teach us and show us new paths that will lead to new lessons.

Buckminster Fuller estimated that there are several hundred generalized principles, and in Buddhism, there are eighty-four thousand teachings—

just to deal with a single concept! A Buddhist teacher once said, "Just as we have many medicines for many sicknesses, so we have these eighty-four thousand teachings for gross and subtle delusions."

Buddhism also offers teachings on metaphysics, ethics, and words of the Buddha. The Buddha lived and taught for a full forty-five years after his enlightenment, so there are many volumes to his teachings. You can devote your entire life to study and practice, and really only scratch the surface.

The journey continues.

ROBERT: TRUSTING IN GOD

When I left Hawaii in search of the proof of God's existence, everyone thought I had lost it. I was leaving paradise, a successful company I had built and rebuilt, friends, and a great lifestyle. On top of that, I was taking Kim with me.

Deep down, I suspected my friends were right: I was nuts.

Part of me agreed with them because I really did not know what I was looking for. I did not know what "proof of God" would look like or how I would recognize it.

This was in contrast to the first time I left Hawaii, in 1965, to go to school in New York. I knew what I was looking for and what I would find there. I had seen pictures of the campus and had an idea of what a military school environment might be like. When I volunteered for the Marine Corps, I had an idea about what my transition would look and feel like. I knew I was committing six years of my life, and if successful, I would emerge a pilot with combat experience. I had seen news clips of the war in Vietnam on television. I had watched a number of John Wayne movies, so I had an idea of what I was jumping into.

Taking a leap in December of 1984 to look for God offered no such clear pictures. It was a leap into the dark abyss of life. As it turned out, 1985 was the worst year of our lives.

Just before we left Hawaii, a friend came up to Kim and me to wish us well on our new adventure. He was one of the few who seemed to understand our search. He did not think we were crazy. One of the original hippies, he had been a searcher for most of his life. Like my sister Emi, he had very little, materially, yet he possessed a deep sense of peace and happiness. Rather than question our sanity, he offered us a gift.

"I will tell you a story that you can use on your journey. This story will assist you when life presents you your biggest tests of faith. This story will give your soul vision when times are darkest." His story turned out to be a very precious gift:

One day there was a man who stood on one side of Niagara Falls with his bicycle. A small crowd gathered as he announced, "I will ride my bicycle across this steel cable stretched to the other side of the falls."

Oohs and ahhs came from the crowd.

"How dangerous!" a young woman said.

"Please don't risk your life," pleaded another woman.

"You're nuts," said an older man. "You're going to kill yourself."

"I know I can do it," said the man as he climbed on his bicycle. Soon he was slowly peddling his way across the cable, dangling and swaying just a few feet over the raging falls. One slip and he would be gone forever. The crowd waited breathlessly as he reached the other side, turned his bicycle around, and peddled back. As soon as he was back on land, the crowd rushed forward, many saying, "We knew you could do it. We had faith in you."

"Should I do it again?" He asked with a big smile. "Sure," replied the crowd. "We believe in you."

"Okay," said the man. "Since you now believe in me, who wants to go with me?"

Suddenly the crowd went quiet. People started to squirm. In the midst of the silence, a few began to leave. Then from the middle of the crowd, a small voice said, "I'll go with you." The crowd gasped as a petite young girl stepped forward and volunteered to be his passenger. As the girl climbed into the basket on the front of the bicycle, many people in the crowd grew angry.

"How dare you risk her life?" said one person.

"I'm calling the police," said another.

Slowly, the man, the little girl, and the bicycle started out across the falls. The crowd was deathly silent. Everyone took a breath as they reached the other side, turned the bicycle around, and headed back. Once safely on dry land, the crowd let out a loud cheer as they congratulated the young girl for her courage.

"What gave you the courage?" asked a woman of the young girl.

"Weren't you afraid?" asked another.

"No," replied the young girl.

"Why not?" asked the woman.

"Because this man is my father," said the little girl. "I don't just believe in my father. I trust him with my life."

Our hippie friend looked at Kim and me to see if his story had made its point. Seeing that we understood the story, he said, "Most people believe in God, but very few people trust in God. When times get tough, go beyond your belief in God, and trust in God."

His gift serves us well, even today.

We all know people who believe in God but do not trust in God. This may be why so many people will cling to boring jobs, low pay, bad people, dead marriages, or toxic environments. As I've said before, "People want to go to heaven, but they do not want to die." Many prefer to hang on to something familiar, rather than let go and let God take them to their next destination. There are many who believe in God, but do not trust in God.

One of the reasons we had trust in God—even if there were moments when we weren't sure of God's existence—is because of what Dr. Fuller called the generalized principles governing the universe. Learning about them preceded our leap of faith.

Kim and I did not just jump blindly. Like my sister, who spent ten years studying and preparing before she became a nun, we also studied and prepared.

Between 1981 and 1983, I had three opportunities to personally study with Dr. Fuller. During those years, I struggled to get through his work. Since he was a generalist, not a specialist, his work spanned virtually all subjects of study, including money, history, religion, and the future. In fact, Fuller was best known as a man who could predict the future. John Denver wrote a song about him titled, "What One Man Can Do." In that song, Denver called him "The Grandfather of the Future."

Each time I was with him, Fuller would begin talking after lunch and continue until two or three in the morning. As long as someone was awake and wanted to learn, he kept on going. In his mid-eighties, he was a lot stronger than many of us who were fifty years younger. His talks seemed to ramble over different subjects. If he ran out of ideas, he would sit quietly and steeple, with his fingers pressed together, under his chin, almost as if he were praying. I assumed he was allowing his brain to fill with the next subject.

In *Critical Path*, Fuller wrote about a few of the generalized principles, what he called the operating principles of the universe. In simple terms, generalized principles are principles that are true in all cases, with no exceptions. These are the principles that literally make the world—and the universe—go 'round. In quasi-religious terms, the generalized principles are the operating principles of God.

One simple example is the generalized principle of precession. Many are familiar with precession as it relates to a spinning top or

In 1985, after we took our leap of faith. We followed our passion
and participated in learning events around the globe, including the "Future of
Business" world event in Aspen, Colorado, which included singer John Denver.
Here, we're with Dr. R. Buckminster Fuller's daughter, Allegra (center).

gyroscope. If the axis it spins on begins to tilt, it becomes subject to
gravity. Gravity, in turn, is a force that acts on one body the same
way it acts on all others. Thanks to the law of gravity, we know if
we leap from a ten-story building without a parachute we will hit
the ground. There are no exceptions. Gravity does not care if we are
rich or poor, college-educated or a high school drop out, Christian,
Jew, or Muslim. We can pray, meditate, and think positive thoughts,
but a fall from a ten-story building will put us in the hospital, if not
kill us. Gravity treats us all the same, no exceptions.

One of the reasons people's lives fail to work is because they vi-
olate one or more of the generalized principles. In other words, they
expect gravity to treat them differently than it treats everyone else.
When Kim and I took our leap of faith in 1984, we were prepared
to use these principles to guide us, to use them in our favor, and not
be crushed by them. Allowing the generalized principles to guide
us would lead us toward the proof of God.

At the second event I attended with Dr. Fuller in 1982, he estimated that there were approximately 200 to 250 of these generalized principles. It seemed to me that if we studied these hundreds of principles, we might be able to tap into the powers of God. At the event, a small group was formed to assist Dr. Fuller in discovering all the generalized principles and put them in writing. I wasn't a member of that committee, but I donated money to the project every month.

Unfortunately, the committee was not able to accomplish much. In 1983, after Dr. Fuller died, I realized that we had lost more than a great man. We lost a great body of knowledge. As far as I know, Dr. Fuller had never completely compiled the 200 to 250 generalized principles.

From then on, all I had to study were the few principles Dr. Fuller had previously described in his books. Although I accessed only a few of those principles, it was the understanding of them that ultimately gave Kim and me the courage to take our leap of faith. The few generalized principles we did study enabled us to go beyond believing in God and allowed us to trust in God.

Like my sister, who read, studied, and immersed herself in the teachings of the Buddha, a small group of us would get together to read, reread, and discuss the few generalized principles we found in Dr. Fuller's books. We would do physical demonstrations, acting out the principles and discussing, challenging, and analyzing their authenticity. We used the same rigors religious scholars have used for centuries to study their holy books. Our discussions would start at 6 p.m. and sometimes go until sunup. I mention this because I will describe only five of the generalized principles we studied. My fear, though, is that my brief and feeble description of the generalized principles will be inadequate and unrepresentative of the power locked within them.

UNITY IS PLURAL

This generalized principle states that unity is not "one." Instead, "one" cannot exist. Unity is, at a minimum, two—meaning two or more. This principle is significant because the concept of only one God violates this generalized principle.

This principle explains why there are arguments and wars. Whenever we think there is only one way, one answer, or one solution, the principle is violated and peace is disturbed. I remember as a kid in church, cringing every time I heard the preacher say, "There is only one God and only one way to God, and that way is through our church and our religion." Even as a kid I knew that statements like this were fighting words. And as a kid, I wondered why there couldn't be more than one way to God.

When a religion claims to follow the one and only true God, that religion is cruising for a fight. Or if they propose there is only one path to God, they are again inviting a challenge—a fight. Today, we are still at war over who is following the one and only God. When I visited Jerusalem, the Holy City, Christians were in conflict with other Christians. They did not need Muslims or Jews to have a fight.

Taking this principle further, man could not exist if woman did not exist. We would not know up without down, in without out, black without white, fast without slow, positive without negative, right without wrong, or heaven without hell. In politics, we will always have, at minimum, a two-party system. We will always have liberals as long as there are conservatives. When dreamers wish for a one-world government, I know they don't understand this generalized principle.

A one-world government is not possible because "one" cannot exist alone.

This principle explains why being politically correct or excessively polite is ineffective. The reason many people want to be politically correct—or nice to everyone—is because they are afraid of criticism.

They try to keep everyone happy. In reality, instead of making people happy, politically correct people are often *too* polite, and therefore, often ineffective.

Every book I write gets criticized. I expect it. I welcome it! Being criticized means I am saying something. I am often asked if I am shocked by what some people say about me in their Web blogs. My reply is, "I'm glad I've upset them. It means I'm saying something." Successful people are criticized. Unsuccessful people are not.

Just think about how many people criticize political or religious leaders such as a president, prime minister, Pope, or the Dalai Lama. Even men of God aren't spared the wrath of an opposing point of view. In the world of sports, professional teams and star athletes wouldn't make the big bucks if there were no opposing teams and no other star athletes. Without disease we might not cherish health, nor would we need doctors. And if humans always agreed, we wouldn't need attorneys—which might not be such a bad thing.

Comprehending this generalized principle explains why there will always be attorneys, police, and the need for soldiers. His Holiness the Dalai Lama is more famous because of Communist China. Without the Chinese, His Holiness might truly be the simple monk he describes himself to be. As my sister stated earlier, the world has had more years of war than years of peace.

In the Bible, we find examples of this generalized principle. In the story of the great flood, Noah loaded his ark with animals marching on board, two-by-two. This principle also explains the reason why inside of everything good lives something bad, and vice versa. Understanding this principle gave Kim and me the courage to take our leap of faith because we knew if we faced the bad, we would find the good.

We opened this book with the quote by F. Scott Fitzgerald: "The test of a first rate intelligence is the ability to hold two opposed ideas in the mind at the same time and still retain the ability to function."

We, as humans, are losing our intelligence. We have hell on earth because too many people think in terms of one God, one religion, one right answer, and only one set of values. Too many people want to make themselves right and everyone else wrong.

The principle of "unity is plural" guided Kim and me toward God by giving us the clarity to not take sides on opposing ideas; rather, we do our best to see validity in *all* ideas. We learned faster because we didn't get caught up in looking for that one right answer, believing all other answers were wrong. We could see right and wrong in all answers. We didn't judge ourselves as good or bad, right or wrong, successful or a failure. After a while, we came to see our weaknesses as strengths, handicaps as advantages, and failures as successes.

Knowing that humans were given a right foot and a left foot—rather than a right foot and a wrong foot—allowed us to keep moving through some extremely difficult times, trusting our intuition, which is the connection between our conscious and subconscious minds.

Rather than argue and attempt to change another person's point of view, we simply moved on, realizing there would always be, at minimum, two opposing ideas. As the saying goes, "If two people always agree, one of them is not necessary." Our job in life is to hold at least two opposing ideas and find our own path between those two or more ideas.

PRECESSION

We have all seen the generalized principle of precession every time we drop of stone in water. The rings or waves that ripple out from the stone's impact are precessional effects.

Many people set goals. Kim and I had set goals, not for the goal itself but for the precessional effect of that goal. In other words, our true goals weren't in front of us but at a ninety-degree angle from the direction we were moving.

For example, many people have wanted to know why we don't take our financial education directly into the school system. This would mean that the school system would be our goal or target. Understanding the generalized principle of precession, we stayed away from schools and allowed our ripple effect to affect education. As I explain the other generalized principles, you may understand more clearly why I do not target schools, even though I want to bring financial education into the school system.

Another visible example of precession, as mentioned earlier, is a gyroscope. When you spin the wheel of a gyroscope, it can stand on a slender pole. The ability for the spinning gyroscope to stand on a point is an example of precession. As a kid building rockets, I soon found out that rocket scientists were using gyroscopes in the nose cone of their rockets to act as guidance systems. While at sea, ships use gyroscopes to guide them and keep them on course across vast bodies of water.

In 1985, Kim and I depended on precession to guide us just as it guides rockets in space and ships at sea. In simple terms, precession is the feedback or echo or the tap on your shoulder you receive from your forward movement. If we were doing what God wanted done, we got positive feedback, feedback such as money coming in, miracles happening, or meeting magical people. If the feedback was negative, Kim and I would use our intuition—that bridge between our conscious and subconscious minds—and change course or set a new goal. Just as ancient sailors used water, air, wind, sun, moon, stars, currents, floating debris, birds, and intuition to guide them across vast stretches of water, Kim and I were using the feedback, or ripple effects from precession, to guide our internal navigation system.

Precession is a massive subject, and I have only touched on it in this short section. Precession explains why the earth revolves around the sun, the moon around the earth, and the stars' motion through the universe. It also explains why some people are more successful than others. For there to be precession, there must be motion in a direction. People who are slow or sedentary—not moving, or doing the same thing day after day—have very little precession. Think of it this way, they have very few of the ripple effects of God in their lives.

Oftentimes, people who are sedentary are receiving feedback, but it's the kind of feedback they don't like. People who are slow often gain weight, experience bad health, and are left behind both professionally and financially. These negative taps on the shoulder are also precessional events.

EPHEMERALIZATION

In very basic terms, ephemeralization means doing more with less. It can also be described as leverage.

Ephemeralization is especially important in business. As a businessperson, if I want to make more money, I need to do more and more with less and less. If I do less with more, I will go broke simply because I am violating this generalized principle. Many times, people earn less because they want to get paid *more* for doing less. Labor unions often subscribe to this idea, which is why so many industries have left America.

Simply said, if you want to earn more you have to do more for less.

Today ephemeralization is easy. The personal computer has leveraged our minds and the World Wide Web has leveraged access to the world. Today, for a few dollars, most of us can be global entrepreneurs, tapping into global markets.

When I hear of people struggling financially, it is often because those people are working physically, rather than ephemerally. One of the reasons we have twenty-year-olds who are billionaires and other twenty-year-olds who are working for $10 an hour is due to the generalized principle of ephemeralization.

From 1985 to 1994, Kim and I ran an education company, teaching entrepreneurship and investing. We were working physically. Once we proved we were practicing what we were preaching and that what we were teaching was working, we ephemeralized by putting information in books and on board games. When we ephemeralized what we knew through books and board games, we precessionally made more money. Notice how the generalized principles of empheralization and precession work together.

In simple terms, ephemeralization is essential for anyone who wants to attain great wealth. As business people, we must constantly be seeking ways to do more and more with less and less, serving more people and at ever-accelerating rates of speed. If you can grasp this last sentence, you are farther ahead of 99 percent of the people on planet earth because your mind is catching a glimpse of the power in this generalized principle.

People who are employing ephemeralization in their lives are getting richer and, unfortunately, those who are not—even though they are often hard-working people—are getting poorer.

LAG

Lag is simply a difference in time. For example, if I throw a ball across a field, the time it takes the ball to leave my hand and reach the other side of the field is lag. Lag is a very important generalized principle.

Different industries have different lag times. For example, the industry with the shortest lag time is technology. New ideas become products and appear in the marketplace one day, and seemingly overnight they are copied, improved, marketed, and sold by someone else. Lag is the amount of time it takes for a new idea to be adopted and implemented.

People have different lag times. Some people are extremely slow to adapt to new ideas. Some people adapt quickly. In their book, *Revolutionary Wealth,* thought leaders Alvin and Heidi Toffler describe the world today through the eyes of a motorcycle cop, standing along a freeway, clocking the speed of nine different cars, nine different groups:

- The first car—the fastest group, speeding along at a hundred miles per hour—is entrepreneurs and businesses.
- The second car, running at ninety miles per hour, is NGOs (nongovernmental organizations). The Tofflers describe this car as one packed with circus clowns, pro-business and anti-business groups, professional organizations, Catholic orders, Buddhist nunneries (like my sister's), manufacturing organizations, cults, tax haters, whale lovers, and everyone in between.
- In the third car, cruising along at sixty miles per hour, is the American family because what we once knew as the typical American family is rare today. Family formats, frequency of divorce, sexual activity, intergenerational relationships, dating patterns, child rearing, and other dimensions of family life continue to change rapidly.

Predicting the Future

As an entrepreneur and investor, I find it important to be able to see the future. Vision is an important aspect of leadership. The way a person can see the future—without a crystal ball—is by being a student of history. Not the study of history taught in school, which to me was a futile exercise in rote memorization of names, dates, and facts simply to be regurgitated at test time. The reason to be a student of history is to use historical events as stepping-stones to the future.

Rather than crystal-ball gazing or fortune telling, Dr. Fuller used the word, "*prognostication*." He used the example of an archer, pulling his bow and arrow back as far as possible—the farther back, the further the arrow would fly, and the farther into the future he could see.

To the study of prognostication, Dr. Fuller added the generalized principle of *ephemeralization*—the process of doing more with less—in conjunction with accelerating acceleration. In other words, the process of change is accelerating, not progressing linearly, not moving in lock step, a set cadence. Dr. Fuller said that the accelerating acceleration of change was catching millions of people completely off-guard, rendering them functionally obsolete, much like dinosaurs or woolly mammoths, unable to handle the changes occurring in the world.

What is Accelerating Acceleration?

In 1500, it took a sailing ship at least two years to circumnavigate the globe. By 1900, with the advent of steam power, that time was cut to about two months. Today, electronically, we can circle the world in less than a second.

A more recent example of ephemeralization is the history of powered flight. On December 17, 1903, Orville Wright flew for twelve seconds, the first successful powered flight in history. On July 20, 1969, the United States landed a man on the moon. In just sixty-six years—less than a lifetime—humans went from a twelve-second flight to landing on an extraterrestrial satellite. That is an example of the generalized principle ephemeralization as applied to prognostication—looking into the past to see the future.

Many people will be caught off guard simply because the rate of change is changing. During the Industrial Age, change took a lifetime. In the Information Age, we will go through five lifetimes of change in one lifetime.

During hunter-gatherer times and through the Agrarian and Industrial Age, we learned to respect our elders because they held a lifetime of experience. For thousands of years, age was respected, age was an asset, age meant wisdom. Today being old is a liability, a sign of obsolescence. People of my generation say, "Fifty is the new forty." It can also be said that mentally and professionally, "Thirty-five is the new sixty-five."

- The fourth car, at thirty miles per hour, is labor unions.
- The fifth car, at twenty-five miles per hour, is government bureaucracies and regulatory agencies.
- The sixth car, at ten miles per hour, is the American school system.
- The seventh car, at five miles per hour, is international intergovernmental agencies such as the International Monetary Fund (IMF) and the World Trade Organization (WTO).
- The eighth car, at three miles per hour, is the political structures of rich countries, such as the United States: Congress, the Senate, and political parties.
- The ninth and slowest car, at one mile per hour, is the law—lawyers, law schools, bar associations, and law firms. While many lawyers and law firms are changing more rapidly, the law is not. One of the reasons for the subprime credit meltdown is that the law and organizations such as the Securities and Exchange Commission (SEC) cannot keep up with financial entrepreneurs traveling at one hundred miles an hour.

When I studied with Dr. Fuller, he said the two slowest industries were education and construction. He said their lag time—the delay from when a new idea appears until the industry adapts the idea—is fifty years. Now you know the reason why I do not target schools for financial education. The lag time for that industry is just too long, and change in that area comes too slowly. Possibly by 2030 there will be financial education in our schools, but I'm not patient enough to wait that long.

In 1927 Dr. Fuller predicted there would be demand for two billion new homes in eighty years. In 2007, eighty years after his prediction, commodity prices were skyrocketing as billions of people in Asia, South America, Eastern Europe, and the Middle East wanted Western-style homes.

Dr. R. Buckminster Fuller and a young Robert Kiyosaki in 1981
at "The Future of Business," a seminar led by Dr. Fuller,
which Robert would find life-changing.

Dr. Fuller is known as a futurist. Two generalized principles he employed to accurately predict the future are the principles of ephemeralization and lag. One of the ways I make a lot of money today is by using these generalized principles to guide my business and investment strategies.

In 1983, during my last class with him, Dr. Fuller predicted that a new technology would appear before the end of the decade. He also predicted that the world's superpowers would begin to fade and lose their domination because of this new technology. Dr. Fuller died on July 1, 1983, and in 1989, the Worldwide Web came up as the Berlin Wall came down. Fuller could see the future and trusted in God simply because he understood the generalized principles—the operating principles of the universe—also known as God's principles.

In the photo on the next page, taken with Fuller in 1981, I am smiling because I am sitting next to the man who gave my life meaning, or at least reminded me of what I was placed here on earth to do. I am smiling and grateful because I found my life's purpose, my mission, the problem I was born to be a solution to.

Up to that point, I had felt as if I did not fit in this world, that I did not belong, that I was an oddball. All through school I wasn't interested in what the school system deemed to be important. I was not interested in going to school to become an employee of the big corporations or the government. I went through the motions of going through school, eventually working for a giant oil company, and fighting for my government, but my heart was never into those endeavors.

Until I met Dr. Fuller, my life seemed a little meaningless, out of synch with the rest of the world. I was marching to the beat of a different drum. I had always been interested in money, ever since I was a little boy, but in my family, throughout school and into the service, to be interested in the subject of money was a sin, a taboo; it was a very dirty subject. So for most of my life—except for the times I was with my rich dad—I rarely mentioned money as a subject I was interested in studying.

While I did want to be rich, I was really just curious about this subject of money. I truly wanted to know why some people were rich and so many were poor. I wanted to know why people like my dad claimed to be not interested in money, yet spent his life working for it and complaining that he never had enough of it. I wanted to know why churches spoke out against the love of money and then pleaded with their congregations to put more money in the offering plate.

I wondered why our schools try to prepare us to get a job but fail to teach us much about money.

TENZIN: HITTING THE ROAD

Of the many teachings in Buddhism, these are the ones that are foundational, and have played an important role in my life:

EVERYTHING IS IMPERMANENT

Our life, homes, possessions, families, and all other relationships are impermanent. Mother earth and all the planets and stars are impermanent. Years ago we would drive visitors along the coast outside Hilo to see Onomea Arch. It was a large, beautiful, natural land arch that stretched into the ocean. Waves would roll in and crash about it onto the rocky shore, and had done so for probably millennia.

One sunny day, an artist was by the shore painting a picture of the arch, and it collapsed before her very eyes. Change such as this is happening to everything, sometimes very suddenly, but more often in constant imperceptible disintegration. All those things we cling to and hold dear will eventually be separated from us.

Even our precious lives are heading to eventual demise. Many people don't like to think about things like this. In my hospital chaplaincy, I sometimes encounter people who are not only physically sick but—as a result of their illnesses—are depressed as well. This mental state makes recovery more painful physically, emotionally, and spiritually. Yet reminding ourselves that everything is impermanent not only helps us understand that our time together is limited, but that we have the power to direct our lives to make the best use of this time.

We can develop loving relationships and work to benefit others. The present, the here and now, is the best opportunity we have to take advantage of this human life. We have the capacity to change even ingrained negative habits because they are impermanent, too; we are never stuck permanently in any situation.

It's funny to think that while we want long lives, we don't want to get old. What a contradiction. I share with people that we are *fortunate* when we have the privilege of growing old. Long life and old age is good fortune when we use our lives to accomplish goals toward betterment for ourselves and others. When we accept that growing old is a normal part of life, our minds are peaceful and content as we age. We develop better relationships with others and have greater purpose and meaning in life, rather than spending time rejecting or fighting the normal aging process.

Simply put, because we were born, we must die; it is a natural course we all face. Sometimes when death is imminent, people think they and their loved ones are being punished. But regardless of how well or poorly we live our lives, we all face death—every one of us. Death is a part of life.

When we're in distress about situations and feel as if things will never change, impermanence can be quite comforting. If you've ever experienced a dead-end job, a relationship that was going nowhere, or a person you care about who is on a bad course, it's natural to feel stuck. Have you ever noticed that when we love something or someone, we never want it to change, but when we feel stuck, time stands still? In a situation like that, we would give *anything* for a little change, sooner rather than later.

Impermanence means everything is in constant change.

And best of all, change provides us with every possibility of achieving our dreams and accomplishing great things with our lives. So rather than attaching your perception of self to what is past—things like a poor self-image or how someone mistreated you—look to your potential and take action to affect your future. If we can purify even one of our faults, like jealousy of others or, in my case, avoidance of conflict, then we can act directly and powerfully.

People grieve at their situations in life—for things that are lost or might have been. If we understand that everything is impermanent, we can focus on what we *can* do, rather than grieve about what is past. The power to change our future pushes us away from reticence, toward doing something meaningful with our lives.

COMPASSION

This is a huge, dynamic force in life. Early Buddhist teachings focus on developing renunciation from the fleeting pleasures of life and attaining nirvana—liberation from suffering. Later, excellent practices and teachings on compassion evolved, adding a powerful dimension to Buddhism. When we develop love and care for others so deeply that we put them before ourselves, there is a change in our inner experience, in our relationship to everyone, and in our relationship with the world around us.

One of the things Mom wanted so much for us was that we would love and care for others, no matter who, and she herself set an example of that for us to follow. Our formative years on the isolated island took place in a safer time, and Mom would help everyone she could: give occasional rides to beggars and strangers, meet visitors to the island, and bring them home to dinner.

Mom was always helping, volunteering on committees, and joining in events. One time she quietly mentioned to me that it was difficult at times to be a nurse of Japanese ancestry, helping in hospitals after the World War II Pearl Harbor attack. To care for men who were hurt, but viewed her and all Japanese people as a hated, suspicious enemy, must have produced a challenging, polarized atmosphere in which to work. Still her friendly, engaging style and her kindness were a natural part of her professional life.

Yet Mom had a painful flaw: while she loved everyone else, she didn't love herself very much. When the door closed to the world, she was a different person, a woman very hard on herself and hard on us. Many Buddhist teachings start with imagining that you love all beings as you have your mother and father. I have used her as the focal point in my practice long and hard, and it wasn't easy.

Now that I am older, I understand her better and have compassion for what she experienced in her own life struggle. We *all* need and deserve love. I think we all have high expectations of our parents, but when I put my relationship with my mother in the light of "given the circumstances, she did the best she could," my heart can embrace her and even move me to tears.

While each of us wants to be loved and oftentimes feels as if we don't get enough of it, we rarely think about being more loving to others. As we develop more openness and receptivity, we lessen our sense of isolation, of being self-centered. In addition, the more we offer others our love and interest, the more receptive we become to their generosity and their gestures of kindness.

Wherever His Holiness the Dalai Lama goes, he says it is like "meeting my old friends." It's so true. We feel that from him and are drawn to his warm friendship. My teachers often say we need to develop an equal love for all beings: friends, enemies, and strangers. Just think about it, if we had that kind of love, then we would be happy to be with everyone we meet, not full of bias, impatience, hidden agendas, or harm.

Compassion is different from love. Compassion is wishing others to be free from suffering, and love is wishing others to have happiness. Develop both, and your life will never be the same. Dr. Fuller understood this in his way, too. He said, "The more people I serve, the more effective I become."

DEPENDENT ARISING OR INTERCONNECTEDNESS

This teaching says that nothing occurs by itself, and everything exists in dependence upon something else. We are all interconnected.

The more deeply we understand this, the more information all life experience brings. The parallel with Dr. Fuller's teaching of "precession" is striking; many of Dr. Fuller's principles connect with this particular Buddhist teaching. Understand, though, that this view is not the psychological concept of dependency, or co-dependency.

It's true that the old adage "nothing occurs on its own" defines our universe. It applies to interpersonal relationships and to the forces of nature. A classic Buddhist example is of a sprout rising from a seed that matures with the right amounts of soil, water, and sun. Remove or overuse one element, and the seed may never sprout.

Dependent arising even provides an explanation for my low bank account! Being poor was in every way the product of the beliefs I had formed in my early upbringing, the decisions I made throughout my life, and my own perceptions of wealth and self worth. I'm not making excuses, but I am saying that many things—internal and external—contributed to my state of affairs.

It took getting cancer to wake me up to the reality that money is useful, not just for the nice things in life, but for the basics like health and wellness. It showed how my physical life constantly informed my emotional, mental and spiritual life. What I do not pay attention to is going to manifest one way or another.

If my first wake-up call was cancer, I shouldn't have needed a second one. I got one anyway, which came in the form of heart disease in 2007. I had been working hard, planning a visit by the Dalai Lama to Los Angeles and enjoying every minute of it; this work and the teachings filled me with energy. The hard part—as with most work of this sort—was the pressure of dealing with people, juggling tough contracts and deadlines. And because conflict situations are my challenge or handicap, I internalized a lot of frustrations. After all, I thought, a nun should not be feeling these things!

Stress—years of it actually, along with perhaps a genetic propensity toward heart disease—landed me in the hospital for angioplasty with only modest insurance and no savings at my disposal. The hospital bills amounted to more than $50,000. I owed $20,000, even after months of wrestling with my insurance company to pay the other $30,000. Reality, dependence, and financial need hit me again.

As Robert's sister, I have a natural window to view a way of life and a way of thinking that's completely different from my own. Working with Robert on this book and participating in his presentations and company meetings, allowed me to change my long-held view of money. Persons of the cloth have their own diverse patterns and beliefs about money and wealth, just as people in

Robert's world have theirs. For me, those two worlds collided, but I see now how the two worlds can co-exist and benefit others.

Have you ever found yourself thinking, "How was I born into this family?" Sometimes, when people find out that Robert is my brother, they ask, "Why aren't you like him? Aren't you rich, too?" We all know how different family members can be. It's remarkable to think how our same parents, roots, and upbringing propelled us in such different directions: Robert toward financial wealth, freedom and happiness, and mine toward inner freedom and happiness.

Serious illness and a reconnection with my brother are what it took for me to change my mental attitude about money and recognize the importance of conflict resolution. It is a beautiful example of inter-connectedness. Even though I live a simple life, I needed to find a way to help myself. Otherwise, what good would I be to others?

Robert and Kim helped me with my medical bills, but they are not giving me money. Rather, they are giving me knowledge so I can help myself and better serve others.

KARMA

Many Westerners use the word karma in everyday conversation. Perhaps you've heard comments like, "Oh, he had bad karma," or "You're going to get some great karma from doing that." It's as if karma is a reward, or retribution for doing something bad.

Karma actually means action and, interestingly, it's not just about what you do, your physical actions. It's more about the *motivations* and *attitudes* driving your action. Ethics and intention determine whether a karma is virtuous or not; that's dramatically different from reward and retribution.

What I'm saying is this: actions from the past determine and inform our present experiences. Our motivations and actions now will determine future results, including our tendency toward doing certain actions over and over again.

Even though I was doing work to benefit others, I was at times full of conflict. Not resolving that conflict affected my relationships and my health. It didn't matter that I was a vegetarian with a meditative lifestyle. I got heart disease—an illness that more commonly affects people like my high-stress, steak-loving brother. How's that for a shock?

I had to make changes.

I now know that because this is the way I have operated most of my life, it would be easy to fall back into old patterns. It's something I need to be aware of, and guard against. My illnesses have been challenging, but I also have great teachers who help me to make corrections in my life.

Just as Dr. Fuller talks of "lag," Buddhist teachings inform us that karma is not instant. Westerners find this challenging. Most want answers and results right now! That is unless, of courses, the results are negative. During a course I attended that was led by the Dalai Lama, an American woman asked, "What is the quickest, easiest, most convenient thing I can do so I can reach enlightenment right away?"

The Dalai Lama wept. He observed that so many people want things instantly. But in fact, we need experience, compassion, and wisdom to attain enlightenment. The process—the transformation that occurs through repeated practice and insight—is indispensable to that goal. And there's simply no rushing it.

If I want my life to go in a certain direction or to produce certain results, I have to direct my intentions and actions. But that alone is not enough. I also must become better informed and gain skills to attain my goals. The Tibetans say, "If you want to know where you came from, look at your life and experience now. If you want to know where you are going, look at your mind."

Robert chided me when I quoted this, telling me I keep getting too deep into theory. He is right from a non-Buddhist perspective. For people who do not accept karma, it is just a theory of the way things exist. Though karma is a theory in some sense, to a practicing Buddhist, it connects causality with behavior. It is the building block of our life experience and who we are. While there are many wealthy and famous people in the world, I observe Robert and Kim having built their wealth through hard work and study, developing themselves, not giving up, building great friendships and connections, learning through their experiences, and teaching others. They are generous and give back to help organizations and their community. All these actions build strength and conditions for future success.

You will find Buddhist masters saying that a karmic act—because of the complexity and subtlety of other actions and motivations involved—is more difficult to fully comprehend than some of the most profound views. Simply said, good karma, not harming others or ourselves, produces happiness, and negative karma produces suffering.

NIRVANA

The word nirvana, like karma, has made its way into Western vocabularies. People use it interchangeably with the word heaven, or even the concept of utopia. Living in India and spending time in study and meditation at my nunnery, sometimes I'd be so happy that there was nothing else I wanted. Some people visit India to study, but run away in horror, afraid of the bugs, disease, and filth. While I have not experienced nirvana, I *have* experienced deep contentment and satisfaction in my life.

But the Buddhist concept of nirvana has a deeper meaning of "freedom from suffering and delusions." Nirvana is a mental state, not a physical place. It is seeing things as they are, without the filters of attachment, aversion, and ignorance. One gains complete experience of the nature of reality.

His Holiness the Dalai Lama says that if liberation from suffering is possible, we should do everything we can to accomplish that and leave no stone unturned. If, in fact, we found that liberation was totally impossible, then he says, why not forget about the effort and live it up? But as long as there is some scent of liberation, of freedom from suffering, then we should work to attain this.

ENLIGHTENMENT

Enlightenment is greater than nirvana; it is a state attained by purifying all traces of delusions such as hatred, anger, jealousy, and ignorance, and cultivating all excellent qualities such as loving kindness, generosity, ethics, and compassion. It includes the powerful intention to attain this state for the benefit of all.

All beings have the potential to attain nirvana and enlightenment. Liberation, freedom, and enlightenment are not just for monks or

We had just moved to the new center in 1997 and the place was still under construction, but we were thrilled when the Dalai Lama accepted an invitation to come and visit the site.

nuns. Because we all possess this potential, we all should have the courage to face life's circumstances, to drive away our feelings of discouragement and low self-esteem. It is those kinds of mental states that deter us from striving to attain enlightenment. This knowledge, that all beings have the essence of enlightenment, can be a powerful inner source for all of us to develop greater tolerance and determination in working with others.

This path as a Buddhist practitioner has filled my life with purpose, direction, and peace of mind. It is like the spiritual family that Robert talks about, that spiritual home where we feel fulfilled, uplifted, understood, and accepted. I must be mindful and make the best progress I can. Meditation gives us perspective and insight regarding the nature of situations and conditions in life. Rather than galvanize ourselves against life problems, we allow more openness and acceptance of others and their differences.

I have dedicated my life to practicing these principles, and they act as both a guide and ballast for me in life.

11

Heaven, Hell, and Happiness

Sunday School taught us that heaven was a place in the sky where people sat around, floating on clouds, playing harps. Hell was the flaming center of the earth, where the devil (with horns, a long tail, and carrying a pitchfork) lived, waiting for sinners.

As adults, we do not know if there is a heaven or a hell after death. There are heaven and hell here on earth, and one person's heaven can be another person's hell. A secure job with the government would be our father's heaven, but Robert's hell. Being an entrepreneur is Robert's heaven. For our dad, having to become an entrepreneur at the age of fifty was his hell.

Marriage can be either a heaven or a hell. Even though we may deeply love someone, life together can be a living hell.

Money can be the reason for heaven or hell on earth. Many financial advisors recommend, "Live below your means." They say this because many people are barely surviving—in a living hell—using borrowed money to live a lifestyle they cannot afford. For others, heaven is having more than enough money to afford their lifestyle.

Since one's heaven can be another person's hell, the question is, what creates a person's heaven or hell? While there are many possible answers, one answer is happiness . . . or the lack of it.

ROBERT:
SELFISH AND UNSELFISH GOALS

As with so many things in life, for every action there is a reaction. If a person is unhappy, he may do something to make him happy, for example, like drink alcohol. Feeling low, he may go to a bar, drink a lot, and feel happy. The next day, he pays for his happiness with a hangover. Do this on a regular basis and that unhappy person becomes an alcoholic, still in search of happiness.

Others take chemical drugs to escape their pain and unhappiness. According to the *Washington Post*, today in America, more than one in every one hundred people are in jail, as many as 20 percent, for drug-related issues.

Being in jail is not my idea of heaven. Some people go shopping to relieve the pain. Money is their drug. The more money they have, the more they shop. Rather than finding heaven, they find hell, living under a mountain of credit card debt.

My drug of choice is food. When I am unhappy, I eat. While I'm eating, I feel happy. The problem is, the more I eat, the fatter I become. The fatter I become, the more unhappy I get, so I eat more, become fatter, and become even more unhappy. In my attempt to reach heaven through food, I wind up in hell. Many people seek to solve their unhappiness through religion. Many have so many problems they feel they cannot solve them, and they seek salvation by hoping God will save them from their hell here on earth.

So what is happiness?

I am sure this question will be asked through the ages. And I doubt there is one answer for all people. Like heaven and hell, one person's happiness can be another person's unhappiness, which is why I'm not attempting to tell you what to do to find your happiness. I have enough trouble finding and hanging onto my own true happiness.

One important lesson I learned from Dr. Fuller was the idea of having "unselfish goals." In other words, goals that follow the generalized principle of "the more people I serve, the more effective I become." This idea fit my mother and father's values of being of service to their community. In December of 1984, when Kim and I took our leap of faith, we took the leap with unselfish goals in mind. As I have already said, it was the worst year of our lives.

It was not a happy time.

Today, Kim and I have found happiness by having selfish as well as unselfish goals. Our happiness comes from being of service, feeling that our work makes a difference in people's lives, and that we are contributing to solving some of our world's current problems. We also have selfish goals, goals such as making enough money to create a standard of living that suits us. We would not be happy being poor, working at a job we did not love, working with people we did not like, living below our means in a dangerous neighborhood, not being able to afford health care or the finer things of life.

Work is an important aspect of happiness and unhappiness. Even though our work is often challenging and filled with problems, ultimately our work makes us happy. We realize that, for millions of people, their work makes them unhappy. For millions, work is just about money.

I have a classmate from high school who is *very* unhappy. Right out of college, she met a rich man, married him, and moved to his large home in Aspen, Colorado. Her husband inherited his wealth and has never really had to work. They have great kids and grandkids. Her days are filled tending to her show horses and doing charity work. Her husband spends his time at his club, putting on events to keep the members happy.

When I asked her why she was unhappy, her answer was simple: "Life seems empty."

When I asked her if her grandkids filled her void she said, "No. I love my kids and grandkids, but I am through with motherhood." When I asked about her charity work, she said frankly, "I do charity work to belong to the right social circles. Charity work is my access to the right charity balls and to be seen with the right people. I know the charities are important, but I am not passionate about the causes."

When I asked her what her soul wanted her to do, she snapped at me and said, "I'm doing enough. I'm good to my kids. I'm a good parent. I'm a good wife. I donate time and money to my charities. What else do you want me to do?"

Our conversation was over. It wasn't the time to get into the differences between selfish and unselfish goals.

One of the most valuable lessons I learned from my mom and dad was the answer to my question, "What is happiness?" The happiest days in their lives were the days they both worked for President Kennedy's Peace Corps. Dad took a break from the education department, and he and Mom spent their days, nights, and weekends working side by side at the Peace Corps training center in Hilo, preparing young people to be of service to the world. As a young man preparing to go to war, I saw the happiness that working together at spiritual work brought my mom and dad. I never forgot that happiness.

When Kim and I took our leap of faith in December of 1984, we were in search of the same happiness. The day we were married, in 1986, we didn't have much money and could not afford a band. Instead we handed out the words to "The Wedding Song" (also known as "There Is Love") by Noel Paul Stookey of Peter, Paul, and Mary. We asked everyone to link arms and sing along with the music. The song conveyed to everyone in the circle the spiritual reason for our marriage, which spread from heart to heart. The following are a few words from this very beautiful song:

Well, a man shall leave his mother
and a woman leave her home
and they shall travel on to where
The two shall be as one.

As it was in the beginning
is now and till the end
woman draws her life from man
and gives it back again.
and there is love, and there is love.

Well then what's to be the reason
for becoming man and wife?
Is it love that brings you here
or love that brings you life?

And if loving is the answer,
then who's the giving for?
Do you believe in something
that you've never seen before?
Oh there is love, there is love.

Kim has been the greatest blessing in my life. We have been together virtually 24/7 since December of 1984. We have been apart only a few days in all those years. Our work nurtures our souls. Our work gives us life. Our work *is* our life.

Like most couples, we do have our rough spots. It is not always peaches and cream. It's not always wedded bliss or the fairy tale of living happily ever after. Through our work we share our love and our reason for being married. While we receive many blessings from our work, we believe the gift of true happiness is the greatest gift, a blessing that brings magic to life.

There are many people who believe the rich are greedy, and many of them are. Yet, I have met many greedy poor and middle-class people. They are simply greedy people with less money. The rich do not have an exclusive domain over greed.

When we were married, Kim and I co-created selfish and unselfish goals. We set four financial goals, and those goals became the four stepping-stones to guide us through the stream of life:

- The first stepping-stone was to build a business that served as many people as possible. We wanted to serve people regardless of their wealth (or lack of it), race, or religion.
- The second stepping-stone was to invest our money to be of service. The majority of our investment money is in apartment houses. We provide safe, well-managed, affordable housing to thousands of people.
- The third stepping-stone of our finances was to tithe, or give money back. Even when we had very little money, we donated to charitable causes that spoke to our hearts. We do not give money directly to people in need. Instead we give money to responsible organizations that have a proven track record of sound money management.
- The fourth stepping-stone was our personal standard of living. Even though we had nothing when we were married, we still wanted to live financially free, at a rich and wealthy standard of living.

All four goals required hard work, miles of travel, a lot of study, and often a good bit of disappointment. From the generalized principle of precession, which is the ripple effect, came the gift of true happiness in our lives.

Today, we have more money than we could ever spend. We have more than we need. This is why today we are focusing more and more on giving the money back, just as Bill Gates and Warren Buffett are doing. Giving money back can be a full-time job. Just as making and investing money creates unique challenges, giving money back comes with its own set of challenges. There is an art and science to charitable giving. Again, rather than give the money to the needy and the poor, which would deplete the money supply, we are diligent in finding responsible, well-managed organizations that will protect our wealth and will use the money wisely for years, long after we are gone.

Kim and I believe in working to create heaven on earth—while we are here and after we have left this earth. We find happiness working together in our life's work, just as working together for the Peace Corps brought true happiness for my mom and dad. Finding happiness by doing our spirit's work is the best gift Mom and Dad have given their children.

This is not to say that our work is uniquely significant, special, or that important. Any work that adds value and is of service to life is important and special. For example, the person who drives a school bus has a very important and special task. I am glad there are people who want to do this job, and I would hope they love what they do.

I especially like comedians, because laughter is vital to a world that so often takes itself too seriously. The gift of laughter is a very important gift.

So what is your gift? When I am asked about how to find one's gift, I simply reply, "If you had all the money in the world, what would you do for the rest of your life? What would make your heart sing?" I also say, "One of the reasons a person does not give or use their gift is because they have been trained to go to school and get a job to earn money. So the question is, What would you do if you did not have to worry about money?"

In 1994, Kim and I had the luxury of retiring. She was thirty-seven and I was forty-seven. I thought retirement would be heaven.

Instead it turned out to be hell. All I did was play golf, and if you've seen my golf game you would know why, for me, golf is the game from hell. In 1996 Kim and I developed our CASHFLOW® board game, I wrote *Rich Dad Poor Dad,* and we got back to work. Our objectives remain the same. We believe that too many people are slaves to money, and one way to financial freedom is via financial education. Our wish is to have you become financially free so you can give more of your God-given gifts and do the work you were born to do.

One of the greatest joys of our work is to have people like you read our work, even if you do not agree with everything we write. I know the world is filled with people with great ideas, great stories to tell, and great gifts to give.

TENZIN:
EXAMINATION

I believe it is important to live a meaningful life. How that is accomplished will be different for each of us.

In my time with Robert and Kim and in reading their books, I'd note their comment about "not living below your means," but I always considered myself not quite a part of this category as they defined it because of my monastic lifestyle. As a nun, living below my means seemed "suitable." There is a difference between "living below your means" and "living suitably." "Below my means" put me in financial and physical jeopardy.

As I worked to find a way to resolve this apparent conflict between my Buddhist practice and my medical debts and health needs, I analyzed my situation based on long held beliefs and my understanding of the practice, and I came up with the following conclusions:

WANT NOT/STRESS NOT

The life of a Buddhist nun should be simple and sublime. Simplicity comes from reducing activities and acquisitions that are focused on self-gratification and the comfort of this life alone. For example, as a nun I don't need extravagance or trendy gadgets, but keeping up with technology is important in today's world. There has to be a balance.

In addition, actions that arise from the motivation to help others find true happiness and become free from suffering make our minds—and therefore our lives—sublime. A contented mind is priceless, and it comes from focus on the happiness of *others*, as well as ourselves.

HELPFUL ACTIONS NEED A HEALTHY BODY

Though we may have many ideas about how to change the world through spiritual action, we can do little that is useful for others if we are physically debilitated. Of course I recognize that there are many forces in the world that can have a negative effect on our health, but there are things we can do to counter some of them. For me, "living suitably" means having at least basic needs met.

Basic needs include proper support in healthy nourishing food, good friends and mentors, shelter, and having a reserve for health care and other life needs as they arise. This is especially true for those who are living on their own. These things are important, and the peace of mind that they provide fuels our happiness and—directly and indirectly—our health.

And, as I have learned from my life experience, most important of all is not having an ongoing inner conflict about our ideas and our reality. This leads to the next point . . .

SOMETIMES WE NEED HELP

In traditional Buddhist cultures, monastics were supported by the lay community. This enabled them to study and practice and, at a certain point in their spiritual maturity, to teach the Dharma to others. In this way the Dharma was maintained through the centuries in the various Asian countries where Buddhism flourished.

My Tibetan teachers and many of my Tibetan monastic friends live within this traditional system, even now while they are in exile in India. I guess it was only natural that I would aspire to this way of life myself when I returned to the United States after being ordained in 1985.

But these are different times, and we are certainly not living in a Buddhist country. Most Dharma practitioners and students are not monastics. They support themselves and in some cases their families, and do not have much left over to help the monastics who wish to spend their days in meditation and study. So, we monastics have had to adjust. For example, I held a job for many years while living in Los Angeles after I was ordained.

Nevertheless, when I was diagnosed with cancer, I was not working and had no health insurance. As I have said, it was due to the kindness of my Dharma friends in Seattle that I had my surgery and recovered so well. Similarly, the emergency procedure to clear clogged arteries took place just after I had completed my work on the visit of His Holiness the Dalai Lama to Los Angeles. I was in retreat and without much income. That time Robert and Kim so kindly helped me pay the extremely high medical bills.

I am certainly not saying that we should expect others to take care of our medical and financial needs. In fact, that is contrary to my aspiration to be in *support* of others. Planning to be dependent on the kindness of others is not a valid life plan, whether one is Buddhist or not. However, there are times when we are overcome by circumstances. Then we have no choice but to ask for help and let others step in.

These situations do not mean that we are failures. It means that there are others around us, our spiritual families as well as our biological families, who are there to help and support us, just as we would be for them. If there is a lifelong pattern of dependence, that is different. Then we must recognize the problem and work to make a change. In my case, even though my health challenges are intermittent, I must be prepared for unexpected circumstances.

CHANGE COMES FROM THE INSIDE

After my last surgical procedure, I realized that I had to come to terms with my need and desire to stay healthy. I became aware of how much I had compromised by living close to the edge and not adjusting to changing needs. Even though I was doing good work, my capacity and reserves became narrow. While striving for happiness, I created hardship by placing some unworkable limitations on myself.

Given my age and medical history it seemed foolish to simply go back to teaching Dharma at a center that would be unable to offer health benefits. I made up my mind that I would move on. In hindsight, what might have been a tough decision required very little soul searching on my part. It was very clear to me: There are many ways to serve in the world. I am trained as a chaplain and have experience as a teacher and administrator for Dharma events. Surely I would be able to support myself in a better way while remaining true to my Buddhist ideals.

In fact, the Buddhist ideal to become the loving bodhisattva—a person who is bound for enlightenment, and serving others—was driving me to resolve my problem related to financing my health care. My dear teacher and some concerned students saw this need, too, and offered me health insurance! It made me happy and eased my mind.

I have come to see that monastics cannot live in America as they had in Asian Buddhist countries. Just the same, I am able to maintain the best part of Buddhist practice by devoting this life to cultivating inner and outer peace in order to benefit others and be a good human being. Through developing inner peace, I create a happier world for myself and those around me. I am vigilant in my life, observing what is supporting growth, freedom, wisdom, compassion, and tolerance.

None of this is in conflict with living in twenty-first-century America, though I have to admit that living as monks and nuns in this place and time is an unusual livelihood.

The principle that *change comes from the inside* applies just as well at the societal level as it does for the individual. As a culture, we Americans are living close to the edge—probably *over* the edge at this point—and we seem to be unable to adjust to changing times and circumstances, either quickly enough or well. We have not faced up to the fact that we have become a country that spends a good deal of time engaged in activities that are often meaningless and, at worst, violent and harmful to life.

I believe that now, more than ever, we must use our creative minds to increase peaceful methods of resolution and cooperation to live on this earth together and restore our planet; to reduce pollution, poverty, and oppression on a global level and to reduce hatred, bias, and selfishness on a personal level. It is up us to resolve and remedy these problems that we humans ourselves have created. Ethical and harmonious religious principles of tolerance and loving kindness are a powerful force, and together with the view of interdependence, our interrelatedness with everyone and all things can help us to bring about these desperately needed changes.

We must develop the ability to look within, to identify faults and shortcomings, and then have the courage and the commitment to change.

12

Life and Death

We all face the final frontier of old age and death. Death and life are intertwined, and death is never too far from our daily lives—as evidenced by the bomb blast so very long ago—even though we kid ourselves that it is not. We all have a waning window of time during which to take advantage of this incredible and precious human life and to live our dreams.

And people don't necessarily handle life—or death—with grace. In life, we often find ourselves seeking out conflict, and not always with a positive goal in mind. When we face death, all sorts of bad behavior can manifest. When that happens, the persons facing death often just make matters worse.

In Vietnam, the issues were both life and death. War consisted of long periods of boredom. Sitting on an aircraft carrier at sea isn't exactly a cruise ship vacation, filled with activities to keep the passengers entertained. There were no big buffets, cabaret shows, or bars filled with happy drunks.

The cramped quarters far below the flight deck were a breeding ground for dysfunctional behavior. There were fights between sailors and marines, or grunts and air wing marines. Pilots and flight crews had an advantage: They flew ashore at least once or twice a week. Yet for thousands of

young men stuck on board the ships, life was cramped, crowded, and con-
fining.

Tragically, there were incidents that went far beyond simple fist fights.
Some few individuals would commit acts of treason, overtly sabotaging
one another's efforts, even endangering lives. In one instance, someone
pumped seawater into an aircraft fuel tank, destroying the entire aircraft.
An aircraft's rigging would be cut, engine hoses disconnected, or rags and
tools stuffed into places where they should not be.

After repeated incidents of sabotage, some crew members took turns
guarding their gunships, 24/7, even though we were all Americans and
were supposedly fighting for the same side.

Dysfunctional behavior isn't limited to wartime, however. Any person
facing death will be dealing with one of the most traumatic events of a
lifetime. Some have prepared for this turning point and approach it with
grace and acceptance. But others lash out, and in doing so they hurt them-
selves and those who might be trying to help them.

This isn't the sort of betrayal that comes from sabotaging an aircraft,
but it still has the potential to cause great pain, and may even destroy
lives.

Yet it needn't be the case.

ROBERT: LIVING IN FEAR OF DYING

In Sunday School I learned about Judas betraying Jesus. It seems as
if the practice of betrayal or treason is a part of human behavior.
Spouses betray their partners, business associates steal from each other,
people lie to protect themselves, gossip destroys reputations, and the
Internet is filled with blogs dedicated to destroying others. The ability to betray is a dark and potent force available to all of us.

During the Vietnam era, there were no women at sea as there are
now. The ships were filled with thousands of young men, all wait-

ing for something to happen. Most of the time the U.S. flotilla sailed back and forth, up and down the coast of Vietnam. On one day the shoreline would be off to starboard—to the right—and the next day off to port.

The grunts—ground marines—spent many of their days jogging laps around the flight deck, cleaning their weapons, or sleeping. Marine flight crews and navy personnel tended to exercise in the late afternoon after things had cooled down—we weren't as gung-ho as the grunts. This self-imposed timetable helped keep the different groups apart, and the fights to a minimum.

Even though we were all on the same side, there were always the few who would find a reason to blow off steam and pit one group against the other.

I crashed my helicopter three times during my year in Vietnam. None of these incidents was due to enemy action. Two crashes were due to aircraft fatigue. Once a tail rotor failed, and the other a hydraulics line failed. Luckily we made it back to the ship as we crashed. Twice we were able to repair the damage and save the aircraft.

The most serious of three crashes was due to sabotage. It couldn't have been the enemy—we were more than twenty miles out at sea, and it would have been tough for a Vietcong soldier to paddle up to an aircraft carrier, climb on board, and stuff a wrench down the jet engine intake.

Our entire squadron was participating in a combined forces strike north of Da Nang. Early in the morning, before the sun came up, my gunship was brought up from below deck, and we prepared to launch. Two gunners, one crew chief, co-pilot Lt. Ted Green, and I went through our pre-flight inspection.

Green and I had gone through flight school in Florida together. After receiving our wings, we were thrilled to be selected for the

Lt. Ted Green and Robert in Okinawa, preparing to join
their aircraft carrier in Vietnam.

gunship program and were sent to Camp Pendleton, California, for
advanced training and transition. As soon as we completed our guns
and rockets training, we were immediately sent to Vietnam together.

Gazing into the intake of the jet engine, I caught a glimpse of
something protruding from between one of the turbine blades.
Since it was still dark, I took my flashlight and peered deep into the
engine. Soon my fingers found the object, and I began tugging and
pulled out a small oily rag.

Shock went through my body, my stomach tightened, and my skin
crawled. Someone had gotten past our defenses. Immediately, I ordered
the entire aircraft reopened for a closer inspection. The crew soon discovered a wrench and some thin wire stuffed into other obscure places.

"Have we found it all?" I asked.

"I hope so," replied our crew chief.

"Hope isn't good enough," said the gunner.

Just then the ship's loudspeaker blared.

"Ten minutes to launch time. Gunship on spot three, are you going to launch, or are you down?"

The five of us looked each other in the eyes, searching for any uncertainty. We all nodded our heads saying, "Let's go," and began buttoning up the aircraft. The engine started without a hitch, and soon we were flying a racetrack pattern over the carrier, waiting for the troop-carrying helicopters to load troops, launch, and join the attack. Although the aircraft seemed to be running perfectly, we remained edgy and nervous, constantly checking gauges and flight controls.

Suddenly, out of the corner of my eye, I saw one of the engine gauges flicker. In flight school we were taught that if this particular gauge flickered, there was something wrong with the engine.

Before I could say anything to my crew, the aircraft shuddered, the engine surged, quit, surged again, and then quit for good. Warning alarms blared and engine failure lights began flashing. With power gone, the aircraft immediately began falling from the sky.

"Mayday, mayday, mayday," Lt. Green broadcasted as he pushed the nose into a steep dive. The crew clung to the aircraft and began jettisoning guns, ammo, and anything loose out the doors.

Watching the ocean coming up at us, I recalled a phrase from flight school: "You look into the eyes of death." That day, I knew what death's eyes looked like. Silently, I wondered if this was my last moment on earth.

Even though there was a lot of noise around us—noise from the ship's control tower warning all aircraft to watch for us, radio transmissions from the battlefield, and the noise of our crew preparing to crash—an eerie silence seemed to fill the aircraft. I wondered if the ocean and the faces of my crew would be my final memories.

In the midst of chaos, I made peace with myself. I asked myself, if I were to die, would I be okay with my life? In about five seconds, I found peace when I reminded myself that had I chosen this life.

No one had forced me to join the marines. When I volunteered to fight, I'd known that I might not come back alive.

So I was fine with my life. If the sight through the cockpit window was to be the last image from my life's movie, I was okay with how the movie would end.

The aircraft was in a stable auto-rotation as we dove toward the water. Lt. Green was piloting the dying aircraft as I shouted the checklist in preparation for the crash.

Green was a great pilot and was doing a magical job guiding us toward the water. He was doing his best to go in as close to the carrier as possible. I was making sure the checklist was followed, doors were jettisoned, aircraft was empty, electrical power was off, and the crew was strapped in. Ted and I had practiced this drill for years, running through the emergency procedure for engine failure nearly every day, over and over again. It had gotten to the point where we could fly with or *without* an engine.

Practice was over, and we would soon know if our preparations would pay off. Our small crew of five was functioning as a team, terrified but not panicked.

Just before we hit the water, Ted rotated the nose and instead of crashing, we glided silently a few feet above the waves. It was a flawless autorotation, flying on momentum.

Everything was going perfectly as I finished the checklist and told everyone to brace for the impact. Then a large ocean swell hit the glass bubble and jade green water swirled around my feet. We began to sink immediately as the aircraft lurched and fought against the forces of the sea, finally tipping to starboard as the rotor blade struck the water at high speed, tearing off the engine transmission and ripping the aircraft in half.

Then I was underwater, struggling to breathe as I tried to climb out of the aircraft, terrified that I might die by drowning. My concern was that a piece of my clothing might be caught, and I would

The moment of the rotor blade impact.
The cause of the crash: engine failure twenty-seven miles off Da Nang.
All of the crew survived.

be dragged down with the rapidly sinking aircraft. Today, I can still see the swirling green water, the aircraft cockpit underwater, and the sounds of water, bubbles, and small explosions as I kicked and clawed desperately to reach the surface.

Bursting through the surface, I took a deep breath of air and screamed for joy. Treading water, the first thing I noticed was that the ocean around the aircraft was boiling due to its contact with the jet engine. Next I saw my two gunners, floating above the frothy and steaming water. Again, I cheered for joy and yelled, "Are you all right?"

Both were stunned yet managed smiles and a thumbs–up.

"Where's Jackson?" I screamed. "Where's Green?"

Both young gunners shook their heads. They did not know.

About thirty seconds went by, and still no sign of our co–pilot or crew chief. As the tail rotor, the last visible piece of the aircraft, slid beneath the waves, gunnery sergeant Jackson broke the surface and the three of us cheered like we had never cheered before.

"Green is still down there," gasped Jackson. "He can't get out of his seat. He never got his door off. I couldn't help him. He was so busy flying—saving us—he forgot to save himself."

It isn't possible to fully describe what I felt at that moment. If I could have gone down to pull Green out, I would have, but the environmental forces were beyond my human abilities. The aircraft was sinking fast, and I was in steel-toed flight boots and a flight suit with an inflated survival vest that kept me afloat. Even though I was a pretty good diver, I was dressed to be a pilot, not a diver. In the time it would have taken to get my boots, flight suit, and flotation equipment off, it would have been all be over.

At the same time, the thought of one of my best friends—just a few feet under water, struggling to free himself and fighting for his life—was a horrible thing. I felt the excruciating pain of helplessness. *How powerless over life are we?* This was the question running through my head. If I could have traded positions with Ted, I would have.

Memories of our three years came back to me as I treaded water, praying for a miracle. For what seemed an eternity, all we could do was stare at the boiling ocean where our aircraft had gone down, hoping for the impossible.

The empty silence was deafening.

Suddenly Ted burst to the surface, gasping and gagging as he took long breaths of air. It was the miracle we had prayed for. The crew immediately surrounded him, assisting him in throwing up the water from his lungs and supporting him to stay afloat. He needed time to get his life back.

"I thought I was dead," he told us. Five grown men hugged, cried, cheered, and celebrated life. Even though we had crashed close to the ship, the overall combat mission was more important than one aircrew in the water. It was about four hours before we were finally pulled from the water and back on board the carrier.

I was tired of death . . . and killing. My career as a marine was over. I didn't want to kill or dedicate my life to killing anymore.

Something inside of me was changing.

Often, we don't fully appreciate something until we lose it, or nearly lose it. Being so close to dying, and even killing, were great experiences because I gained a deep appreciation for the precious gift called life. Instead of living in *fear* of dying, I do my best to live a fearless life. I believe that one of the reasons I do not succumb to the fears of job security, fear of failing, fear of criticism, and fear of not having enough money, is because to me those fears are fears not worthy of dictating how I live my life. Rather than live in fear, I choose to live life with excitement, gratitude, and giving back, in exchange for this gift known as life.

When I was in Sunday School I learned about the crucifixion and the resurrection. In Vietnam I learned that we did not have to die to be resurrected. One of the great things about war was facing death. While it is normal to fear death, it is also important to know that death is a transition, and there *is* a resurrection—a transformation, an evolution, a reformation—if we choose to see it that way.

One of the problems I had with some of the churches I attended was the literal interpretation of the resurrection message, the belief that there was only one type of resurrection and that it was the final one that happened after death, with an ascension into heaven. I realized that life itself is a daily process of birth, death, resurrection, and evolution or reformation.

In war, I found life in death. After Vietnam I also realized that I did not have to sit in a church to get the message. The message is all around us, every day, no matter where we are.

Today, I meet many people who live in fear of dying rather than with the joy of living. Many cling to job security, inadequate pay, abusive relationships, and live below their means, oftentimes in poor health and facing other challenges that seem insurmountable. In my opinion, many live in fear of some form of crucifixion, not realizing that their fear is already crucifying them.

Living in fear, living below one's full potential, is a form of cru-cifixion. To get beyond crucifixion, it takes faith that there is always a resurrection, an evolution, and a reformation, as long as we are open to it.

When I lost my first big business, I was crucified. The Hawaii busi-ness press wasn't kind; they went after me like sharks. Bill collectors hounded me. Some of my friends stopped being my friends. My first wife filed for divorce. My Harley-Davidson was repossessed. My credit cards were taken away. I had no real estate left. I sold my Porsche because I could not make the payments. I took the bus, rode a bicycle, or walked.

I did not know how or when I was going to get back to life again, but I knew I would. From Vietnam, I understood the message of life after death. From church, I understood crucifixion and resurrection. I also understood evolution—not from the biblical or Darwinian sense but from a financial historical sense. I knew that most successful entrepreneurs failed before they ever succeeded, that it took a cru-cifixion before they could rise again.

I've never understood faith-based messages that say you don't have to do anything for salvation. The ones that profess that all you have to do is be a good person, attend church, pray, and put money in the offering plate. Simply do those things and God will solve your problems. I know—firsthand, I might add—that miracles happen, and that just sitting and praying works for some people, but per-sonally, I'd rather take an active role in creating my future.

I connect with the Sunday School lesson, "God helps those who help themselves." In my life I have found that the more I help oth-ers—and myself—the more miracles I have in my life. The Marine Corps instilled in me the value of willingly giving my life for a higher purpose. That's why Ted Green nearly died. He thought of his crew before he thought of himself. I know many people talk about giving their life to a higher purpose, but talking about it is very different from actually doing it.

As stated earlier, many times we do not appreciate what we have until we lose it or come close to losing it. I did not appreciate the gift of life until I nearly lost my life. I did not appreciate my freedom until I nearly went to jail. I did not truly appreciate my rich dad's advice until I lost everything. I did not appreciate the love of my first wife until I lost her.

The crash put me face-to-face with death, and with someone who was prepared to give his life so others could live. That crash profoundly changed my life by giving me a deeper appreciation for the gift of life. I am against killing. My samurai heritage still runs in my veins, but today I would rather use that heritage to fight for life rather than take it.

"Why do bad things happen to good people?"

After something is lost, or something bad happens, I often hear people ask that question. I follow Dr. Fuller's idea that "good and bad are meaningless." I now know that all things—good or bad—are blessings. For example, crashing into the ocean gave me life. Going broke made me rich. Losing my first wife made me a better husband for Kim. Getting fat made me a healthier person today.

Our lives are continual crucifixions, resurrections, evolutions, and reformations, and each of these is as vital to life as food, water, sun, and exercise. If one of the four is missing, existence is incomplete. For example, not being able to breathe, and thinking I was having a heart attack was my crucifixion and my blessing. Changing my diet, exercise, knowledge, and discipline was my resurrection. But just diet and exercise were not enough. I had to evolve on the inside, too—from a fat person to a healthy person. If I did not evolve, it wouldn't be long before I became an obese person again.

My evolution—from fat person, which I had been for most of my life, to a healthy person—required a reformation, a changing of my rules. In other words, when I was fat it was because I was breaking the rules of my body. I was being unethical and immoral to myself.

When people say, "I've found religion," to me that means they've found the discipline to follow the rules. One of the reasons I would lose weight and gain it back was because I never found the religion of health. I'd cheat or pretend the rules of my body didn't matter. My near heart attack was my crucifixion, my wake up call, which led me to choose a resurrection.

The same idea of finding religion was essential to becoming a wealthy person. I had to follow the rules. In my marriage to Kim, I definitely want to follow the rules. She is the best thing that has ever happened to me.

Evolution and reformation are essential to the process of finding heaven on earth. Those of us who are old enough may recall *The Beverly Hillbillies*. It was a TV program about a poor mountain man who struck oil and packed up the family and moved to Beverly Hills. Even though Jed may have been wealthy, living in a wealthy neighborhood, he was still a poor hillbilly, and that was the source of the program's humor. He may have been resurrected from his crucifixion of poverty, but he hadn't evolved or reformed into a rich man. He just remained a poor man with a lot of money.

A reformation of life requires mental, physical, emotional, and spiritual transformation.

Many people move out of poverty, but bring their poverty with them. For example, many immigrants move from their homeland and join other refugees from the same homeland. This is why most big cities have ethnic communities, as well as ethnic gangs. When I was preparing to leave high school to go to college, many people advised me to attend school in California, Washington, or Oregon. When I asked why, their reply was, "Schools in those states have strong Hawaiian clubs."

As much as I love Hawaii, its people, and its culture, I was leaving Hawaii to evolve and reform. So I chose a school in New York and made sure it did not have a Hawaiian club. If I had stayed close to my Hawaiian culture, I doubt I would have made New York friends such as Donald Trump or Steve Forbes. I wouldn't have come to understand their world. I had to evolve and reform if I wanted to have New York friends, as well as Hawaiian friends.

I have a great marriage today because I was a horrible husband in my first marriage. If I hadn't gone through a personal evolution and reformation, I know Kim would not have married me. When we were first dating, I knew I loved Kim, but I still wanted to fool around—and did so once. When I realized I was doing the same things to Kim that I had done to my first wife, Janet, I immediately confessed and told Kim the truth. Although hurt and disappointed, she gently said, "You know I will not stand for that type of behavior. I will not marry a man who cheats."

Since then I have not betrayed her trust. I do not want to lose her respect or her love. I know I wouldn't have such a great soul mate if I still had a corrupt soul.

Marriage and entrepreneurship are very similar when it comes to legal, ethical, moral, and spiritual rules. As you know, in business, there are many crooks, liars, fools, and thieves, just as there are in marriages. One of the great things about being an entrepreneur is that I get to choose who I want to do business with. This does not mean I only work with friends. As an entrepreneur I let everyone know that if they do not perform, support our mission, work as a team, and continue to improve, they will be looking for another place of employment.

But most of my friends are just like me—wealthy entrepreneurs who love their work because it challenges them. They work because they love what they do, even though what they do is often difficult and trying. Many have earned my respect—most would not be *my* friends if I was unethical, immoral, or illegal. They would probably still love me, but they would lose their respect for me.

Over the years, I've had the blessings of doing business with some very smart crooks, liars, fools, and thieves. I say they were blessings because they taught me business lessons I would never have learned from a textbook. Every one of those crooks, liars, fools, and thieves showed me the crook, liar, fool, and thief in me. If I weren't one of them, I wouldn't have been hanging out with them. I am a stronger, more honest businessman because I know firsthand the pain that comes from being a crook, liar, fool, and a thief.

Earlier in this book I wrote about character and character flaws. Whenever I find myself not as successful, rich, or as happy as I want to be, I focus on my character strengths and the character flaws that are the flip side of the coin. For example, when I become successful I often become cocky.

Many character flaws are those we hear addressed in church, also known as the seven deadly sins. They are: pride, greed, envy, lust, gluttony, rage, and laziness. Humans have struggled with these sins—or flaws—for centuries. If we do not evolve or reform, those flaws diminish our power.

Saving the Middle Class

In 2008, during the presidential primaries, many of the candidates were promising to change things and to save the middle class. At the time of this writing, Barack Obama had just been elected as our next president, and I am pretty much certain that he will not be able to save the middle class. As most of us know, if your future wellbeing is in the hands of the government, you're in deep trouble.

In 1900, it was possible for the government to protect you. Since the year 2000, that is less and less possible. Neither governments nor religions can protect people from the global accelerating acceleration of change.

In 1974, when I saw my dad sitting in front of his TV set, I was grateful that the U.S. government had financial safety nets in place to cover his cost of living and medical care. By 2020, these government safety nets will probably not be adequate to accommodate the millions who are expecting medical and financial salvation.

In John Lennon's song "Imagine," a line goes, "Imagine there's no country, it isn't hard to do."

Actually for most people—including me—it *is* hard to imagine a world without countries. Few can imagine a world without the United States, or England, Japan, Mexico, Brazil, Canada, Australia, and South Africa. Since we've all been born into an era of nations, it is difficult to imagine a world without countries and governments to protect people. Yet, a world without nation-states is what many prognosticators are predicting.

One of the reasons Lennon's song may come true is that the idea of a nation is an Industrial Age idea. Prior to the Industrial Age, there were kingdoms with kings and queens. Today, there are only a few kingdoms left. Could a world without countries be next? That is what Lennon's song is asking.

If the idea of nations and governments is obsolete, what will happen to the millions and billions of people counting on a country and government social programs to take care of them? I believe the answer to that question is only a few years away. Who will they turn to for food, shelter, and medical care? God? Their church, temple, mosque, or synagogue?

In more explicit terms, what happens if national governments go broke and cannot afford to keep their promises? What will you do if you are one of these people who has been counting on the government to take care of you?

When I meet someone who isn't living up to his full, God-given potential, I begin to look for the sin or sins that have not been resolved. I know *I* still struggle with these seven deadly sins, and I invite you to go through the list and see if you can recognize any of them in yourself. If you can't, you may want to apply for sainthood or seek membership in the "Sacred Order for the Holier than Thou." It's a very popular club, with many members, some of whom you probably know.

During one of his talks, I listened as Dr. Fuller said, "We as a humanity are starting to work out that we are not making it by killing everyone." As he spoke, my thoughts drifted back to the atomic blast I witnessed, my experiences in Vietnam, and my kill-or-be-killed attitude in business. I began to realize that the more I tried to kill my enemies, the harder they fought to live.

After facing death in Vietnam, I began searching for another way to live. This search led me back to the values of my parents, family, and my church. I finally heard what they were trying to tell me. By 1981, I had evolved and reformed enough to where I could finally hear Dr. Fuller asking the question, "What would happen if we began working for everyone to live?"

With that question, my evolution and reformation began. Instead of focusing only on making myself rich, I began focusing on building a business that made *everyone* richer. And that is what I do today. It's why I have good fortune and financial success.

TENZIN: LIVING—AND DYING—
WITH GRACE

My work as a hospital and hospice chaplain brings me face-to-face with death more often than most people. Perhaps I was meant for it. I was there when my dad died. I was there when my mom died. Their deaths left permanent impressions on me as a young adult and left me resolute to search for spiritual pathways to peaceful living and peaceful dying.

We all face the final frontier of old age and death. As a Buddhist, I have been studying and reflecting on these subjects for some time. However, now that I am older, and especially after having faced serious illness, I see how death and life are intertwined, and how death is never far from our daily lives, even though we kid ourselves that it is.

I am keenly aware that I have an ever-narrowing window of time to take advantage of this incredible and precious human life and to live the dream of increasing my ability to love and be compassionate to others. In the end this is what we really have. As important as our wealth, our friends, our family, even our doctors are to us during our lives, the only thing that can help in our final hour is a peaceful mind. And from my observations, as well as personal experience, graceful dying comes only from graceful living.

Graceful living is defined as a spiritual and ethical life, resolving our inner conflicts with ourselves and our outer conflicts with others. Living well is the secret to dying well.

Robert claims that my work with dying isn't the kind of subject matter that makes for great dinner conversation; most people would rather just avoid it. He faced death in Vietnam and saw his buddies die in horrible situations far from home. He says he's not afraid of death, and maybe that's what gives him amazing vibrancy every day of his life. For me, facing the reality of my own death is part of my Buddhist practice.

We are trained to contemplate how our bodies change over time, how we grow old. There is also the practice of considering that most of us alive today will not be alive one hundred years from now. However, I don't need to think about death in such an abstract way because I have lost so many friends and family members. My experience with death has come firsthand.

The final transition of death is an intense time of life for all of us, and it usually carries a powerful emotional charge. Death has the potential to make everyone it touches wiser about life. I am preparing for my death by leading a life grounded in Buddhist principles. You may wonder how that can be of any use at the time of death, especially if you accept the scientific thinking that humans are without a consciousness or a spirit, and that all our thoughts and ideas come only from chemical reactions and electrical responses in the brain. According to this view, when our brain dies, that's it. Nothing of the person continues.

But my years of practice and study have convinced me that life does not end at death.

One evening I taught a class and read a piece by the Japanese haiku poet Jakura, who passed away in 1906. He was part of a tradition in Japan of Zen monks, poets, and samurais who composed short works just before their death, to capture their thoughts and their states of mind at that crucial moment. Just before his death Jakura recited, "This year I want to see the lotus on the other side."

After a few moments of contemplation, a new student in the class asked, "Does he mean, from under the dirt?"

Our bodies will be "under the dirt," perhaps, but our consciousness—no longer supported by the body—will separate from it and continue on, sustaining the very subtle imprints and propensities of a life.

Some scientific studies are beginning to support the Buddhist teaching that consciousness is different from the physical organ we call the brain. Consciousness exhibits the qualities of clarity and knowing. It is not a material object and therefore isn't subject to deterioration when the body dies. At death, this consciousness continues to exist and, in fact—according to the Buddhist view—it becomes the basis for a new body and a new life.

This is one reason why I do not accept the position that life is meaningless. Life is *full* of both meaning and purpose. We are on a long journey toward ultimate happiness. The road we must follow is based on ethics, and an ethical life, generally speaking, is one that is focused on the happiness of others, as well as our own happiness. Following an ethical lifestyle brings peace of mind, which can be helpful at the time of death.

Living an ethical and disciplined lifestyle is important, even for those who do not accept the concepts of a separate consciousness or rebirth. Everyone wants to be happy, and we pursue that in many different ways. Some believe that happiness is found in money, fame, power, and the other trappings of our twenty-first-century world. And it's true—as I have learned from my own journey—that it takes a basic level of wealth to maintain health and happiness. But money alone does not bring happiness, no matter the quantity.

The pursuit of happiness without an ethical foundation is certain to change into the pursuit of *unhappiness*. Ethics and good will toward others compose the essential state of mind that will bring about happiness in this very life, and it is this state that is the real human treasure, the true wealth.

We prepare for death by being mindful of how we live.

Of course, to develop the essential state of mind, we must first take care of our basic needs, and attend to healthy and conducive living conditions, but once we have these things in place, we can achieve whatever we put our minds to. This is the true way to put poverty behind us.

Dying with grace is a function of being prepared and accepting of it. Ultimately, we all would like to be prepared and accepting of death—our own and the deaths of the ones we love. For me, whether we die with ease and grace or die with emotional suffering depends upon our level of acceptance and our preparation for death. While we cannot choose *the way* we die, we can choose *how* we die. These are our basic choices:

Prepared but unaccepting	Prepared and accepting
Unprepared and unaccepting	Unprepared but accepting

UNPREPARED AND UNACCEPTING

When I was teaching at a Dharma center some years ago, a man who was about forty years old started attending my classes. He had fatally damaged his liver through drug and alcohol abuse. In fact, he was in hospice but was stable enough to be released for a couple of hours to come to class. He enjoyed the meditations and the company of the students, and we all rallied to befriend him. We visited him in hospice, transported him to our classes, and helped him with errands.

One day the hospice doctors gave him some astonishing good news: His health was improving, and he was getting better. Then they gave him the bad news: He would have to leave hospice.

At first he stayed with his brother and sister-in-law. When that became a problem, he found an apartment on his own. Soon after that he stopped attending our classes, and we lost track of him over the next few months. Later we discovered that he had returned to drinking and carousing, and was living a life that exacerbated his physical illness. He quickly succumbed to liver cirrhosis and was found dead in his apartment. While he had been a model patient and sincere seeker at hospice, out on his own he returned to his old ways of life, even though he had been given a second chance.

It seemed our friend had no faith in himself and no understanding of his human potential. Without a positive view of self and the world, he was lost and confused, and so he lost hope. Some try to become free from depression by turning to drugs or alcohol or some other poisonous substance or activity. Perhaps they have no one to help them, or maybe they are unable to seek help when they need it. Such social isolation is a serious problem for many people. Like my friend, they live their lives in a numbed state, one that has a kind of spit-in-the-eye-of-death carelessness.

But as the Buddhist teachings say, "Do not seek misery as a means to happiness." Even though our friend was interested in spiritual teachings, he wasn't able to incorporate them into his life. Perhaps his habit of "seeking misery" was too strong. In any case, he seemed to sacrifice his life to escape from his problems, rather than choosing to live and try to transform his suffering into a healthier life.

PREPARED BUT UNACCEPTING

Mom and Dad were both intellectually prepared for but unaccepting of their deaths. They had both dealt with dying more than most people during their lives; Mom through being a nurse, particularly at the time of the attack on Pearl Harbor, and both of them through tidal waves, fires, and the deaths of many family members and friends. Mom performed CPR to try to resuscitate her brother at the time of his untimely death, and Dad actually forced himself into a burning building to pull out someone who was trying to retrieve his belongings.

There was a time when Dad had to identify the body of a very close friend's son after he had been in a head-on collision with a large truck. Dad refused to let the boy's grandparents see his body because he had been badly mangled and disfigured.

Both my parents had many encounters of this sort, and looked death in the face to help others. Facing their own deaths, however, proved more difficult.

Mom was a faithful woman. She attended church and was very active, but even as children we could tell that her faith seemed to

273

offer her little relief from the deep, personal sorrows of her life. Particularly, Mom was unable to accept the medical prognosis of her heart condition. She went from doctor to doctor, searching for a different answer, simply unable to deal with the truth that her heart had been damaged years earlier by rheumatic fever.

Her denial of the medical realities wasn't uncommon, and the attitude was portrayed by example in the eighth-century writings of the famous Indian Buddhist saint Shantideva, who wrote, "I lull myself by thinking that today, at least, I will not die. But the time of my death will arrive inevitably."

I was the only child at home in Hawaii when Mom's heart finally failed her. She died so quickly that none of us even had a chance to say goodbye. She was young, and it was a complete shock. In retrospect, it should not have been.

Being a nurse, Mom knew more than the average person about her condition. She was prepared through her Christian faith to go to heaven; she just wasn't accepting that because of her condition, her time might be near. In our home there was little constructive communication about the inevitabilities of sickness and death—not at least of the kind we could respond to. Mom in her own way did communicate her condition to us, but she did so through her lack of acceptance and, as a result, her words were painful, hurtful, and pushed us away.

We didn't know how to help her, and when she died that truth affected us all; we all loved her, and wished we could have done more.

It's something to consider when we are faced with serious health conditions: How do we cope? As a sick person, spouse, relative, or close friend, we can turn a deaf ear to the doctor and all the signs, pretend the illness doesn't exist, and hope the situation will change. We can submerge ourselves in the suffering of it all and cause misery to ourselves and those around us.

Or, we can find ways to cope and people to help us through, perhaps with counseling. Mom was gripped by the suffering of a serious sickness, and we didn't have the proper tools to help her—or ourselves. Moreover, being the stoic Japanese family, we did not *seek* help. Today we can research our ailments extensively, online and at libraries, so that we know much more than we ever could have known years ago.

But while there is constant research, and there are advancements appearing every day to help us live healthier and longer, we still head toward the same end.

One way Dad prepared for his impending death was by cleaning out his home. I was disappointed later to find that he had thrown away almost all of his paperwork: speeches and documents he had written, projects that he had participated in, all gone. In the last few years

Emi with her dad at Robert and Kim's wedding: "Robert and Kim got married in 1986, and I had recently returned from India after being ordained in 1985. I chose to wear lay clothes to their wedding as I was getting adjusted to life in the West as a nun. Notice Dad still holding a cigarette."

275

of my visits, he would encourage us to take things that we wanted to keep—artwork, dishes and silverware, and other mementos for keepsake. In this and other ways, he was intellectually prepared for his death, but nevertheless, the last months were tumultuous.

When Dad became sick with lung cancer in 1990, I was studying in India, but my daughter Erika went to help him many times. Dad struggled with his decline. He would become very upset, seemingly unable to accept his situation. Erika called me to say his condition was getting worse and that I should return if I wanted to see him before he passed away.

I spent two weeks with Dad, the last two weeks of his life.

Suffering is never easy to watch, particularly when there isn't much we can do, and that was the case with Dad. The lack of oxygen that is the result of lung cancer causes suffocation, and Dad was scared. During the course of his illness, the doctors had removed one lung, and Dad received radiation treatments on his other lung, which made breathing even harder. The doctors told us he needed to return to the hospital because he wasn't getting enough oxygen from the portable tanks.

He did so, and initially the oxygen tent at the hospital provided relief, so Dad relaxed a little bit. He asked me to bring Robert Frost's book of poems and wanted me to read "The Road Less Traveled" again and again. He gained a brief sense of peace and acceptance from that.

Eventually, his lung began to fail, and the oxygen infusion was at the highest they could administer. As his condition worsened, Dad's breathing became more strained, and he would become so agitated the nurses had to tie his arms and legs down to keep him from harming himself or others. He had a tube in his throat so he couldn't talk. In calmer moments, he wanted to write something to us, but being sedated and having his arms tied down, he could only write an illegible scribble.

That we couldn't hear or read his last words was terribly hard on him, and on us. What did he want to tell us? What words were left unsaid? He wanted desperately to communicate, so much so that even at the end with family members around him he fought against his dying, tossing in bed until death overcame him. He didn't want to die; he wanted to communicate and was frustrated in the end.

Dad was not religious, but he was a philosophical man. He had experienced tragic losses in his life. It had been twenty years earlier when he had experienced the compounded tragedies after the 1970 election. All of this was a tremendous shock, coming as it did at age fifty and all at once. Although he read and studied and took care of so many people during his life, I don't know how much time he spent preparing himself for personal loss, sickness, and death.

With or without a spiritual path, difficulties come to us during our lives and can take a toll on us. The question is, can we pick ourselves up and start again when our world has collapsed around us? Can we transform our problems so that we can rise out of devastation and turn our suffering into wisdom and compassion? These are the essential questions and personal challenges that Buddhism addresses.

In short, the answer is yes, we can transform ourselves—if we make an effort to use our intelligence and emotional strength to analyze our lives, our situations, our behavior. We must determine which of our problems we can effect change upon—or not—and move forward. I quote Shantideva's amazing support, "If there is a remedy when trouble strikes, what reason is there for despondency? And if there is no help for it, what use is there in being sad?"

We can paraphrase by stating this: If there is something you can do about it, why be upset; if there is nothing you can do about it, why be upset?

In my father's case, the events that occurred at mid-life were massive life lessons that changed him forever. The brilliance and dynamism he had possessed before then never really shone again. Somehow, he never came to terms with the crushing blows of that time. That he hadn't done so may have been the reason he was un-accepting of his death some twenty years later.

Our death is definite, and with that knowing, we can develop some determination and resolve to use our life well while we have energy and time. Whether with the help of spiritual practice or just by our own observations and reasoning powers, we will be better able to accept the inevitable.

UNPREPARED BUT ACCEPTING

Ashley and Shasta were building their dream home in Hawaii. They were deeply in love, and their young daughter was the delight of their lives. They wanted to settle in Hawaii and raise her on a beautiful tropical island.

Ashley was finishing a few more things on the roof one morn-ing before coming down to join Shasta and their daughter for a lit-tle holiday on the other side of the island. All of a sudden Shasta heard him scream. She raced outside to find that he had fallen off the roof. Rebar sticking out from a temporary electric pole damaged his carotid artery. Shasta cradled his head in her lap as he said, "Oh, Shasta I love you. I think I blew it."

He was conscious for a while and tried to follow what Shasta was telling him, "Just try to breathe. Remember your teachers, keep them in mind."

Shortly after, he breathed his last breath.

Ashley and Shasta had been studying Buddhism with teachers in California. They created a beautiful family together, and it was un-folding with great plans for the future. All of this changed. With the unfinished house, a new family and their future ahead of them, Ash-ley's untimely death was not something he or the family had pre-pared for.

But Ashley and Shasta accepted that it was the end, and acknowledged the most important part of their relationship—their love for each other—in those last moments. Shasta returned to California and is raising their daughter surrounded by loving friends and familiar places.

PREPARED AND ACCEPTING

Given the diverse fabric of life, it's not surprising to find that many people who live their lives peacefully, gently, and kindly also have peaceful deaths. They aren't particularly famous or accomplished but are like our grandparents or neighbors, who can be trusted with anything: private words, a listening ear, or a lending hand. They live ordinary lives and are all among us. They don't need all the fireworks and dazzle of fancy things and associations and live in friendship with everyone.

My friend Mamie's mother was an amazing example of this. In her last months, Celia was so peaceful and a joy to be with. I'd stop in to visit her just because of that. Even during her life, she had a remarkable, loving attitude about people and about living. One time she told me about a young burglar who had entered her house when she was already getting on in years. He wanted money, so she went to get her purse and gave him everything in her wallet. Then she asked him to wait a minute while she got her other purse to give him some more money.

Then he said, "Do you want to make love?" But she calmly told him, "Oh no, you wouldn't want to do that. I'm sick, and you don't want to catch that. I gave you all my money, so go and don't come back." So he left.

Even though when all this happened while she was ill and recovering from cancer treatments, she was calm and cool in fending off the young predator. It's not that she possessed a life without problems. In fact, she was from a wealthy family in China who had become refugees, leaving only with what they could carry in order to escape during the Japanese occupation. She raised her family in the United States, was forced to learn English, and worked in a toy factory, at one point, to make some extra money.

In the end, Celia spent her days quietly in her apartment, saying her prayers, visiting with family and friends. She was very comfortable, and comforting to others. She didn't complain, and passed on very peacefully.

Such people are quiet teachers, persons who instill us the knowledge that people are essentially good and kind. These are the people who are the real fabric of humanity, who allow us to drop our guard of fear, paranoia, or competition, who allow us to feel trust and honesty in ourselves and among others, knowing that we can be friends, simply and without demands.

We experience peace of mind, ease, and a warm heart around people like Celia.

These four stories are in truth our four choices, not of death, but of living. One final story exemplifies a truly enlightened life, and therefore an enlightened death.

It's the death of a Dharma Master Kirti Tsenshab Rinpoche in December of 2006. A lifelong monk, Rinpoche began a fifteen-year meditation retreat at age forty-five. His retreat took place in a small stone hermitage in the mountains above Dharamsala, India.

Rinpoche ended his retreat because His Holiness the Dalai Lama requested him to come out of retreat and teach. And teach he did. For the next twenty years he traveled the world, giving Buddhist teachings. The Dalai Lama includes himself among Rinpoche's students.

In the summer of 2006 Kirti Tsenshab Rinpoche was diagnosed with liver cancer. Because he was eighty years old and the tumor was quite large, the cancer was not treated. After the initial diagnosis, Rinpoche gave a short talk to a small group of students. Among his comments were the following:

> *I am fully aware of the fact that the disease, especially at this stage, is incurable. But I am not sad or disappointed in any way. When [the doctor] informed me of the presence of a tumor in my liver, I thought immediately that he was so very, very kind. He was extremely kind to me. [I have been practicing taking on the sufferings of others and giving them my happiness for many, many years.] But it was more or less mere theory for me. When I was told that I have cancer, I did not feel sad or upset. On the contrary, my mind was uplifted, and it felt light and open. I thought: "Finally, I have the chance to put this theory into practice now! My prayers have come true. How wonderful!" I intend to use whatever time I have left in order to deepen my practice of [giving and taking].*
>
> *"I don't want you to be sad. I want you to be happy and inspired since I now have such a wonderful opportunity to practice in a way that all bodhisattvas do. My doctor has been so kind to me. Why would I ever want to hide the fact that I am now practicing in the footsteps of the bodhisattvas?*

Rinpoche wanted to record his experiences as the disease developed further. He believed that would be useful for other cancer patients and their families, and hospices as well.

In September, one of his doctors said that he never met anyone with a tumor that large who was still alive. He also said that living with such a tumor would cause great pain. But Rinpoche was not in pain. He was able to meditate, and take long walks every afternoon. The doctor also said that Rinpoche's face, and especially his eyes, were very alert, which indicated that he was fighting the cancer very well.

On December 3, Rinpoche's student and translator wrote the following in an e-mail:

Rinpoche has not been able to consume anything orally for a number of days, and he continues to lose weight and strength. Even so, his blood pressure, temperature, oxygen intake, pulse, and other parameters remain within the normal range. Perhaps this is the most extraordinary manifestation of "normality" while the cancer is at such an advanced stage. Rinpoche continues with his daily practice and prayers, and all attendants continue to offer their services tirelessly, around the clock.

On December 16, Rinpoche entered his last meditation session, which ended four days later on December 20, at which time Rinpoche passed from this life.

This is the record, in brief, of one who exemplified the life and death of a sincere and accomplished Buddhist master in the Tibetan tradition. Rare to even hear of such a thing, but because of the times in which we live, it was recorded by e-mail and posted on a Web site, where it remains today to be a source of incredible inspiration.

While death may not be dinner conversation, it should be conversation; not in a morbid or sad way, but in a positive way much like Rinpoche demonstrated. And I believe the conversation should occur sooner than later. After all, it is through a realization of our own mortality that we have the potential to become fully human and embody the compassion and love that are within us. But we must do the work to resolve our own internal and external struggles.

And that practice takes a lifetime.

Where am *I* on the grid? Through all my practice, study, and meditation, I feel intellectually prepared for my death. Contemplating death helps, as do certain meditations that work to transform our clinging to life and the negative perception we have about death. I say that now, but when the time comes, I'll know then the extent of my preparation. I trust I won't be a coward.

Teachings I've heard say that it is best to be in a quiet, calm place at the time of death so that we can prepare ourselves, and our minds can be peaceful. I believe this because of some close calls I've experienced. One time, I was on a late flight to India, and the plane suddenly went into a free fall. People slammed onto the roof of the plane and crashed down again as the plane shifted to stop the fall. The screams were frightening, as was the shuddering of the wings, which I thought would break off.

Then it happened again. People were thrown into the air and crashed onto the seats and floor; I thought it was the end. When we finally landed, people had to be wheeled off; one woman had a broken leg, others had bad scrapes. It would be hard to have a peaceful mind in such an accident. I certainly did not.

Death will be a measure of how I lived and how I resolved the issues of my life—both internal and external. How empowering it is to know that we can shape our final moments by the way we shape our present ones. It's not that we should live our lives solely so that we may have peaceful deaths, but rather, know that if we desire a peaceful death, then we must live our lives accordingly.

It was difficult to look at the deaths of my parents in this stark way and especially hard to admit to myself that my parents struggled as they did. I have always held Dad high, with utmost respect. He was brilliant, commanding, and accomplished. My Mom and I were often at loggerheads, but recollecting who she was shows me what a delight she was as a friend and member of the community.

My journey from childhood, to the mountains of the Big Island of Hawaii, to motherhood, to India and beyond—with all the learning, the realizations, and the beliefs formed, shattered, and formed again—has been one I would not trade. It's been a spiritual journey, and whether we know it or not, we are all on spiritual journeys. Like everyone, I'm learning as I live. And every day I learn more, understand more, and have more questions.

But I'm happy in the process and thankful for all my teachers and life experiences.

13

Finding Your Spiritual Family

As we've said from the beginning of this journey, our spiritual family is our true home, an environment where we can live the life we are born to live. There are many paths to finding the spiritual family: marriage, education, religion, career, friends, teachers, and even crisis and despair. Our paths took us to an abandoned temple in Hawaii, the war zone of Vietnam, the mountains of Colorado and India, the streets of New York and Calcutta.

Many people search for—but few ever find—their spiritual families. Many times along the way it seemed as if we might not find ours, as well. Our barriers included failed marriages, family tragedies, and catastrophic health issues, and had we allowed them to be, they could have been insurmountable.

But by accepting that each barrier, each setback offered a lesson, we were able to emerge from each situation having learned. Each trial led us to better understand what it was inside of us that might have led to failure and allowed us to embrace the mental, physical, emotional, and spiritual aspects of transformation.

As defined by the generalized principle of unity, every down led to an up. As expressed by the teachings of Buddhism, each "death" became the basis for a new body and a new life. And with each relationship, we discovered more about what would make up our spiritual family. We found those persons—including Dr. R. Buckminister Fuller and His Holiness the Dalai Lama—who inspired us, transformed us, and ushered us into our spiritual families.

ROBERT: FINDING BROTHERS

One advantage I had was going to Vietnam twice.

The first time, in 1966, I was a student on board a merchant marine ship, carrying bombs between California and Vietnam. The crew of the merchant ship was made up of civilians. Most signed up for these bomb runs because they were paid a 100 percent bonus. For example, a third mate who would normally receive about $5,000 per month could sign on to board an old, beat up bomb carrier, without air-conditioning, to sail into a war zone and receive about $10,000 a month. That was a lot of money back in 1966.

The second time I went to Vietnam was in 1972. I was on an aircraft carrier and the crew was military. Rather than earn the $10,000 a month, which I could have earned as a third mate on a civilian ship in the war zone, I received about $600 a month as a Marine Corps pilot.

Being in a war zone with civilians is not the same as being in a war zone with marines. There is a different level of intensity. There is a different reason for going to war. As an old riddle asks, "What is the difference between bacon and eggs?" The answer: "When it comes to bacon and eggs, the chicken is involved—but the pig is committed." The men on the merchant ship were involved with the war, but the men on board the warships were committed to the war.

Christmas 1972—one last strike before going home. Robert is seen here with fellow pilot Lieutenant "Gentleman Joe" Ezel.

Knowing the difference between money and mission is important when seeking one's spiritual family. In the war zone, I learned there are three types of people. They are:

CORPSE-MEN

Corpse-man was a name we gave to the walking dead. For whatever reason, these people had lost their soul. Their spirit had departed their body. For them, dying was probably easier than living. While I was in the war zone, there were two pilots who were given the label corpse-man. In both cases, the pilots panicked, and their panic cost lives. Under pressure, they saved themselves but lost the lives of others.

One of these pilots lost his nerve flying into a hot landing zone. When rounds came through his cockpit, he panicked, pulled his aircraft up rather than push it lower to the ground, flying toward the enemy fire. Going higher made his aircraft a giant target, floating aimlessly in the sky, the "sitting duck" for a new battlefield weapon—

a handheld, heat-seeking rocket still used in combat today. An enemy soldier pointed, pulled the trigger, and the rocket did the rest.

I wasn't on that mission, but my friends who were said it was horrible. Sixteen young men—Americans as well as Vietnamese troops in the back of the aircraft—lost their lives. Most burned to death when fuel poured into the cargo area and burst into flames. Another pilot in the area claimed he could hear the screams of the dying men over the radio as the pilot who lived radioed for help.

This pilot turned into a corpse-man. He was a dead man walking. He was often seen talking to himself, defending what he had done, even if there was no one there to listen to his defense. Mercifully, his commanding officer transferred him back to Okinawa, and he was given a desk job. Although he wasn't directly blamed for the deaths, we all knew what he had done. We all knew that when push came to shove, he had panicked. In an intense situation, his true character emerged. He knew it, and we knew it. Saving yourself at the expense of others is not part of the code of honor within a band of brothers.

No one wanted to fly with him again.

In the early 1990s, I was invited to deliver a talk to a group of international corporate trainers in Hong Kong. The subject they gave me was "Putting the Spirit Back in Business." When introduced and called to the stage, I silently walked to my flip chart and wrote the words "Corpse-o-Ration." Turning to the group, I pointed to the word corpse and asked, "As trainers, how do you raise the dead?"

In the crowd of approximately five hundred, only a few laughed.

My talk went downhill from there as I spoke about my experiences in Vietnam and about dead men walking. I also talked about my experiences at the Xerox Corporation in the mid-1970s, relating my experiences to dead people working for spiritless corporations.

"Corporate trainers would come in and try to raise the dead. They try to tell us about mission and team spirit.... At Xerox, we all knew that if someone came along and offered a promotion, more pay, and better benefits, most loyal Xerox employees would leave. That is what happens when you hire people who sell their souls for money." Before long, I was politely told my time was up. For some reason, I have never been invited back to speak at their corpse-o-rate conferences.

Many marriages turn into corpses. I have a number of friends who have been married for years, but the spirit of their marriage is long gone. They have secrets that have remained secret and things they should have said that will never be revealed. The couples remain together in their loneliness. It seems as if their marriage is simply two bodies living together, waiting "till death do they part."

LIFERS

A lifer in the military is someone who is there for the job security. They are there for a secure retirement. Lifers seem to like the military hierarchy and structure more than the mission. Many lifers are there because they like looking down on people of lower rank. For example a lifer major would take pleasure in looking down on new lieutenants, and a lifer sergeant would receive vicarious pleasure in ordering new recruits around.

I suspect many of the lifers I met had doubts about whether they could make it in the real world, so their job was to keep a low profile, not make waves, and retire safely.

Corporate and government bureaucracy are also breeding grounds for lifers. These are the people who go to work, do their jobs, go home, eat dinner, and watch TV. The merchant ship I was on was full of lifers. The only difference was they couldn't go home at night, so they hid in their rooms instead. The work ethic of a lifer is to work hard enough to not get fired. If you want them to do a better job, they expect to get paid more. Many lifers are good, solid people. They go to church, raise the flag on the Fourth of July, vote on election day, and avoid risk at all costs.

Lifers also exist in our prison system. They have no hope of getting out. They are held prisoner by bars of steel. Lifers *outside* of jail are held prisoner by minds of steel encased in doubt.

In the war zone, we quickly learned to tell lifers from the real career officers and noncommissioned officers. A career officer was in the war zone because they wanted to be there. They were mission-driven. Most lifers were in the war zone to make an appearance. They were there to get their dance card punched, which helped in getting their next promotion.

In our squadron, many lifers were poor pilots because, as they grew older, they didn't strive to become better. Many were dangerous in hot situations. One night, my friend Lt. Joe Ezell had to take the aircraft away from his co-pilot, who was a major, because the major panicked during a night carrier landing. My friend was nearly brought up on charges of insubordination. Luckily, the flight crew backed up Lt. Ezell, saying they were grateful that he took the aircraft away from an incompetent major.

BROTHERS

In the war zone, the word "brother" took on a special meaning for me. I believe one of the reasons African Americans use the word brother is because many of them grew up in a war zone, and many are *still* in a war zone. When living at the boundary of life and death, it's crucial to know who your brothers and sisters are. Life is about being spiritually related, spiritually connected. Life depends upon knowing who would die for you, and you for them.

In the war zone, we were all marines, but not all marines were my brothers.

In many religions, calling someone a brother or a sister carries similar intensity. "Brother" or "sister" isn't something you call just anyone. One of my favorite people in the whole world was Brother Duane, a Catholic. Although I wasn't Catholic, he remains one of my favorite spiritual teachers because he taught via his actions, more than his words. He was a model of spiritual integrity. He had given his life to God.

You still may be wondering why I use my lessons from war and fighting to describe the process of finding one's spiritual family. After all, war and fighting are not pleasant subjects. The reason I use the background of war is because most of us are in some kind of a fight, if not with others, then with ourselves. For example, for most of my life I have been in a fight with my weight, the everyday battle of the bulge. Losing more than fifty pounds and keeping the weight off has been one of the biggest battles of my life. I have also been in a lifelong battle for wealth. For me, getting rich was not easy. If not for my spirit, I doubt if I would have achieved wealth or health.

Without spiritual strength, I would be a fat, sickly, unhappy, and poor man today.

When I hear people complain about being poor, saying "I can't afford it," I know their spirits are weak. When I hear people saying that the government should help them with their finances, help put their kids through college, forgive them their bills or debts, pay for their medical expenses, and pay them after they retire, I suspect again that these people have weak spirits.

When I hear someone complain that life is unfair, I know that their best is not good enough. They have been beaten by their own life. They lost the battle with themselves.

My reason for using the metaphor of fighting is because there are things in life worth fighting for. For some reason it seems as if God has created fighting to be part of our existence. Everything in God's universe is in some sort of fight for survival. For example, as I write this, there are three sparrows fighting outside my window. There is plenty of food in my yard, yet for some reason these tiny spirits want to fight.

While it's ideal to dream of peace and pray for peace, the reality is that fighting is part of life, and peace is worth fighting for. Going to war and fighting for peace made my spirit stronger. The same is true in my fight for health and wealth.

While most fights are best avoided, there are some worth fighting.

My sister learns a lot in her spiritual training. As a marine pilot, I too was a trainee. Some of my best friends in business were former trainees. A number of my business associates were former Mormon missionaries, and others sold religious books door to door. When I ask them about their experience as missionaries, they all tell me it was a priceless spiritual experience. Being missionaries tested their faith and strengthened their characters. Today they are better able to handle the challenges of life.

Having sailed into a war zone twice, once with civilians and later with marines, I found that mission is more important than money.

The following are a few steps that may assist you in finding your spiritual family, if you have not already found them. The first step is to ask yourself, "What am I willing to give my life to?" The answer to this question may take some soul searching, but the moment you begin to find your answers, you will begin to find your spiritual family.

The second step is to ask yourself the following questions:

- If money were no object, would I continue to work at my job?
- If money were no object, would I work at my job for free?
- If the answers are "No" to the first two questions, then what would you work at forever and for free?

• If you are not willing to work forever and for free, then the chances are you have not yet found your soul's purpose for your life. If there is something else you would rather do, maybe you should do it.

I continue to work, even though I no longer need to work. I have retired twice, and yet the work keeps calling me back. Today, I realize that I am doing my spirit's work. So even though the work is challenging, often difficult, and sometimes exhausting, I keep working.

It is very rewarding work, financially as well as spiritually. I suspect there may come a day when I stop working, but for now, my work is my life. My work nourishes my body, mind, emotions, spirit, and my wallet. I know I would do this work for free because I started out doing this work for free.

The third step is to ask yourself the following questions:

• Am I working with people I love as much as I love my biological family?
• Do I respect the people I am working with?
• Do I trust the people I work with to have my best interest at heart?
• Is the product or service of the company I work for a product or service I am proud to produce?

For example, since my dad died of lung cancer, I could never work for a tobacco company. To make money selling a product that killed my dad would be the death of my soul. This is not to say I am personally against tobacco. If you want to smoke, that is your choice. I smoked for a few years and then quit. I still enjoy a good cigar now and then.

Life is about relationships. The quality of one's life is directly related to the quality of one's relationships. If you are working in a corpse-o-ration, selling products you do not believe in, be very careful. Just as there are vampires and werewolves in the movies, there are bloodsuckers in the real world. If you spend your life in a corpse-o-ration, you, too, could lose your soul.

The fourth step is the most important step. It is the step that strengthens your spirit.

The reason strengthening your spirit is important is because spirit is the difference between successes and failures. For example, the world is filled with talented people. It's the people with talent *and* the strongest spirits who win. In sports, there are many gifted athletes. Again, it's the athletes with the strongest spirits who win. The world is also filled with smart people. Yet, as we know, there are many smart people who are not successful. In other words, if you want to be successful with your God-given gifts, focus on strengthening your spirit.

The fourth step is to work for free.

Giving your God-given gifts to people or organizations that support your spirit's work—and doing so for free—is probably the best way to strengthen your spirit. For example, if your religion is important to you, then work for free for your church. If you are good at marketing in the business world, offer to assist your pastor in increasing your church's attendance. Working for free and not expecting anything in return strengthens your spirit. It works because you are giving your gift to a higher purpose.

The more you give, the more blessings will come your way. I am certain most pastors will welcome *real* brothers and sisters with generous hearts and gifts to give. Most churches are filled with corpse-people and lifers who show up only to take more than they give.

If a charity is nearest your heart, then give more than money to the charity. Give your God-given gift. If it's accounting, then offer to assist with bookkeeping and records. If it is mowing the lawn, do it for free, expecting nothing in return. If politics is important to you, then work your heart and soul for the candidate you think will be the best leader. You will be blessed in many ways.

Playing on a sports team is also a way to build your spirit. I loved team sports because I learned to count on my team as they counted on me. For years, I played baseball, football, and rugby. One of the toughest of team sports was rowing—a sport I participated in for four years at the academy.

As I've said before, many network marketing companies are places to build your spirit via business. Donald Trump and I support network marketing companies because they are training grounds for entrepreneurs, and most of us know that successful entrepreneurs run on spirit. If you want to be an entrepreneur, find a network marketing company with a great personal development program. Then invest at least five years developing yourself by helping others develop themselves.

The Rich Dad Company has a franchise program for people who want to learn to do business the Rich Dad way. A franchisee's job is to create CASHFLOW Clubs and each club's job is to make financial education available to as many people as possible. It is a great franchise for people who love to teach as they learn about investing and entrepreneurship. In many ways, the Rich Dad franchise is modeled after the missionary program of many religions. Our message is not religious. Our message is a message of financial freedom via financial education.

It is about teaching people to fish.

As you know, there are many people who give with all their heart and soul but remain financially poor. One reason is that they may have rich spirits, but poor minds, and poor minds are the result of the lack of financial education in our schools. One of the purposes of the CASHFLOW games and CASHFLOW clubs is to create rich minds and rich spirits. Raising a person's financial IQ allows a rich spirit to give their gifts to the world and make this world a better place to live.

By giving from your heart, you gain much more than money. I know because I have worked for free. I have gone to companies and worked with their sales teams, teaching them to sell better. I asked for nothing, yet somehow *my* sales skills increased. When a friend's real estate company was having difficulty with partners, I mediated the disagreement for free. A few months later, one of the best real estate deals of my life came across my desk, and that investment continues to make me money today.

One of the better lessons I learned in church is found in the saying, "God does not need to receive, but humans need to give." I have found that the more I give, without expecting anything in return, the more I receive. When I meet people who do not have enough love, money, or happiness, I know it is because they fail to give enough.

Today, I have the great pleasure and honor to work with people much like my brothers in the war zone. Many of the people I work with I have grown to love. They are members of my spiritual family. We share the same mission and I trust them with my life.

In summary, in a war zone I learned:

- Corpse people are alive but afraid of dying. They live not to die.
- Lifers are alive but afraid of living. They may find dying easier than living.
- Brothers and sisters, and mothers and fathers have found something worth dying for, and this gives them life.

In 1981, after meeting Dr. Fuller, I had a change of heart that changed my life. Instead of using what I knew to make myself rich, I began to use what I knew to make other people rich. Once I made that switch, I began to find my spiritual family.

In 1984, the most beautiful angel appeared in my life—my wife Kim. When she and I took our leap of faith, we began to pass through the eye of the needle. As some of you know from my previous books, our passage through the eye has not been easy. There were many highs and lows, wins and losses. We met many great people, as well as false prophets. Interestingly, we learned as much from the false prophets as we did from great people.

False prophets can be angels also. Kim and I grew strongest when times were darkest because in the darkness we found our true spirits and the love to carry on. It has not been an easy journey, but it is a journey worth taking.

In the year 2000, another angel named Oprah Winfrey invited me to be a guest on her television program, and my life has never been the same. Oprah gave me her gift—the gift of her voice and the trust she has earned from people around the world—in the process of communicating Kim's and my gift, the message of financial education, to the world.

In 2004, I met Donald Trump and found that we shared the same concerns for people and financial education. Meeting Donald was like meeting a spiritual brother, related by a common mission. In 2006, our book *Why We Want You to Be Rich* was released and endorsed by Steve Forbes, another person concerned about the need for financial education.

And now, through *Rich Brother Rich Sister*, my life comes full circle with my biological sister Emi, now my spiritual sister Tenzin. I know I would never have met such great people, including my sister, if I had not made my life's changes in 1981.

When you find the things in life worth dying for, you begin to find your spiritual family.

Finding my spiritual family has been a challenge. I doubt if being with *any* family is ever really easy. In many ways, family relationships

Joining forces as teachers. ...

can be more painful than social or business relationships. So before you rush out and start finding long-lost spiritual relatives, let me pass on a few lessons I have learned along the way.

Out of everything bad comes something good.

I start with this because many people hang on too long to bad relationships. If you have a bad relationship, it's tough to make the space for a good relationship. Sometimes you have to let go, even if you love the person, so you both can move on. At work, many people hang on to a bad job too long. If you have stopped learning and growing, it might be time to look for new opportunities to learn and grow.

It is difficult to earn more if you have stopped learning and growing.

Remember the generalized principle of unity is plural. You cannot have a bad without a good. The most important thing is to be morally, ethically, and legally sound. If you are sound spiritually, the "good" in the good–and–bad will come to you. If you are bad and do not admit it, the bad will make you worse, and your situation will worsen, as well.

Remember, our jails are filled with "innocent people." I realize that the system does put a few genuinely innocent people in jail, but for the most part jails are filled with people who did bad or foolish things. As long as they do not come clean, their situation gets worse. This happens even to people who do not go to jail. Remember when President Bill Clinton could not admit he had sex with Monica Lewinsky. Rather than come clean, he lied to the world, and his situation got worse, not better. And what impact did his lies have on his wife's path to the White House?

When I was caught with women in my helicopter, flying drunk, my lying made a bad situation worse. Not only did I disgrace myself, I dishonored my fellow marines. It was only after I found the courage to come clean that I was physically, mentally, emotionally, and spiritually set free. Today, I realize that telling the truth turned a bad situation into a priceless lesson.

Telling the truth takes courage. Lying is for cowards. Even worse, life becomes tougher for liars and cowards because they have a habit of making bad situations worse.

Fear means new opportunities.

Whenever you feel fear, it may mean you are approaching the boundary of what you know and what you do not know. If you back down or step back, your growing stops because learning stops.

Fear gives us the opportunity to test our spirits. Fear gives all of us the opportunity to grow stronger or grow weaker. In Vietnam, the fear of dying made me a better pilot. I had to become better than my enemy. In war, I learned to respect my enemy, not hate them. Hate makes us all blind.

In the world of money, many people prey upon your fear. For example, the mutual fund industry has been rich because most people think investing is risky. While there is risk in investing, investing does not have to be risky. What is risky is remaining financially uneducated and turning your money over to a salesman whose job it is to keep you fearful and believing they know more than you.

I was recently sued by a former business partner. Rather than give in to my fears, which I believe my former partner was counting on, I simply said, "Bring it on. This is a new opportunity for me to learn and to grow."

Today, I look back on that experience as one of the best experiences of my life. Though emotionally painful, it has been spiritually revitalizing. Because I love to fight, I have personally learned a lot and become a better businessman in the process. If I had given in, I would not have gone beyond my own boundaries, my own comfort zone. If I had given in, in the war zone of business, I would have lost my soul, and my spirit would have departed.

Don't work with corpse-people.

If you are working for a corpse-o-ration—government or business—be careful. There are people who feed on your fear of losing your job and your need for money. Oftentimes these people give you the creeps or heebie-jeebies. That's your spirit talking, telling you to be aware. If you stay too long, working only for a paycheck, promotion, or retirement, your soul will be long gone.

Most of us have seen or met people who stayed too long and became corpse-people. These people are often burned out, do not like what they are doing, and are just hanging in there. These are people who live for the weekend or retirement. They show up at work, put in their time, and go home. Their *body* shows up at work, but their spirit has departed.

At times people become upset because I mix my days in the war zone with the life I've lived since then. In our society, many people think war and fighting are bad, and, in some ways, they are. Yet if you look at life, most of us have personal battles to fight. For example, when I realized I was poor, I had to fight and claw with all my heart to become rich. When I gained a lot of weight, becoming clinically obese, I had to fight *that* battle in order to regain my health. In my life, my wars to gain health and wealth were priceless battles.

Today, I see too many young people who expect their moms and dads to give them everything. I meet poor people who complain that the government or their boss does not pay them enough. I meet obese people who buy the magic pills that will make them thin. Often I meet baby boomers my age who have nothing set aside for retirement and just pray that God will send them a miracle.

War and fighting are not good for most people. Most people would rather be nice and polite. Most people would rather get along and be peaceful. And so, generally, would I. The difference for me is that I have been trained to recognize a fight. And if there is going to be a fight, I fight to win. There's no sense praying for peace when you are in a war zone. If someone breaks into your house with a gun, intent on robbery or rape, I would rather fight now and pray later.

War made my core stronger. If not for war, I would not have had the courage to find my own spiritual family. If not for war, I would not have had the courage to withstand all the criticism I have received for my work. If not for war, I would be defending myself on the Internet blogs, rather than doing my work. If you are going to find your spiritual family, you must be willing to develop a spiritually stronger core because your spirit will be tested. I can promise you that.

In 1981, when I crossed the line from greed to generosity, miracles happened. So did disasters. Some of the miracles were life-changing. I became a student for the first time in my life. I found out what I wanted to study. Money did not matter as much. Being of service was more important.

Rather than be someone who gave up because I didn't have the money, I simply found ways to create the money. I discovered that human beings need money, but our spirits do not. I found that when I focused on serving others, blessings other than money came to me. Sometimes the blessings came in the form of bad people or disasters, which is how I learned that something good always came from something bad. Actually, I found I learned more—if I was humble enough to learn—from my disasters than my miracles. Instead of running from fear, I *took on* my fear, not because I am a daredevil, but because I wanted to test the strength of my spirit and further strengthen it.

Since 1981, I have been in a process of strengthening my spirit. It is a process without end. It's not a process where I can suddenly jump up and say, "Hallelujah! I found God! My life is now perfect." It is a lifelong process of discovery and learning. It is a process of highs and lows, wins and losses, good and bad. It is a process that makes life better—not instantly, as many people might wish or even pray for, but eventually. It is a process of testing my will. It is a process of mental and spiritual stress, much the same as the stress we put on our bodies when we go to the gym.

It has been my process to find out if there is a God or a great spirit, and I've discovered a few other things along the way:

- Work for free. The more I work for free, the more money I make. The more you *need* anything, like love or money, the less you will have.
- The more I give, the more I receive, but not instantly.
- Truth is harder than lying, but the more I move toward truth the less I have to lie.
- Our soul has a price. For many people, that price is too low.
- The more I teach, the more I learn.
- If I want higher-quality spiritual friends and family, I need to increase my own spirituality. When a person cheats on a member of their spiritual family, life changes and often goes downhill.
- Know that what you sow you too shall reap. Be willing to accept the consequences of what you sow, as well as what you reap.

- Know when to turn the other cheek, and know when to fight. Know the difference between revenge and justice.
- If you don't fight when it is time to fight, you may fall victim to a predator. Remember, for there to be a predator, there must be prey. If you are weak and never prepared to fight, then you become prey who needs to pray a lot.
- Live life according to your own standards. Many people say that money is not important, yet your standard of living is. Personally, I love my home, vacation home, cars, and the finer things of life.
- Learn to laugh on the inside, especially when there is misery all around you. When my first major business failed, I was miserable for a year or two. I got happy when I could see my losses as blessings because they held valuable lessons.
- Choose your friends carefully. One of the great things about being an entrepreneur is I get to choose who I want to work with, and most are just like me—wealthy entrepreneurs who love their work because it challenges them.
- In the world of spiritual families, respect is often more important than love.
- Just because someone is tough on you does not mean they do not love you. Sometimes the hardest thing a spiritual friend can do is to tell you things you do not want to hear. Feedback is often tough on the giver, as well as the receiver.
- My spiritual family includes my professional advisors. For example, through adversity, I have met the best lawyers, doctors, and accountants.

Recently, I had trouble with my heart. I was very disappointed with the traditional cardiologists' advice and mannerisms. All they did was recommend surgery–immediately. One even suggested I stop exercising immediately and go into surgery that night.

That was six years ago.

Rather than go through the surgery, I sought out other points of view. In the process I met a medical doctor—through a friend of a friend—who understands alternative health and did not put down my desire for more natural medicines and cures. While I still needed the heart surgery, today I am healthier because I found doctors who are members of my spiritual medical family. In other words, I have found that my spiritual family can be a very extended family involving all aspects of my life.

All of this begs the question that I am frequently asked: "What happens if I do not find my spiritual family?" There are two answers that I know of.

One is you could remain an orphan—an orphan alone or an orphan with a lot of friends and family. There is nothing wrong with this. Most people are happy with a life like this. Most people do not even know they might have a spiritual family somewhere in the world. For many it is a painful and soul-searching process that they choose not to undertake. For many, the loneliness or emptiness is a small price to pay for not feeling the stress of pushing outside of what's comfortable for them.

The second answer is that God or the Great Spirit may force you to find your spiritual family. For example, a friend of mine lost his eight-year-old daughter to cancer. Sharing dinner with him a few months ago, he quietly said, "I would have traded places with her. I would have given my life so she could live." Today, rather than live a life of grief, he works tirelessly and gives generously to the Make-A-Wish Foundation and other charities and hospitals that work at finding cures for cancer. Through the loss of his daughter, he found a purpose for his life and his spiritual family.

What is the life you were born to live? What special gifts do you bring to your world and how are you using them to serve? What is worth giving your life to, even worth dying for?

Only you can answer those questions, and those answers can only be found in your heart.

TENZIN: EXPANDING THE PLAYING FIELD

My spiritual quest started with the classic "leaving home" adventures. It took a lot of propulsion to do so because being a single mom with a young child, few skills, and little money made it hard to venture out. Leaving Hawaii takes a lot more than driving across the state line. The flight from Hawaii to the nearest landmass takes five hours, and one arrives in something very different than the tropical islands with balmy sea breezes. I had to plan and save to make it to California with enough money to find an apartment, put Erika in school, and find a job. For the first two years, I took the bus and often walked to save the bus fare. The situation was similar in moving to Colorado, Alaska, and India as well. While change is constant, we have habits and patterns of living, doing things. I was determined to explore spiritual paths, find excellent teachers, find my spiritual family. That was the start, and the journey continues.

This challenge of finding your spiritual family and then committing to the path, hanging in through thick and thin, holds in many ways the same problems and challenges as being with one's biological family. Participating in a church or spiritual center is another kind of family; it's not that different. We still have to deal with difficult people, hierarchy, bureaucracy, and daily schedules. There are joys, wins, blockades, stalls, and emergencies in spiritual life too.

There really should be no separation between one's life, livelihood, and spiritual endeavors. The entire world becomes the classroom, and everyone becomes someone we can learn from, someone to practice patience with and to develop tolerance and compassion. This does not mean we ingratiate ourselves and let everyone walk all over us, but it means that we develop skillful and loving ways in dealing with every person and every situation. Some people are role models and teachers for us; others we must teach and help as we can. Still others are challenges for us. Because we are too involved, attached to situations and persons, or caught up somehow that we don't know how to deal with certain people, we get angry, irritated, stuck, and depressed or become dominated by the situation. It overwhelms us, and rather than rising up out of the ashes of loss and despair like a phoenix, we sometimes spend our life in a rut.

One couple I worked with in hospice was so remarkable that I eagerly looked forward to every visit with them. The husband was in the hospice program and the physician, nurses, and social workers made regular visits to his home. Our first exchange was very cordial and both husband and wife shared with me how every day was a blessing for them. Having been diagnosed with two months to live, the husband had by now lived six months longer than that. They said to me, "If we get upset or depressed because of failing health, we lose a day, and we don't want to waste our time together that way. Now every day is a blessing so we appreciate every day together. We are so happy we have another day."

As the months went on, the wife was diagnosed with cancer too and had to go for chemotherapy and radiation treatments. Still, they took every change in their condition in stride. They had to have a caregiver come in to help because the wife had to be away every day for treatments, and the husband's condition was getting weaker. On the first or second day, the caregiver took out the trash and accidentally locked herself out of the house. She was at the bedroom window outside knocking and calling to the patient to help let her in the house again. He had to struggle to get out of bed, into a wheelchair, and to a room with an outside door. The caregiver was mortified that the patient had to help the her. "I'm supposed to be helping you! I'm the caregiver," she said in embarrassment.

The couple thought it was so funny, they later told me. "These kinds of things happen," they laughed in reply. They continually thought of others while slowly cutting down on the number of visits with their friends and neighbors and the amount of time they spent with them because it became exhausting. Still, every step of the way, with every visit I made to see them, I kept thinking to myself, "I must remember what they say. They are a model for dealing with the inevitability of death," for their attitude and way of being with others was remarkable. It was inspiring to be with them, and it made me wish I could share their story to help others. In their way, they were teachers for me.

Sometimes we get caught up in unhealthy, co-dependent relationships. In needing friendship and love, we sometimes start out with wonderful connections, work situations, service organizations, churches, and spiritual relationships and later on realize that we've enmeshed ourselves with unhealthy people and work. People often attract romantic partners and business partners that hook into their own neurosis and needs. What a minefield we can get into! From roommates to lovers, family members to work and church, every individual has the challenge of cultivating healthy, happy relationships that build personal growth. We make choices every day in all our interactions with others. All we wanted and needed was love.

I had to forgive myself, my family, and the culture of our times after years of carrying unexpressed shame and guilt about getting pregnant and getting "caught" without being married. There was and still is, depending on family, church, and culture, such a stigma for girls and young women who get pregnant before they are married. Even though I rejected the shame and the stigma and loved Erika, I still internalized the shame that had been running my life and cut my personal power and confidence. Such "sins" are a cultural blaming of young women who get caught; as if no one does *it* unless and until sanctified by marriage.

Without counseling, encouragement, and discussion, these kinds of "views" about sexuality, marriage, money, culture, and religion get impressed upon generation after generation and diminish people. It layers guilt upon an already difficult challenge.

Proactive and preventive discussion and education help tremendously before situations like this occur. It is unbelievably tough and a handicap to enter early adulthood not knowing how to fend for oneself in life while already strapped with the responsibility of raising a child for eighteen years. This points to the reason for marriage in the first place for it implies gaining the support from the other parent and the greater family. In a more liberal world today, there is greater tolerance and openness, but many still carry the subtle weight of guilt and damning from having made a "mistake."

Too often we enter arrangements and contracts backward, wanting to allay our guilt and somehow make it right, legal, or pure. While marriage, family, church, and temple are places of joy and belonging, sometimes they hold their members by guilt and fear. Sometimes people hold it on themselves, even though the environment does not. I had to release that in myself.

Robert spoke of Lifers in the military world. We find Lifers in churches, temples, and spiritual centers too. People get baptized or go for refuge—the Buddhist equivalent of baptism—and hope that doing so will keep them out of purgatory, hell, or lower realms. You can tell by the way people talk about their religious affiliation with their church or organization how they are connected to their faith. People often take dogma they hear and then impose that on everyone they meet. Their minds lock into a particular set of beliefs, and it becomes their perspective on life. Their world becomes black and white, and they conduct their lives based on these beliefs. You can hear in their speech how they've classified you. They've battened themselves down and see life through the prism of their dogma. Wanting not to do anything wrong for fear of retribution and going to hell, their lives become rigid.

Monastics, too, can hide from life challenges, like Robert named the Corpse-man and Lifers. Monastic life was intended to deepen one's spiritual life, and no matter where we live or what we engage in, lessons and choices present themselves. If a monk or nun does not take these opportunities when they arise, they too may be hiding, not utilizing the chance to grow. Whether in an office, family, church, or monastery, whether we stick with one job or change jobs a lot, live in one house, one town, or many, there is the pattern of the Lifers who seek "job security" by never challenging themselves within the walls they create.

At a teaching event not too long ago, I questioned some attendees and practitioners about their view of health and medical insurance. After my heart incident and the struggle with insurance, I wanted to know how others were dealing with this very real problem. Here were some of their answers: One person said she was well and so didn't think about coverage. (That's how I thought.) Another said he was waiting to be eligible for Social Security. I noticed as we chatted that he needed some serious dental work. A third person I spoke with said they had no insurance and added that, "If you practice meditation very well, you can even cure cancer when you are sick." I shuddered to think of my own experiences and that if I had tried to cure what I had by sitting on my cushion I would probably be dead by now. While I do think it is possible in rare cases for someone's cancer to disappear perhaps with the assistance of sincere prayer, I would not want to experiment with that on myself. Additionally, I don't think I would have a calm mind at all if I knew sickness was progressing and did not seek help.

At another interfaith event, I met a Catholic monk who shared with me similar concerns from his monastery. It had been founded in the 1950s, and some of the monks were elderly. He said none of them had medical insurance, and a recent health incident for one monk almost depleted their funds. He said he didn't know what they would do if it happenead again or they could possibly lose their monastery! A good health plan needs to be established for these precious communities.

After these conversations, I thought about how I have sometimes lived with people who hold these kinds of views, and I know there are many faithful and sincere followers in different faiths who believe these ways. This is a view of the "faithful" that can get people in trouble, but it is not the view of the Dharma teachings. Remember, the Buddha's first teaching was that we get sick, get old, and die, and that we must take care of our needs. I love being around different spiritual friends and communities but will seek skilled and broader options regarding health elsewhere.

There are those who utilize life in retreat well, sincerely working with their meditation practice and consulting their teachers and fellows. There are others who support the system: the cooks, managers, disciplinarians, teachers, and scholars. I think in every kind of system though, whether office, family, or monastery, we find drones, who find a way to live in passivity. While it seems the system supports them, in fact it does not work for them, they become Lifers.

Because the path I found is so precious to me and finding it was hard won, being immersed in the Buddhist communities, I spent many years feeling content and in the right place. It worked and was incredibly fulfilling. But I have new lessons to learn and have to make my world larger to avoid stagnating as a Lifer and to infuse new life into my practice. Robert talks about how we can't change people but we can change environments. My lessons must include a larger community of people. For a while, I stuck to a style and format that did not fit for me anymore.

I still have much to learn and practice in the Teachings that have meant so much to me and have been the main direction in my life. I was truly nurtured by the incredible teachings and teachers I have

Tenzin Kacho with actor Richard Gere (left) and Fred Segal. My friend Irenka, Fred, and I planned the entire celebration of His Holiness the Dalai Lama's birthday at Peace Park in Malibu. We found a Bodhi tree for the Dalai Lama to plant to commemorate the event, but we forgot the shovel! The Dalai Lama used some cardboard to scrape a little soil over the tree, and then when he wanted some water to moisten the ground, we had forgotten that too! Someone handed him their bottled water. Notice the tree isn't properly planted yet.

met over the years and I sustain great appreciation and respect for the tradition I am nurtured in. I must expand and take these teachings with me. I feel a big part of my future work is in creating better bridges for our spiritual life and livelihood.

Robert's teacher, Buckminster Fuller wrote of his own self-discipline: "I recounted that the larger the number of humans I undertook to serve, the more effective I became, wherefore I concluded that if I committed myself to serving everyone, I would be optimally effective." And, "In undertaking our critical-path development of a practically realizable means of bringing about all humanity's spon-

taneously realizable escape from fearfully ignorant self-destruction ... we are being taught ... to immediately 'undertake the greatest task with thorough commitment of attention to every detail.'"

Robert is my biological brother, but he is also my spiritual brother
in that he is a friend who continually exhorts me and most everyone
he meets to be bigger, to embrace the larger field of people, to give
our gifts more.

Now with age and years creeping up on myself and my generation, we are quickly becoming the elders, even though we are tiny
in the shadow of some of the great masters we have studied with.
We had particular lessons due to the times we grew up in. We have
to step up to the task of serving others. We must reconcile our lives,
its sobering experiences, and the fact that we have a finite number
of years left. I don't hold a division between preciousness and ordi-
nariness in people so much anymore. Can we cultivate our excellent potential and let go of limitations?

Learning to fish is about learning to find a viable balance between
spiritual and material needs, and cultivating one's spiritual life while
living in the world.

EPILOGUE
Tenzin: Karma, Nirvana, and Past Lives

Robert has presented many important ideas for living a better, more spiritual, and more financially secure life by focusing first on what we can do for others, all for the sake of making the world a better place—creating a "heaven on earth" for ourselves and those who surround us.

This approach is reflected in the Buddhist concepts of karma and nirvana, both of which I have addressed earlier. Both are central to everything that makes us who we have been, who we are, and who we will be and warrant further discussion.

When discussing the generalized principles put forth by Dr. Fuller, Robert was concerned that he wouldn't be able to represent them faithfully or adequately. As with the discussion groups he organized to analyze Dr. Fuller's concepts, there are those of us who have spent long hours discussing the teachings of the Buddha, and the learning will never stop. What I offer you here are additional aspects of these central ideas, so that you may begin to see how they operate.

KARMA

Karma is created by mind. Intentional action is like planning and building a house. Karma can be actions that occur without intention, such as accidentally stepping on your pet. To create a complete karmic action there are four parts:

Intention
Object
Action
Completion

Here is an example: I was going to the market one Saturday evening and saw a man standing outside looking at the display of beautiful bouquets of flowers. Suddenly, he grabbed two huge bouquets and ran off into the night. My assumption was that he was stealing them to offer his date. In the act of stealing, he went to that store because the flowers were outside and easily accessible (intention), determined which bouquets (objects) he wanted, took them (action), and was content that he stole flowers without getting caught (completion).

The four parts are complete, which makes a strong karmic act of stealing. If one of the parts was missing, for instance, if he later sincerely regretted stealing or got to the store and decided not to steal, then it would not be a complete karmic act.

The same formula is applied in creating virtuous karma: setting the intention, perceiving the object, engaging in the action, and feeling satisfaction at completion. The main factor driving creation of karma is *intention*. It's possible the man who stole the flowers could have been broke and was taking flowers to a neighbor in the hospital. Here the intention is benevolent, but it is still nonvirtuous to take something that is not yours.

If intentions are good and actions are virtuous, there are harmonious relationships and environments. Otherwise, when they are around someone who steals things, people become wary, suspicious, and protective of their belongings.

Sometimes our actions may appear good to others, but in fact the motivation is self-serving and may be filled with negative intent to deceive or harm others. At other times, our actions may *appear* harmful but in fact have the intent and result of benefiting others, as when a parent or mentor is disciplining us. And sometimes even when our intentions are good, we don't get the desired effect.

One day at my nunnery in India, I invited my teacher's niece, a young Tibetan, to attend class with me at the Library of Tibetan Works and Archives because I thought she would enjoy seeing how a Buddhist class was conducted for Westerners. Our nunnery is situated high on a mountain ridge, and the library is down the mountain and was reached by an eroded, cliff-hanger road. We took a shortcut down the mountainside below a construction site and unfortunately got caught in the middle of a slow landslide on the steep slope. The mud and earth were literally sliding down all around us, and we couldn't turn back. We had to keep moving as the mud and earth slid, cutting across the slide as quickly as we could to reach stable ground.

We made it, but things could have been bad. It wasn't what I had intended, yet our interactions and activities are sometimes a gamble, and we're not able to predict how things will turn out.

Pleasure and pain in your life come from previous intentional actions. Simply stated, if you act well with a good motivation, you will experience pleasant effects. If you do not, you will not. We each commit virtuous and nonvirtuous actions through our body, speech and mind; we create karma all the time. Virtuous intentions and actions create pleasure and happiness in the future, as well; similarly, harmful intent and actions create causes for experiencing pain and suffering in the future.

Karma is not a simple equation of $x = y$, nor does it imply that because of x you will experience y. There are numerous gross and subtle causes and conditions that continually converge and bring about effects.

Karma manifests in everything around us through our experiences, relationships, and all phenomena. The ways we perceive things—the ways we interpret and act on our experiences—are dependent on our karma. All of these have an effect. In addition to what is occurring in the present, what we experience is a result of our previous actions. We also are influenced by our society, generation, family, body, school, friends, neighborhood, and numerous other factors, and we engage in actions as a result of those influences.

There is no single, original cause in Buddhism because everything arises out of karma.

Some people think that karma is fated, with little or no free choice. All happiness you experience in your life came from positive actions you engaged in previously. Karma has definite qualities—for instance, you will not experience something you did not create causes for. However, it is not definite that karma will absolutely come to fruition because karma can be purified, and changes in circumstances can also prevent karma from ripening.

How you deal with situations and act on things is where you find choices. Your actions in the now create the causes for what and how things will manifest in your later life. When we engage in virtuous actions that benefit everyone, it results in happiness now and in the future. Sometimes actions may be painful and unwanted, but we undergo them because the outcome will be beneficial—for instance, going into surgery for the sake of future good health, or disciplining our spending habits so we aren't swamped in bad credit.

People will undergo mental and physical suffering if they see that it is beneficial or important to do so.

Events occurring now are the result of conditions we created in the past; if we did not create the cause, we will not experience the effect. Events in our current lives give us a glimpse of what we were like and perhaps involved in during previous lives. We Buddhists do not accept that this is our first life and that we are born a "blank slate," pure, without faults or karma. In fact, we have had numerous lives,

In 1992, Tenzin was at the United Nations in New York, on tour with the Gaden Shartse Monks, and met Rigoberta Menchú Tum, winner of the Nobel Peace Prize for her work in social justice and ethno-culture reconciliation.

and we remain in *samsara* or unenlightened existence and are continually reborn until we directly comprehend the nature of phenomena and existence—and attain enlightenment.

When people hold the view that this is our only life, they tend to think we are innocent from certain occurrences that take place in our lives. When something negative occurs, we try to discern how we were connected to it—where we had something to do with it. When we don't find any memorable link to having caused or committed actions that would precipitate such an occurrence, particularly if something is perceived as bad, we are surprised, offended, and confused as to why bad things could happen to us.

When something good happens, we are thrilled, think we have had a windfall, that luck was with us, or that we experienced grace. These ideas or attitudes are very different from those who accept karma.

Within the concept of karma, when something difficult occurs—even if we have no recollection of having done something or having been connected with such difficulties—then that should make us content, even happy.

Why? Because it could mean that negative karma we created in a previous life is coming to fruition, and ending. And when something wonderful occurs, it shows us that we engaged in virtuous action in the past.

Even while we practice living ethically today to create good conditions for later on in life—and future lives—we experience the results of past actions. This explains why good people have negative experiences and bad people can have positive experiences. We no longer have control over what we did in the past but lend a hand to our future by what we do in the present.

Creating good causes, we experience good effects. If karmic results were instant, I think we would all be more conscientious about our actions.

The Precious Garland, an Epistle to a King, as translated by John Dunne and Sara McClintock, was written by the first-century Indian teacher Acharya Nagarjuna as advice to a king who wanted to learn how to conduct his life and rule his people well while remaining in the world without giving up his kingdom:

> *From nonvirtue comes all suffering,*
> *likewise all negative rebirths.*
> *From virtue comes all positive rebirths,*
> *and the happiness within all births.*

As mentioned before, we want everyone to know when we do something positive, yet we seek to hide our actions when they cause harm. But when a karmic imprint is left on our mental continuum, we will experience the result of that act in one way or another in the future. Karma has no physical weight or form, but there is an imprint upon you psychically. My teacher says, "If karma had weight, we could not stand up!" There is no one out there keeping a tally on you but you, yourself, are creating your own causes and conditions. When we act with full intention of doing something positive or negative, and rejoice when the act is completed, we create a force, a propensity to do it again, enjoy doing it, and feel that it is okay to do; we justify our actions.

We gravitate toward and attract people who are likeminded, and it compounds the situation, for not only do we feel right about what we do, our circle of associations justify it and encourage our behavior. Those mental attitudes become our worldview. Our actions, positive and negative, continually influence us.

When we find that we have done harmful actions in ignorance, and regret those actions, it is a sign that we are moving in the right direction. To refrain from negative actions, to regret having done hurtful things, creates positive energy or good karma. Regret is not guilt; regret is acknowledging that certain actions were bad, not helpful to yourself or others, beneath our best potential, and we see it as negative.

Don't linger in guilt, obsessing that you are a bad person and hopeless. That depletes your energy and depresses you, rather than purifying any negativity. Moving past your feeling of guilt does not give you license to continue negative actions, though. It is powerful if the regret is sincere, and impels you not to engage in that negative action again.

I conducted myself poorly with my mother. She had poor parental skills, and as an adult and parent myself, now I understand that clearly. Most parents do not have any training, and we tend to do as we were done to when we become parents. In my ingnorance, I imposed some erroneous ways on Erika, too: not helping with homework or encouraging her in other ways. Still, she surprised me by earning her master's degree before myself or any of my siblings. I was stuck in the way I related to Mom, and because she died so suddenly and so young, I did not have the chance to outgrow or change my behavior.

Repetitive actions or those that follow what others do without thinking are done in a fog, lacking attention, so we are only partially present. I don't blame myself for how I acted. I had no tools to deal with her complaining, and our family rarely had discussions together. But it was a powerful lesson in the impermanence of life and how— if we want to change the habitual, negative way we interact with oth-ers—we had best change now. I don't wallow in remorse, although I know my actions were not kind. The heaviness of the negative ac-tion is lightened somewhat by sincere regret, knowing now my huge loss and understanding my uncaring actions.

How does karma operate here? My unkind actions were reactive, fighting back against her unloving words. I hope my lack of know-ing how to interact with her takes the edge off that unkindness be-cause the teachings say the ignorance of our actions minimizes the power of a full karma. It does not mean that I want to remain ig-norant. Now I know better and must practice with this knowledge. Sincere regret also lessens the heaviness of the karma. Were Mom still alive, and my actions did not change, I would be creating a heav-ier karma; if I were cruel with the full intention of harming, that would be the heaviest karma.

Our actions are driven by our emotions, and the intentions be-hind our actions compound the power of the karma. Our practice is to observe the mind and work to become better persons. Today I find myself "adopting" many of my friends' mothers, enjoying the opportunity to respect and appreciate them, especially because I missed growing into an adult friendship with my own mother.

Here is one way we work with our negative actions in meditation.

Rather than burying or ignoring what we did, we bring it to light. Call a specific event to mind, recall what you did, who you did it with, and observe the motivation that was driving you.

Develop a sense of regret for having performed that negative action. This is not guilt that rotates around self-pity and makes you feel worse. Guilt does not alleviate the problem or the habitual actions. Guilt still focuses on yourself and how bad you are, instead of the people you harmed!

Regret acknowledges that you hurt the other person and yourself. Negative actions diminish who we are and cause suffering. Allow both the experience *and* understanding to arise. Then make a promise not to engage in that action again. If it is a habitual action, this may be difficult, so begin by making the promise to it for a specific amount of time. That way you can keep your promise and begin to build positive strength to counteract doing it again.

Next, having made the promise, consider what you can do to take this resolve into your life. Determine some positive action you can do within the next few days or weeks. For example: apologize sincerely to the person you harmed. If that's not possible, do something else to bring this promise into the world around you. You don't have to tell anyone why, but it connects your promise to your life.

Offer flowers to a friend. Help a neighbor do an errand. Do something *doable*. If the person against whom you committed the negative action has passed on, you can apologize sincerely in your meditation. Call that person to mind and imagine actually sitting with that person before you and apologize.

Another point of this meditation practice is called "rejoicing." This brings natural energy and buoyancy to your practice and life. You can also bring to mind the person you hurt or offended and think about their good qualities. I can recall how my mother had so many friends who loved her and what a remarkable singing voice she had that friends would always ask her to sing at parties. She also gave me my life and took care of me when I could not as an infant or when I was sick. Even though she was difficult, I know she loved us. Take a moment to rejoice in kind actions and events around you.

Recall your teachers, mentors, and parents—people who really helped you in your life. Acknowledge them and thank them. Recall ordinary people around you, too, and things that occurred that were beneficial, caring, and fun—for yourself and others, today, this week, or last month.

We all want happiness, and we know when we are acting poorly and causing others unhappiness. A pattern of ingrained slights, accusations—any way we act without love—is not caring. We fall into habitual ways of interacting with one another and become hardened to the persistent, abrasive rub of disrespect and lack of kindness. Bad habits can be changed to loving, caring habits.

With my mom gone, my father became even more precious to me. Living for a few years on another island, I would fly to Oahu to spend a couple weeks at a time with Dad at his home, working in his garden, gathering fruit and flowers and distributing them to friends, cleaning the house, and spending time with him. I loved sharing the Hawaiian music that was becoming so popular then, and we'd listen to music together. We took time to talk now that he was alone and not working so much.

Sometimes the conversations were an effort because he would be focused on endless televised golf events or puttering on a project. He loved to cook for Erika and me, so we would hang out in the kitchen chatting then, and again around the dinner table; I found ways to engage him.

When I was busy raising Erika in California, I spent my vacation time each year staying with Dad. Several times, I chose a room to paint as a project during my stay. Dad would get involved, too, and the visits were happy times. During my stays in India, I would write to Dad every week or two. I poured my love into Dad, the remaining parent.

Dad passed away twenty years after Mom, when the kids were all adults, and I still felt the twinge of what it is like to be an orphan. I missed him terribly and felt as if we had lost the buffer our parents provided us. We became the elder generation, faced with increased aging and inevitable demise. This is the natural way of things.

As a nun, I am fairly protected from nonvirtue as my vows keep me out of trouble. I am responsible for my actions at every moment, and life as a nun helps me stay more aware of how I conduct myself all day long. I promise to watch my vows, even in my sleep. Of course, I still blunder and upset people. I even upset myself. I forget to acknowledge others and can say things distractedly or forget things.

But I reset my resolve and move forward. We already have the good result of this precious human life and need to prepare for the circumstances of our next life. We do that in the way we conduct ourselves with body, speech, and mind, in relating to everyone: friends, enemies, and strangers.

As I finished writing this book, I found this passage from the Buddha, quoted from the *Dhammapada* (*Sayings of the Buddha*) as recorded by the Venerable Sri Acharya Buddharakkhita:

> *Those who in youth have not led the holy life, or have failed to acquire wealth, languish like old cranes in a pond without fish.*

This analogy had a strong effect on me as I embarked on the new adventure of writing and collaborating with my brother. I know this book will bring me into public view, and my life will be changed because of it.

Venturing back into the working world and doing hospice work has also brought changes. After decades of living on the edge and seeing the impact of economic poverty firsthand through medical concerns, it was a relief to be generating some positive cash flow to handle my needs and not be entirely dependent on people's kindness. It was also a relief to find myself still employable and reentering the work force at age sixty. I am sure someone would have always helped me out, but I want to be of service to the community, and to create positive cash flow; that is my motivation. It's also about looking at ways of right livelihood and balance for monastics.

The image of the old crane languishing in a pond without fish was powerful. I interpret it personally and globally. For thousands of years, monastics and mendicants of every tradition have been supported by their communities. Generations past had the time and resources needed to support monastic and faith communities. They do now, as well, but the time and economic capacity for the masses have been compromised, given today's economic crunch, the declining power of the dollar, and even the longer commutes on congested freeways. Also, our world supply of air, water, oil, food, and land are becoming depleted and polluted. This is the pond we live in.

One Sunday morning I went with Robert and Kim to a lecture they were giving to eight thousand people. Robert told me that most of the people in the audience were Christians. Why weren't they in church? I wondered.

With both parents working too many hours and not finding enough financial ease to enjoy life—let alone have the leisure to attend church every Sunday—people are looking for ways to make their financial lives better. I find that people are naturally generous and want to support beneficial causes, but they need the facility and ease to do so. Of course, there are many other reasons people aren't attending churches in numbers as they used to. Problems within organized religions have caused people to be more cautious. Yet being cautious helps us clarify our spiritual goals and question what we engage in.

We can affect change on what occurs in the present. When difficulties, sickness, and other problems arise, it may be irritating and unfortunate. But rather than be depressed or overcome by our problems, we can check our mental attitude and use the problems to help us grow. We develop fortitude, patience, and compassion when we see that others around us also face difficulties. If life were always pleasant, we would have no wish to change.

But change comes regardless, and with it, aging, sickness, and death. This view has a deep effect on the way I conduct my life on a daily basis.

Karma is powerful, subtle, and pervasive. As a reflection on our conduct, and given the impact karma has on us individually and collectively, it should impel us to be more mindful of our conduct and care for others and the world around us. Although we have improved communication devices and live in a time of excellent global technology, we must conscientiously work to improve our relations with our world neighbors.

Living on a burgeoning planet with diminishing resources and global warming, we must learn to get along with others and practice moderation and conservation. It is imperative that we develop the inner technologies of tolerance, cooperation, and friendship in our increasingly dependent world.

MIND, NIRVANA, AND REBIRTH

Mind has the qualities of clarity, knowing, and apprehending objects with awareness. While dependent on the body and physical brain, the mind is not physical. Intention, for example, is a mental act, and mind cannot be seen. Mind has no physical weight and is not limited to time and space. You can sit here reading this book and think back to being five years old just entering kindergarten, or what you did at age eighteen, thirty, or sixty-five. This demonstrates continuity of mind.

Tenzin Kacho in January of 2002, with the reincarnation of her
first teacher, Venerable Ling Rinpoche. His predecessor was the senior
tutor to the Dalai Lama.

Because the mind is not physical and has continuity, it is the basis for the Buddhist teachings on rebirth and reincarnation, the
continuation of a person from one life to another.

During life, we grow from children into adults and then into old
age. Our body ages, and there is a limit to our physical longevity.
Today the average lifespan of Amercians is about eighty years, but
with global warming, pollution, and other conditions, it is uncertain how much more we can improve or extend our lives. Given the
right conditions, however, the mind can continue to improve. It does
not age like the body does, and while there can be problems such
as brain disease, intoxicants like alcohol, or too much television, given
the right conditions the mind has the potential to excel limitlessly.

Impermanence and change work with us. If things could not
change, there would be no room for transformation. It is possible
to overcome the overwhelming gravity of sluggish, unproductive bad
habits. We have to conscientiously change our mental attitudes and

actions to cultivate compassion and wisdom, love and kindness for others and ourselves, overcoming greed, and bias and self-interest. We cannot control or change what has already happened in the past, but we have the capacity to determine and direct our motivations and actions now—in this life—creating better causes and conditions for our future.

Life being impermanent, we have a window of time to accomplish our goals.

Even when situations are uncomfortable or difficult, with a strong and virtuous mind state, we can endure a lot. The opposite is not true; when one's mind is disturbed through jealousy or hatred, even when the best physical circumstances surround a person—health and beauty, friends, wealth, and good food—it often cannot help a disturbed mind.

This shows how the inner condition, a buoyant mind, and emotions, are important in our daily interactions. Life can be difficult, but the mind can be happy.

Our body and ordinary mind—or "sensory consciousness"—are impermanent and changing. They came from causes and conditions. It is important to inquire where we came from, why we are here, and where we are going. Generally, we don't question why we are who we are, although we may have done so as little children. I remember wondering, "Why am I part of this family and not another? Why do I have this kind of body?" Most of us, at some point in our lives, question where we go after this life, after when we die. The body dies and disintegrates, but it is difficult to say definitively what happens to the "person" or consciousness; because mind is not physical, there is no tangible, physical evidence.

The strict, radical, materialistic view believes that once we die, there is nothing left. According to that view, our mind is a chemical reaction contingent upon our body and stops when the body dies.

But even from the materialist's view, you can see that phenomena continue on in changed forms. Just as water becomes ice and vapor, even our body components become dust and earth again; there is gross and subtle transformation of physical phenomena. What the Buddhists propound is that there is gross and subtle transformation of nonphysical phenomena, too, particularly the mind.

The body gets old, sick, and dies. Buddhists hold the view that the mind separates from the body, and the connection with this life is finished. At the time of death, all gross familiarity with that life diminishes, and the mind loses recognition of the things and people of this life. What continues is a subtle mind with propensities and predispositions toward certain views, tendencies, and emotions; our habituated tendencies to respond in certain ways are retained. The gross level of mind ceases with the body and life, while the very subtle mind continues and becomes the basis for the next life.

Accumulated karma from past lives will determine where one is reborn and what kind of body and initial life circumstances, parents, and relationships one will have. Notice how over a lifetime, people's actions are often predictable; some people tend to be very thoughtful, kind, generous, and relate with others in cooperative ways, while others may be caustic, steal or hurt others, or cause divisions between friends. People constantly change, but we tend toward recurrent behaviors that become ingrained and mostly unexamined habits.

What is carried forward is the continuity of subtle propensities to do and act as we always have.

In the Buddhist view, the world came from causes and conditions, intentions, and actions. Ask yourself, "Did your current life come from causes or no causes? If it came from causes, what kind of causes? If there is life after death, are there causes for that? If someone constantly maligns others, steals, and hurts others throughout their life, what kind of congruent effects does that create for one's future life?"

Actions created do not just disappear; just as at the end of life all of the physical objects we created do not simply disappear, either. Good actions bring good results, but like seeds depending on many circumstances, they may not ripen until a later time, they may be compromised; there are many factors.

Culturally, the idea of reincarnation is quite thoroughly accepted in India and many Asian countries. Depending on where we are born in the world and in what culture, we are inclined to believe in reincarnation or not. In the Western world, people tend to believe that this is our first life, while Eastern traditions lean toward belief that we have had many lives. When our views don't coincide with our birth culture, we often question them and seek out people with similar views.

Even though Robert and I were raised Christian, when the view of reincarnation was introduced to me in high school and college, I was immediately drawn to the idea. It seemed natural, as well as intriguing. How did I come to have the life I have now? What was I to do and accomplish in this life? These questions became woven into my spiritual search.

His Holiness the Dalai Lama has mentioned meeting two Indian girls who remembered their past lives. They spoke of where they were born and what their lives were like in the past and what happened in their deaths. The Dalai Lama said the similar factors that these two girls mentioned were that in their previous lives, they were relatively young at the time of death, and they died suddenly. I think accidental or sudden death may leave a stronger imprint on the mind, enabling the person to recall the past while the condition of being aged—with slow decline and going into mental eclipse—would not impel strong retention.

It was my Buddhist study that gave me a more logical view of how reincarnation worked, revealing the nature of the continuity of mind, traversing from life to life, and how we create causes and conditions through our motivation and actions. In the Tibetan tradition, some people are recognized as reincarnations of previous teachers or special persons. They are an integral, vibrant part of the community. As I immersed myself while living in India, I came to accept reincarnation as a natural part of life, a process in life cycles.

His Holiness the Fourteenth Dalai Lama is considered a human incarnation of the Bodhisattva Chenresig (Tibetan), Avalokitesvara (Sanskrit), or Kuan Yin (Chinese), although the Dalai Lama himself would never admit to that. An advanced Bodhisattva such as His Holiness is a being who has achieved high levels of attainment, has gained insight into the nature of existence, and has developed compassion and wisdom to a high degree. This type of Bodhisattva is also a being who has liberated himself or herself from suffering existence but because of his strong compassionate wish to benefit others continues to return to the world again and again to guide and teach.

The post of the Dalai Lama is considered the highest for the Tibetan people, and the Dalai Lamas have been revered for several centuries. The person who holds the post is recognized as the reincarnation of the previous Dalai Lama. To test and find each incarnation is a task conferred upon esteemed teachers and meditators who were close to the previous Dalai Lama. The present Dalai Lama is the fourteenth recognized incarnation. When we speak of congruent causes and conditions creating certain effects, it becomes evident in observing the quality and ability of the Dalai Lama to accomplish all he does in this life. He is a scholar, meditator, teacher, head of state, and Nobel Peace Laureate. He exhibits incredible physical stamina, strong mental fortitude, and brilliance in teaching and guiding his people and disciples.

His teaching and traveling schedule is exhausting, but he goes where he is invited and where he feels his visit will benefit others. This is complemented by the receptivity of his people and many friends around the world.

In the person of His Holiness the Dalai Lama, with whom I have studied and from whom I have received teachings since first meeting him in 1975, I continue to be inspired by his incisive and compassionate teachings and his remarkable personality. In the early years of my study, my father remarked a couple times that although the Dalai Lama had all these titles and was celebrated and honored everywhere, the amazing thing about him was his command of English.

"Where did he have time and opportunity to learn English in all his busy activities?" Dad wondered.

In the Buddhist view, we have had countless lifetimes, and teachers say, in fact, that we've had it all and done it all. Our life gives us the opportunity to modify our actions of body, speech, and mind and in this way it can create excellent conditions for our future lives. We have the potential to attain freedom from this endless cycle of repeated birth and death and attain enlightenment.

Attaining nirvana means liberating oneself from unenlightened existence. It is not some airy high or magical place. It means you are no longer in suffering existence. Your mind is no longer contaminated with negative views and thoughts, and you have cut the causes for unhappy existence. A person seeking nirvana continually works to purify their mind and cultivates meditative concentration and insight into the nature of existence.

There are two levels to this nirvana. The first is that a person is freed from endless rebirth in cyclic existence, and the other is full enlightenment, completely free from subtle illusions of the nature of phenomena and reality. The first level includes the advanced bodhisattva, the person who chooses to be reborn in cyclic existence to work for the benefit of others, but is untainted by delusions. All their actions are for the benefit of others. The second level is the fully enlightened, completely pure being. Buddha means someone who is "awake" to the nature of existence, free from all delusions and harmful actions, and sees reality as it is without the veils of misperception and ignorance.

In the Tibetan Buddhist view, all beings can attain this freedom through purifying negativities and delusions and cultivating all excellent qualities.

Reincarnation and nirvana are complex and subtle—not easy to comprehend. These topics can challenge our personal views, but they are not something anyone must force himself to believe. There are other, more important, even indispensable qualities we must cultivate in our lives that will benefit ourselves and everyone. Here is a comment to that effect by His Holiness the Dalai Lama, drawn from an incomplete text of *Activating Bodhicitta: The Awakening Mind*. It comes from a section called "Exchanging Oneself with Others":

> *As sometimes I say (although perhaps I am being controversial but in a way I'm getting to the crux of the matter) that, even if one does not believe in reincarnation, it does not matter, and even if one does not believe in the law of actions and their consequences, it may not matter, but for as long as one lives one must maintain a noble and virtuous mind—a good heart and an altruistic attitude. Because, even though one may accept reincarnation completely and understand all the ins and outs of the law of karma, of what use is such understanding if one keeps a poisonous mind? Someone who knows nothing about such topics yet keeps a noble and virtuous mind and helps others according to his ability need have no fear of his rebirth when the time of death comes. It will surely be beneficial. There is nothing superior to the thought of cherishing and benefiting others, the thought concerned with their welfare and happiness. This is what I usually think and say, so that whether or not one accepts doctrines and religious beliefs, the essential practice is to maintain a good heart and to consider others before oneself. If one keeps that state of mind, it is always helpful and most beneficial.*

While our spiritual study can take us along refined and wonderful paths that titillate the mind or give us the opportunity to converse in lofty circles, we need to be grounded with our feet here on earth. Rebirth is about past and future lives, but we must check how we work and live with the neighbors around us now—in this life. Cultivating love and caring for others is what will truly expand the depth of our learning and help us become good people.

EPILOGUE
Robert: The End of Greed

We all have two financial statements. One is our personal financial statement. This statement shows our personal assets and liabilities: how much we earn and spend and owe. The second is the social accounting statement that shows us how much good we have done here on earth: how many people, places, or things we have served.

The lesson I learned in 1981 from Dr. Fuller is to use my personal gift to serve myself and as many other people as possible. If I do this, I will tap into the joys and abundance of the Great Spirit. If I use my gifts only for my personal interests and gain, then my returns on the second financial statement are limited.

I suspect many people who are rich suffer in other ways because they accumulate personal wealth at the expense of others.

On the flip side, there are many people who are tremendously generous on their second financial statement, their contribution to life here on earth, but they neglect the first financial statement, their personal financial statement. My dad, who I have called my poor dad, was in this category. He spent his life dedicated to the education of kids, but did so at the expense of his own family.

A problem I had with church was that it taught the love of money is the root of all evil. Although money is one of the subjects most referenced in the Bible, it seemed to me that the desire for money was evil. I am not saying this is true. All I am saying is that was my perception as a young boy at church and Sunday School.

One of my mom's Church Lady friends was very rich. She did not work because she married a rich, older man. He died and left her a fortune. Even though she was rich, she seemed to criticize me for wanting to become rich. Years ago, when I first introduced my educational game CASHFLOW, she repeated to me what she had been asking for years: "When was the last time you went to church? You should not teach people about getting rich. You should teach people about the Bible and what Jesus said."

Personally, I do not know why some people think you cannot be both—a lover of God and a lover of money. I personally do not think that loving money is evil. Money is just money. It is no different than my loving my home or my cat. It is how money is earned that can be good or evil. And how we use it.

For example, if I robbed banks or sold illegal drugs, that would be evil and illegal. If I worked at a job I did not like or with people I did not like, that would be evil. Or if I wasted my money on silly things while my family suffered, that would be evil.

To me, money is just money. What is really evil is that our school system does not teach people about money, and it brings in bankers and financial planners to teach kids about money. That is like letting a fox into the henhouse. In the last few years, it is these very institutions and the people who work for them—the banks, investment bankers, mutual fund companies, financial advisors, mortgage brokers, stock brokers, and real estate agents—who have caused much of the global financial mess of 2008. Many people blame the subprime borrowers. To me, it is the subprime investment bankers who are the real cause of this fiasco. The word "greed" comes to mind. It is these financial representatives and the organizations that prey on people and profit from their lack of financial savvy. It is these same people, who only want to recruit future customers, who are invited into our schools to teach our kids about money. This is more than evil. This is criminal.

In church I was taught that Christ's last words from the cross were "Forgive them Lord for they know not what they do." As I have said throughout this book, the Lord may forgive, but in the real world people are punished severely for not knowing what to do with their money.

I believe there is a coming apocalypse, an end of times. The end I am concerned about is not the same apocalypse I learned about in Sunday School, but it is best described by what Dr. Fuller called, "the final examination." One of the reasons I found it easy to follow Dr. Fuller's teachings was because we shared the same view of the future—that humans were on a path to self-destruction.

When I saw the atomic blast on Christmas Island in 1962, I wondered why humans were focusing so much time and energy killing each other. I wondered why we did not spend more time and money on making life better.

Listening to Dr. Fuller talk about the final examination, his ideas were very similar to the ideas of the Apocalypse expressed at my Sunday School. But rather than predicting the appearance of the horsemen, heavens parting, the rapture, and the second coming, Dr. Fuller talked about greed and that the final examination would test whether or not we as humans could use our minds and God's gifts, our resources, to create a sustainable life for all—not just for the rich, those of a chosen religion or race, or those from a chosen country. In so many words, he said that if we did not change greed to generosity, then life on earth—for humans—was over.

After my meeting with Dr. Fuller, I began to examine my own greed and the greed of others. It became apparent to me that too much greed is toxic. Greed is poisoning our planet, and our planet is becoming toxic to life. Greed causes us to deplete our oceans and cut down our forests—and trees and oceans are the lungs of our earth. The loss of the lungs of the earth—when combined with carbon emissions—is causing the air we breathe to become poisoned.

Greed also creates toxic governments and toxic government policies. For example, the U.S. government pays farmers *not* to produce food, just to keep food prices high, while much of the world is still on the brink of famine. Instead of feeding the world, we deny the world God's abundance.

Greed has caused the money supply to become toxic, keeping the middle class in debt and the poor dependent upon government support. The money supply is toxic because governments can print as much money as they want, and this "funny money" discounts the efforts of working people while rewarding, instead, those who play the money games.

Many religious organizations are greedy, too, claiming that heaven has space for only one religion: *their* religion. I do not know if there is a heaven, but if there is, I am sure there is plenty of space and more than one key to the gate. Claiming to have the only key to heaven is greedy and has been the cause of much pain, misery, and violence here on planet earth.

So what is the solution to greed? The obvious one is to be more generous. When Dr. Fuller talked about "cosmic accounting," he was referring to God's generosity. He said that the only reason solar power was not the primary source of energy on planet earth was because greedy people had not yet found a way to put a money meter between you and the sun. They had not yet found a way to charge you for what God was giving all of us for free.

Today, instead of harnessing God's abundance, we spend billions of dollars and kill thousands of people for oil. Why not spend that money on improving solar power? Why not turn every home into an electrical power plant? The reason is greed.

We now have the technology to create heaven on earth. The question is, do we have the willpower? Will we work with our minds and adapt new ideas, or try to run the world with old ideas

Very few people know that the rules of money changed in 1971. That year, President Nixon took the U.S. dollar off the gold standard. The dollar replaced gold—which is money made by God—with man-made money, which is also known as *fiat* money, or money that is not based on a physical commodity. In 1971, the dollar became a currency, and it was no longer money.

The word currency comes from the word "current." A currency, like a river current or an electrical current, needs to keep moving. This is why parking your money in a bank or in a mutual fund reduces your wealth. Your wealth declines because your money is not moving. Sitting in an account, your money is moving for your banker, financial advisor, investment bankers, and mutual fund companies—but not for you.

Personally, I do not save money, nor do I have a retirement account. I do not park my money. My job is to keep my money moving. Since most people leave school without much financial education, their money flows out.

The reason I created the educational game CASHFLOW is because every financially smart person knows they need to control the flows of their money, their currency. People with high financial IQs know how to keep more money flowing in than flowing out. My game teaches people how to control their cash flows. That requires financial IQ.

You can choose to blindly turn your hard-earned money over to a so-called "expert," or you can take steps to become financially educated yourself. There are two reasons I am against the idea of turning your money over to a financial expert. One is you do not learn anything. If you make money, you still have not really learned much. The second reason is that if your expert turns out to be a fool, and all your retirement or your child's college money is gone, then you may not be able to recover from the expert's mistakes.

Warren Buffett, America's richest investor, has these things to say about financial experts and their advice:

"Pension fund managers continue to make investment decisions with their eyes firmly fixed on the rearview mirror."

"Risk comes from not knowing what you are doing."

"Diversification is protection against ignorance. Diversification makes very little sense if you know what you are doing."

"Wall Street is the only place that people ride to in a Rolls Royce to get advice from those who take the subway."

John Bogle, founder of the Vanguard Funds, is a strong critic of mutual fund managers. He points out the following:

• Investors put up 100 percent of the money, take 100 percent of the risk, and earn 20 percent of the reward.
• Mutual funds put up 0 percent of the money, take 0 percent of the risk, and earn 80 percent of the reward.

As stated earlier, the Lord may forgive those who know not what they do, but the real world punishes and steals from the same people.

In 1974, the rules of money changed again. That year, the U.S. government passed ERISA—the Employee Retirement Income Security Act—which today is known in America as the 401(k). In simple terms, ERISA changes the rules of employment. Until 1974, the rule was that an employee working for a company would be paid a paycheck for their working years and continue to receive a paycheck into retirement for the rest of their lives.

Due to global economic competition, U.S. companies found that paying employees for life was too expensive, so the companies asked the government to change the rules. Today, workers are on their own. If an employee does not have enough money to last them a lifetime, it is that person's problem, not the employer's. Today in America— once the richest country in the world—there are millions of workers who need or will need the government to take care of them, medically and financially, once their working days are over. This is what happens when people and their leaders believe the quasi-religious idea that money is the root of all evil. Money is not evil. *Ignorance* about money is evil.

The reason I decided to work with my sister on this book and assist her in becoming a multimillionaire is because I know she has a very strong spirit. One of the definitions of the word "integrity" is "wholeness." It is my belief that for a person to be truly rich, they need be rich spiritually, emotionally, physically, and mentally. Also, getting rich is easier if we are legal, ethical, and moral. I can assist Tenzin in becoming a multimillionaire not because she is my sister, but because I know she has spent years strengthening her spirit. I know how well she can control her emotions and continue to have a joyous outlook, even when facing tough personal, financial, and physical challenges such as cancer and heart disease.

With a strong spirit and a little financial knowledge, she will be unstoppable. All she needs is to train her mind to think like a rich person. Let me explain with the following diagram. It is a tetrahedron, an object known for its structural integrity and strength.

Many people struggle financially because one or more of the four parts that make us human are weak. For example, I have met many people who have very smart minds, but they fail to have a strong spirit, or they are run by their emotions. I have a friend who has her MBA. She is very smart at business, but she lacks emotional and spiritual strengths. Today, she is a baby-sitter. This isn't to say that baby-sitting

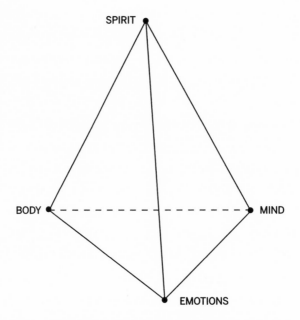

People who succeed financially have all four of these components intact.

is not an important job. All I am saying is that her financial struggles are spiritual and emotional, not mental. Financially, she is a mess, even though she knows what to do.

Some of the most successful entrepreneurs I know got their training in church. Some are former Mormon missionaries; others sold Bibles door to door. All of them stated that it was the best business experience they could get. It taught them discipline, determination, and drive—the process strengthened them mentally, emotionally, physically, and spiritually. My best friend, Lari Clark, got his training in Northern Ireland, converting Catholics to Mormonism at the height of the turmoil in that country. The building in which he lived was destroyed by a bomb. He was shot with rubber bullets because he got too close to riots.

Years later, Lari was selected as one of *Inc.* magazine's "Entrepreneurs of the Year." He owes much of his financial success to his work as a missionary.

I did not serve as a missionary for a church. I served as a missionary for the U.S. Marine Corps. The marines focused on developing me mentally, emotionally, physically, and spiritually. I was taught that the mission of the Marine Corps was more important than life. This may be why the marines say, "And on the eighth day, God created the marines." This may also be why there are only seven days in a week.

In traditional companies, if you do not perform, you are fired. One of the reasons Donald Trump and I recommend network marketing as a starting place for people who want to become entrepreneurs is because many network marketing organizations have tremendous training programs designed to develop people mentally, emotionally, physically, and spiritually. As long as you are willing to learn, they are willing to teach.

Many individuals have a rich mind but a poor person's emotions. As I've stated earlier, we are both humans and beings. If a person's emotions are weak—if they react in a human way—they may desire wealth, know what to do, but lack the emotional fortitude to achieve wealth. These people often say, "I need job security."

"What if I fail?"

"It sounds so risky."

"I can't afford it."

These are words that stem from poor emotions. As Warren Buffett often says, "If you cannot control your emotions, you cannot control your money." When it comes to money, many people are human because they have emotions, emotions which overpower the being.

When it comes to money, it's easy to understand why people would be overwhelmed emotionally, physically, and spiritually. Consider, again, the tetrahedron.

Mentally, a person with limited financial education will always live in fear, afraid of making a mistake, spiritually weak, praying and hoping for salvation, and physically clinging to any form of security, such as a safe job that may not pay enough. A financially weak person will fall prey to false prophets—people such as bankers, brokers, and bandits, all appearing to have their best interest at heart.

Many people are spiritually poor, even though they may go to church and pray every day. Spiritually poor people depend upon hope rather than faith, which is why my rich dad often said, "Hope is for the hopeless."

When I lost my first business, my surfer wallet business, it was faith—not hope—that got me through one of the roughest periods of my life. Not only was I broke and out of a job, I owed nearly a million dollars to my investors. Rather than quit and declare bankruptcy, I had to choose between being a human or being a being. A human would have quit and declared bankruptcy. Going back to face my creditors and rebuild my business was one of the worst experiences of my life, as well as one of the best experience of my life. It tested my *being*, who I was at my core. It strengthened my spirit.

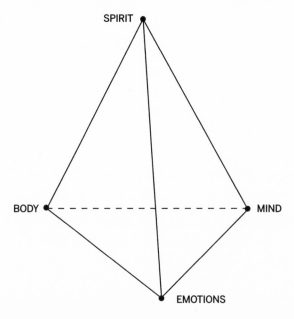

The structural integrity of these components is so important, I've included the diagram twice. If one part is weak or missing in us, our attitudes around money will collapse.

It made me a better human being—a person who makes mistakes, learns, and *grows* from the experiences.

We all know that a coin has two sides. Yet when it comes to money, many people see only the bad side of the coin. That is why they do not become rich. These same people often fail to see the good *and* the bad that exist in everything. My bad experience of failing in business not only strengthened me mentally, it strengthened me emotionally, physically, and—most of all—spiritually. Today I know that failing in my first business was one of the best experiences of my life. It was painful and the pain lasted for years, but it was my faith—faith that I could learn from this—that kept me going.

Today, when I meet people who are terrified of failing, I know they are looking only at the bad side of the coin, not recognizing the possibility of a good side. These people may go to church and pray a lot, but unless they take the first step and take a risk, their spirits will never be tested, nor will their spirits have the opportunity to grow stronger if they let the emotion of fear dominate their spirits, their faith in God.

Schools reward people for having the right answer and punish people for making mistakes. In real life, there are no right answers. Real life is a multiple-choice test. Sometimes we guess wrong. The problem with many mentally smart people is they *need* to be right and then become paralyzed emotionally, spiritually, and physically because in real life no one is holding up a sign saying, "That was the right answer."

George Soros, one of the greatest investors of our time, says this about investing, yet it applies to all areas of life:

> *You have got to make decisions, even though you know you may be wrong. You can't avoid being wrong. But by being aware of the uncertainties, you're more likely to correct your mistakes.*

In the real world, the smartest people are people who make mistakes and learn from their mistakes. In school, the smartest people are those who do not make mistakes. My poor dad—a smart man and great teacher—lost everything when he left the school system. Although a smart man academically, he wasn't prepared for the real world, a world that does not care what your grade point average is. He did not know how to make mistakes and grow richer.

He fell victim to crooks and con men who preyed upon his lack of financial knowledge. Rather than enjoy his retirement, he struggled financially until the day he died. Without a steady government job, he was the proverbial fish out of water.

While many people dread being sued, I have looked at the process as an opportunity to learn and to test myself. I am richer today—mentally, emotionally, physically, spiritually, and financially—due to the experience.

The same is true with health. I was born with a birth defect. I was born with a defective heart, apparently passed down from my mom's rheumatic fever. All my life, this faulty heart bothered me. I was told I could not play football, yet I did. I was told I would not be accepted to military school, yet I was. The same was true with flight school. Rather than give in to the physical weakness, I called on my mind, spirit, and emotions to make me stronger. Rather than causing me to become weaker, my weak heart made me stronger.

After passing the age of sixty, I decided it was time to fix my heart and am scheduled for heart surgery to physically make my weak heart even stronger.

We cannot forget that we are born as both humans and beings. Life gives us the opportunity to strengthen both our human side and our being or spiritual side. Unfortunately, many institutions prey upon our human or weak side.

In school, I was emotionally battered because I did not fit in mentally. Academically, I was very weak. I am not good at reading or writing. Once again, I used the act of failing to become stronger. In school I failed writing, accounting, and typing. Today, I make a lot of money writing, teaching accounting via my board games, and I spend a lot of time typing at the computer.

Although I became very rich via my weaknesses, I continue to be a writer who is not always grammatically correct, would never be an accountant, nor would anyone hire me as a typist. Although an "F" student in traditional terms, I make more money than many "A" students.

Most of us know that the two most dangerous words in business are, "Trust me." When you hear those words, grab your purse or wallet and hang on tight. Over the years as an entrepreneur and investor I have heard variations on the words "trust me." I get ready to run when I hear these words, as well: "I am a good Christian."

Whenever a person leads with their faith, I become very suspicious. When I hear those words, I know the chances for losing money or winding up in a bad relationship are pretty good. Just because someone is a good Christian, Jew, Muslim, Buddhist, or whatever faith does not mean they are honest, trustworthy, or competent in business.

"I have integrity."

If you have to tell me you have integrity, you probably do not. I prefer to let actions do the talking.

"I'm here to help."

When I hear these words, I wonder who they are trying to help. Are they here to help you, or help themselves?

"I'm behind you all the way."

My rich dad often said, "People like to stand behind you because it's easier to get into your pockets. On top of that, if they are standing behind you, you cannot see what they are really doing."

As cautious as I am when I hear such statements, this does not mean I have not been taken advantage of because I have. I have been the sucker and a fool many times. Now older and wiser, every time I lose or trust someone who is not trustworthy or make a mistake, I remind myself that every coin has two sides. Personally, I have learned a lot from bad partners, crooks, con men, and mistakes. In fact, I am a richer person because of bad partners, crooks, con men, and mistakes.

I am grateful when I lose money. The memory may be painful, and the process of straightening things out may be a tough one, but the lessons are priceless. As my sister often reminded me during the writing of this book, "His Holiness says that Mao Tse-tung is his greatest teacher." Experiences good or bad are all food for our spirits.

One final thought on God and money is this: I believe money goes to those who are most trustworthy, and money stays away from those who are not trustworthy. This does not necessarily mean they are bad or dishonest people. What I mean is that money stays with people who care, respect it, and know how to grow it. Money stays away from people who either abuse it or do not know how to care for it.

This is why the four points of the tetrahedron are crucial to being rich.

If we are unethical, we can do business only with unethical people. The same is true with morality. For example, it would probably be hard for a person with strong moral values to do business with someone in the pornography business. And people who follow the rules will stay away from those who break the rules. As with anything in life, birds of a feather *do* flock together.

One of the more valuable lessons I learned in Sunday School is that the word becomes flesh. In other words, we *are* our words. In the ideal world, we all know we should tell the truth, keep our word, and not make promises we cannot keep. In the real world, lying often takes less courage than telling the truth face-to-face. It is easy to not keep our words, and it is easy to not keep our agreements. All of these events detract from our spiritual financial power.

For example, I have a friend who constantly makes promises and does not keep them. He isn't a bad person; he just has a bad memory. Since he does not keep his agreements—his words—people do not trust his word, despite the fact that he is a good person. Instead of business getting easier, he has to work harder to keep finding new customers. His old customers soon learn not to trust him.

One of the more valuable lessons I learned from rich dad along those lines was that if our word is no good in the present, then our word will be no good in the future. Every time we do not keep our word, we lose power. On top of losing power, we have the weight of a broken agreement hanging around our neck, which means we need to work harder. If no one trusts me and I say, "I'm going to build a million-dollar business—will you invest with me?" chances are most people, even your friends, will say "No."

On the positive side, when a person is as good as their word, they gain the power to speak into the future and have things come true. If you are trustworthy, which means you have the integrity of mind, body, spirit, and emotions, and you say, "I'm going to build a million-dollar business—will you invest with me?" chances are more people will be willing to invest.

We have all had people break their promises to us. A friend of mine borrowed $25 and has never paid it back. Today, I would never invest with him. His word became flesh, and it is not good. If you want to be rich, then keep your word.

You are only as good as your word.

One of my reasons for writing this book is to stress the importance of being in mental, emotional, physical, and spiritual integrity. I have not always been in integrity, which is what caused so many financial and personal challenges in my life. I lost my first business because while I was strong spiritually—I had the courage—but lacked the *knowledge* of business. When we were successful and grew rapidly, I was not able to manage the growth, or my partners.

Going back to my investors and apologizing for losing their money was trying and spiritually demanding, but telling the truth brought me back into integrity.

I do not want you to think that I think I am perfect. I assure you, I know I am far from perfect. I know that every day I live in human form I will have my being challenged to learn more.

I say this because I do believe in a God or a Great Spirit. I also believe we all have great spirits inside us. When we can face all events, good or bad as good lessons, we will have more good in our lives. When we can face all events good or bad as lessons for our spirits, we can grow to become more spiritual, grow richer, happier, and closer to God.

So is there an answer to greed? One path is to be more generous. When Dr. Fuller talked about "cosmic accounting," he was referring to God's generosity. If we do, indeed, all have two financial statements—and the second "social" statement is measured in Fuller's "cosmic accounting"—we can contribute to the end of greed by focusing on the good we have done here on this earth: how many people, places or things we have served, how well we have used our gifts to create a life that is rich in all things—spirit, mind, body, and heart.

AFTERWORD
A Change of Heart: A True Story

On September 3, 2008, I was admitted to the Mayo Clinic, in Phoenix, Arizona, for open-heart surgery.

From birth I have lived with two weak heart valves, but that did-n't keep me from fighting hard and living harder. On top of that, I had always used stress as a motivator, a driver. I've always believed that stress is how intelligence grows, and I've lived my life that way: pushing myself hard, then pushing still harder. And fortifying my-self with a diet of red meat and vodka.

My heart surgery came off without a hitch, and I went roaring into recovery and rehab, as fearlessly as I've attacked most challenges in my life. Three weeks after surgery I had resumed my exercise rou-tine and was back in high gear.

Four weeks after surgery I was back in the hospital. The doctors' orders: reduce the stress in my life, stop getting so worked up about things, meditate, do yoga.

For years—sixty-one, to be exact—I've listened to my heart, the surge of my lifeblood, and been all too aware of its flaws—my labored, ragged, often erratic heartbeat. Today I am lulled to sleep at night by a steady, sure heartbeat, a novelty, but a comfort after these sixty-one years.

I think about my doctors' advice, about stress, yoga, a healthier diet, and meditation. Could this hard-living, hard-driving leopard change its spots? *Would* he?

It's surprising to me that I am actually considering a few changes. Time will tell.

One thing I know for sure: It's amazing what a change of heart can do.

—ROBERT KIYOSAKI, OCTOBER 2008

OUR WISH FOR YOU

We wish you all the joy life has to offer.

We wish you love and happiness and kindness.

We wish you love for you and your biological family and love for your spiritual family.

Thank You.

I remember the days when it seemed no one wanted to listen to what we had to say.

A wise person once said, "The greatest gift a person can give you is their time."

As you know, time is a very precious commodity.

So thank you for giving us your time. And thank you for reading this book.

"I Am The Rich Dad Company"

I am the Rich Dad Company. Welcome to my world. A world of possibilities, a world of learning, a world of understanding. A take-charge world. Through me, people of all walks of life, from around the globe, have a chance at their dreams. See, I am not just a company; I am an awakener. I am a teacher. I am a community builder and an empowerer who has changed lives and is resolute to keep changing lives for decades to come. I won't stop. I am the Rich Dad Company, and my mission on this earth is to elevate the financial well-being of humanity.

Is my task daunting? Hell, yes. Am I afraid? Never, because the Rich Dad Company thrives on leaps of faith. These leaps are the fires that ignite, and they are the catalysts of change. And with change comes growth. I believe that following the status quo is what got so many people into the mess they are in. It's going to take unwavering, fearless actions and words to awaken the hearts and minds of people who unknowingly have been following the blind, with the hope and belief that they have been following the enlightened.

I know otherwise. I've lived through the lies and saw the future with my own eyes. I am the Rich Dad Company, and I don't believe hope gets anyone anywhere. Why hope, when you can learn, understand, take action, achieve results, and get stronger? I am not a helper. I am a teacher, a tough teacher who some won't be able to handle. I don't mind minced words, I rock most boats, I profess action, and I demand hard work today for freedom and happiness tomorrow. But I also simplify the path and keep it fun, entertaining, experiential, and unforgettable. That's what good teachers do.

I know some people won't step up. They are simply too lazy, too scared, too comfortable, or are basking in the lull of false security to take charge of their lives. Some will come around. And when they do, I'll be there with lots of entry points: books they can read, games they can play, videos they can watch, seminars they can attend, and coaches they can hire, just to name a few. I have many doors, and every one of them is open to the willing, no matter their standing in life. Taking control all starts with a dream.

Like those whom I teach, I am learning and growing, too. (I recognize that finding true happiness means expanding beyond a mission of financial well-being to a mission of complete well-being—in health and wellness, spiritual awakening, philanthropy, business building, and purpose.) In essence, a Rich Life. And that is my next transformation. If we are not growing, then we are dying. Those who have transformed their lies through me have tremendous stories to tell. They are stories of strength, optimism, power, spirit, and winning. These people are going beyond the basics of the Rich Dad principles. They are emerging into The Rich Life, and so am I.

Best-selling Books by Rich Dad's Advisors

Sales Dogs
by Blair Singer
Reveal the five simple, but critical, revenue-generating skills

Own Your Own Corporation Updated and Revised 2008: Why the Rich Own Their Own Companies and Everyone Else Works for Them
by Garrett Sutton

How to Buy & Sell a Business
by Garrett Sutton
Strategies used by successful entrepreneurs

The ABC's of Real Estate Investing
by Ken McElroy
Learn how to achieve wealth and cash flow through real estate

The ABC's of Building a Business Team That Wins
by Blair Singer
How to get rich quickly and stay rich forever

The ABC's of Getting Out of Debt
by Garrett Sutton
Strategies for overcoming bad debt, as well as using good debt
to your advantage

The ABC's of Writing Winning Business Plans
by Garrett Sutton
Learn to focus your plan for the business and format your plan
to impress about building a multimillion-dollar business

The Advanced Guide to Real Estate Investing: How to Identify the Hottest Markets and Secure the Best Deals
by Ken McElroy

Guide to Investing in Gold and Silver
by Mike Maloney
Everything you need to profit from precious metals now